Edited by Benno Heisel, Theresa Spielmann,
Andreas Wehrl, Christina Wehrl

The 2051 Munich Climate Conference
Future Visions of Climate Change

THIS BOOK WAS PUBLISHED AFTER THE OCCASION OF THE 2051 MUNICH CLIMATE CONFERENCE, WHICH TOOK PLACE ON 18–19 SEPTEMBER 2021 AS A COMBINED ONLINE AND LIVE EVENT AND WAS OPEN TO THE GENERAL PUBLIC.

The German National Library lists this publication in the German National Bibliography; detailed bibliographic data are available from http://dnb.d-nb.de

BÜRO GRANDEZZA TEAM
T2051MCC directors: Benno Heisel, Theresa Spielmann, Andreas Wehrl
Academic Advisor: Sebastian Schindler
Chief Technician: Lionel Dzaack
Embodiment Facilitator: Io Cohn
Project Management Assistant: Jennifer Zoll

COLLABORATING ARTISTS
Scenography and Arts at Bellevue di Monaco: Susi Gelb
Costumes: Martha Pinsker
Executive costumer: Marlene Rösch

ADDITIONAL TEAM
Moderators: Nabila Abdel Aziz, Souad Alfa, Zahra Akhlaqi, Sebastian Schindler
Performers: Diana Marie Müller, Robert Spitz
Communications: Christiane Pfau
Online Spaces and Website: Moby Digg (Maximilian Heitsch, Sebastian Haiss, Ines Huber, Susanne Janssen, Lisa Duespohl)
Streaming: Markus Kink / MediaBox TV
Mobile Camera: Pablo Lauf, Moha Ebrahimi
Concept and idea (2018–2020): Nikolaus Witty
Project Management: Laura Martegani, Rat & Tat Kulturbüro

SPONSORS
City of Munich, Department of Arts and Culture
Allianz Kulturstiftung
Edith-Haberland-Wagner Stiftung
Franz Kriechbaum Stiftung
FutureCamp Climate
Bürgerstiftung München
Aqua Monaco / Good Monaco
OmniCert

PARTNERS
Bellevue di Monaco
Moby Digg
MediaBox TV
Rehab Republic
HochX

PUBLICATION
First published in 2023 by transcript Verlag, Bielefeld
Publishers and Editors: Benno Heisel, Theresa Spielmann, Andreas Wehrl, Christina Wehrl
Design Concept: Sebastian Haiss
Print: Printed by Friedrich Pustet GmbH & Co. KG, Regensburg
ISBN: 978-3-8376-6384-6
Set in Public Sans, Custom T2051MCC Font

The production of this publication was made possible by Allianz Kulturstiftung.

The 2051 Munich Climate Conference
Future Visions of Climate Change

**Benno Heisel, Theresa Spielmann,
Andreas Wehrl, Christina Wehrl**

THE 2051 MUNICH CLIMATE CONFERENCE (T2051MCC)

Future is weird. But there is an undeniable need to talk about it. Therefore, let's talk about the past: We are a performance art collective called Büro Grandezza and in the year 2021 we organised an international conference on the subject of climate change. It was held September 18th and 19th in a hybrid online and in situ setup at *Bellevue di Monaco* in Munich (Germany). We had invited the academic community to contribute to a climate conference in an imagined year 2051. To do so we had spread an open call through the usual channels of the academic world and received comfortably enough contributions to fill two days worth of programming. This book is the conference proceedings of that event: The 2051 Munich Climate Conference or, in short: T2051MCC.

This introductory chapter will outline what happened during the event, share insights into the creation process, discuss why we set it up the way we did, and present the conclusions we drew on artistic, academic, and structural issues.

WHAT TOOK PLACE

T2051MCC was a two-day academic conference. It was open to the public and participation was possible on site or via a virtual conference centre. Admission was free. Within two days, 45 scholars gave 25 academic presentations in 12 sessions. Four international experts and activists gave keynote speeches. The program also included artistic contributions and performances, and speeches by local activists.

Our venue in Munich was the *Bellevue di Monaco*, a cultural and residential centre for refugees and other citizens of Munich. T2051MCC took place in all publicly accessible rooms and areas of the Bellevue.

The visitors entered through the café, where they were admitted, received a costume (designed by Martha Pinsker) and were provided with information on the program. In the café, visitors could also hang out, eat and drink throughout the days. The café was also the main sluice to generate the narrative idea of a venue where the future was perceptible (room design by Susi Gelb). Two lecture rooms, "mycelium" and "vivarium", were the main places to follow the presentations. The mycelium focused on networks, otherness and nature, while the "vivarium" was centred around knowledge, transferal and action. There were always two different presentations running at the same time and the audience had to choose which they wanted to attend.

There was also another conference centre: a digital version of the various rooms – albeit in an artistically heightened transformation –

Benno Heisel
Theresa Spielmann

Andreas Wehrl

Introduction

could be accessed online. We used the Mozilla hubs platform to offer the possibility to get in touch with other participants while listening to the presentations. Our website (designed by moby digg) served as another point of entry. Visitors had the choice: just watch the Livestream of either of the rooms via YouTube and hang out in the respective chat or the T2051MCC website, or watch them embedded in an interactive auditorium via the hubs (designed by moby digg and Benno Heisel). All three ways to participate (in situ, live chat and Mozilla hubs) were also monitored to allow for the audience to ask questions and participate in discussions. This very complex streaming setup was only possible by the support of mediaBOX TV, a movie production team including contributor Markus Kink. They provided skills, team members and equipment far beyond what we could expect or afford.

It is important to note that T2051MCC took place during the second year of the Corona pandemic. Throughout the production phase we did not know whether a live audience would be allowed to attend and what the regulations would be. So the target audience for the elaborate online version was not only the international public but also the local one.

THE IDEA OF T2051MCC

Our idea was to motivate scholars from a broad range of disciplines to (intrinsically) work within a fictional setting. Most fields of research that are even tentatively connected to the climate will produce narratives of the future – e.g., in forms of models, projections, simulations and so on. Fictionality however invites a different kind of depictions of the future and those scholars that answered our call told us that this indeed was their reason to apply: An opportunity to be playful, harsh, direct or even wrong without being disconnected from their usual academic environment and convictions.

The year 2050 is central to discourses and legislatures on climate change. It is the year by which the task to limit global warming below the catastrophic 1.5°C is said to have succeeded or failed. So, the year after 2050 was the one we went for as a setting of our conference. However, to accommodate the greatest variety of imaginations we decided to have the two days be set in a different world: One below and one above 1.5°C of global heating. In contrast to usual calls for papers, an acceptance meant that we would enter into dialogues with all participating scholars to develop a common understanding. And starting from the ideas that were presented to us we set out to build a coherent but unrestrictive framework for the presentations.

CLIMATE AND THE ARTS

While climate has become a mainstream topic in the arts today, the methods of engaging with climate change in the artistic realm are still being developed. Climate change as a problem for society is intangible. As theatre makers especially, the engagement with climate in 'our' medium is confronted with hurdles such as the inherent anthropocentrism in theatre and the difficulty of fitting such a vast and complex issue within a dramaturgy that is portrayable and, to put it simply, makes sense and adds to the discourse in a productive rather than redundant way. If you want to make theatre that engages with the climate how do you do that? Do you focus on making theatre sustainably? Or do you tell a story about climate change? But which one and how are you not just reproducing news cycles? How do you use the medium theatre without being limited by its supposed boundaries? For the audience and visitors of T2051MCC the experience might not have felt like a theatre experience seeing as it is breaking out of so many conventions associated with said medium. As theatre makers in this project we had to ask ourselves the same questions as in any other theatre production: Where will the project take place? Where does the narrative take place? When does the narrative take place? What is and defines the narrative?

HOW WE APPROACHED T2051MCC

As independent artists we commission ourselves. We develop a convincing idea first, then we seek funding and set up the team.

In this case, the idea also needed to convince others: scholars who should develop and present the contributions, as one more extra task among the many they would have already. So the concept had to be attractive for people who neither knew us nor T2051MCC.

Therefore, we had an unusually long run-up for the project: starting in 2018, we travelled to two United Nations climate conferences to discuss our concept with actual scholars and see how they would respond to it. The reception was generally positive and encouraging.

So we conducted a series of interviews with experts from different disciplines to understand, how a fictional setting and academic work could come together. This project phase was particularly entertaining because it brought up a lot of actual science fiction. Surprisingly for us, we ended with a very simple fictional framework (to be discussed in the dramaturgy chapter). In the course of this conceptional phase we also had the chance to discuss our idea in different expert fora and at research institutions. After a number of scholars had stated their intention to hand in a paper we applied for funding.

Benno Heisel
Theresa Spielmann
Ar̲̲̲̲ Wehrl

By February 2019, the cultural department of the city of Munich had granted us a first, substantial funding within a program to support independent theatre projects. The difficulty with this sort of funding is that the decision is either yes or no and there is only one deadline a year to apply. At this time, we planned to stage T2051MCC in early 2020.

After we had secured basic funding, the actual project phase started. We hired Rat & Tat cultural bureau's Laura Martegani as a project manager who quickly became the backbone of the project. We realised we would need more funding and were lucky to meet Mandana Mansouri. With her communication skills and her profound understanding of artistic work she helped us to expand our funding base. In the digital design studio Moby Digg we found a partner who was interested to accompany us in a month-long process of developing not only a website but also a concept for an entire virtual conference centre, and who was capable of putting all the avatars and virtual meeting rooms into action. The whole thing kept growing and the technical requirements did so, too. To ensure that our aesthetic and technical approaches would work, we created a prototype ("Displaced by climate change", Büro Grandezza 2019). Due to the Corona pandemic we had to change the date of the conference twice so that it took place more than a whole year after we had originally planned. It was a particularly difficult time for people working in arts. From our original team of directors, Katharina Wolfrum had moved on to a new job and Nikolaus Witty had followed the call of the sea. We are grateful for their support in bringing this idea to life. Benno Heisel and Theresa Spielmann then joined and together with Andreas Wehrl (formerly: Kohn) formed the team of directors.

In early 2021, the deadline of our Call for Papers came closer. This was a moment of truth. After hundreds of hours of work and particularly presentations on presentations to many different audiences we would find out: Would we actually receive abstracts? Would it be enough to put together a whole conference? And would they be good enough? It was a pretty exciting time, and our first meeting after the deadline was among the most joyous experiences within the project.

From that point onwards, even more work was to be done. We asked all contributors, as we called them, for an online meeting. This was unusual for an academic conference, but it was necessary to attain a common understanding of the fiction we built and the way we would get it to work, both technically and performance-wise. The meetings proved very useful and we learned a lot about all sorts of disciplines. With most contributors we had more than one meeting. Since many were in different time zones, we had to set up a booking system where contributors could book slots in our calendar. In the morning we would simply check which meetings were planned for the day. Since we mention work: everybody in the team was paid the same amount of money per month (except for some with whom we agreed on a lump sum). There were no strict working hours, particularly not for ourselves. It is worth noting that during the preparation phase we also tried a lot that did not work out in the end, proved too complicated to pursue or was too difficult to integrate into the conference. For example: Setting up intergenerational dialogues of activists (of today and the '68-Protesters) became it's own project called "play \ rewind" (Büro Grandezza 2020).

When the conference drew closer one of the biggest tasks was to manage our growing team. The streaming team by mediaBOX TV alone would include 10 people at a time on the conference days. In total, we coordinated more than 100 people. To ensure everybody had a space to address their personal well-being during the process Io Cohn had the position of Embodiment Facilitator as we called it. Everybody in the team was invited to use this offer of open-ended consultations.

In the final phase the project became more familiar in shape, albeit very large. The conference organisation had to be finalised in parallel to the complex live-streaming, programming tasks and rehearsals. Finally, we could welcome our audience and scholars to T2051MCC at the 18th of September 2021 10 a.m. CET.

DRAMATURGY

Reception and creation of aesthetic experiences both rely on coherence: the possibility to relate elements of the work to one another. The most organic way to create (or wantonly break) coherence is world-building. In our case however we did not want to constrain our contributors to a diegetic fantasy-setting we forced on everyone. During our interviews with scholars in the conceptional phase of the project we came to the conclusion, that this kind of an approach would cost us more interesting thoughts than we would gain from it. Particularly as it would imply predictive powers and thus limit the narrative openness that was needed if T2051MCC should serve as a platform for scholars within which they could develop their contributions.

So what does that mean for the audience and our scholars? What we decided on was the idea of an unreliable transmission from the future. There would be no live presentation in front of the audience but rather a live-stream to our lecture halls and our online audience at the same time. Meaning: the scholars who participated in person in Munich held

Benno Heisel
Theresa Spielmann

their presentation in a studio setup. This way we also wanted to make sure there would be no emphasis on the presentation in situ. What the respective year 2051 would look like should be decided by the contributors themselves stated during their presentations more or less explicitly. We only asked everyone to decide if their speech would come from a world that went though more or less than 1.5°C of global heating and bundled them together accordingly: The first day would be transmissions from a catastrophically overheated planet and the second day from a world with limited global heating. It was a joy to see that there were quite a few statements which broke the initial intuitive idea that this would also mean our first day was dystopic and the second day utopic.

But to give our audience something to connect everything together we needed to provide them with a narrative that would allow for these transmissions to occur. So we set up all the communication in a way that made a mysterious "Department" the organiser of the conference (e.g. with the print materials on site, with our website online and in advertising). The omnipresence of science fiction narratives makes it very simple to reference overbearing organisations that feign benevolence. But because of that it is rather tough to find aesthetics for a conference that do not clearly reference known franchises and give presentations a meaning that infringes on the content.

FRACTALS AND FUNGI
What we chose in the end were two main sources for aesthetic choices: fractals and fungi. Both presented us with enough scientific and metaphoric connectivity to climate sciences, the philosophy of science, and very particular aesthetics. To date, for example, there are very interesting applications of fractal analysis being developed with the computing models to match. But applying those to climate research and action will still take years. However the promise of fractal mathematics in future applications is very real. And as far as the fungi are concerned: yes, there are slime molds being used as biological computers. But the omnipresence of mushrooms in research fields as different as nutrition, building materials, waste management and – in a more metaphorical manner – humanities goes far beyond that. So we created a science fiction around T2051MCC that was full of fractal imagery and mycelium structures. This gave us imagery that allowed us the refer to growth, mathematics, and networks in a very sensual manner without being too sinister or simple. This was rounded off by the team of Moby Digg designing an alien typeface which can be interpreted as being derived from dimensional coordinates which in

turn was used to generate fractal geometry. (See image block pages 81-128) This typeface accompanies the design of the book as well as being an important part of the "corporate design" of the fictional hosts.

STAGING T2051MCC AT THE BELLEVUE DI MONACO
The above was a solution for another major question: How would we relate T2051MCC back to our venue, *Bellevue di Monaco*? A few words about this organisation: Situated in the very centre of Munich it stands on land which is arguably amongst the most expensive in the world. Not long ago the buildings that now comprise the *Bellevue di Monaco* were marked for sale and about to be torn down and replaced with luxury apartments. A small but strong civic movement prevented this from happening and managed to turn the place very publicly into a cultural and habitational centre for refugees run by a cooperative. Apart from offering apartments for mostly unaccompanied minors it offers language and legal courses, asylum and migration counselling, tuitions, food, work and a broad variety of cultural events. And while in another world the place could host a fantastic penthouse for the perversely rich, the *Bellevue di Monaco* has the only rooftop soccer place in Munich and using it is free for everyone.

Our on-site staff, our stage hands and – most visibly – our moderators have direct links to the *Bellevue di Monaco,* e.g. living there, visiting courses or just being a frequent visitor. The ways in which climate change is connected to migration are manyfold. But there is a clear disconnect of the discourse in both artistic and academic fields from the realities many people who have been forced to leave their homes live in.

Overall: we chose this venue as it is associated with migration and flight. Climate change is a deciding contributing factor in both. Additionally, it is a strong statement within the urban development of Munich and evokes all kinds of questions related to economic and political issues. It was important to us that this context would be seen and felt by our contributors and our audience.

PERFORMING THE CONFERENCE
Whilst it was important to us to lend the main focus to our contributors we are still very much coming from a theatre background. So we wanted to use theatrical means to connect our on-site audience to the themes and issues of the conference. Therefore, we invited the actors Diana Müller and Robert Spitz to improvise with the audience throughout the two day span of the conference. They were pretty much playing an open ended escape-the-timeline-game: two agents from the

Benno Heisel
Theresa Spielmann

Introduction

future whose only connection and way back to their time is the transmission of the conference, need to find out what makes this timeline special and how to get back to their original timeline. Of course, they need to keep their mission and identity secret whilst understanding what made them get stranded here in the first place. Simply put: What – here and now – has any influence on the future? This was not only meant to get the audience involved and talking in a non-intrusive manner but also provided us with a string to follow along with a camera to document the whole project further.

Many smaller and partly spontaneous bits (like an unplanned concert by Io Cohn on the roof or questionnaires our helpers had to strike up conversations with visitors) helped keeping the venue alive during the intermissions. But overall, the main stage was given to the presentations. In-between we made room for the conference feature most frequently asked for by scholars in out preparatory talks: Time to get talking with other contributors and visitors.

THIS PUBLICATION AND ITS STRUCTURE
Throughout the preparation process for the conference we spoke with our contributors about the possibility of a printed publication and started fundraising for different options. The scope and form of this book are a bit of a foreign body in the usual portfolios of both scholars and publishing houses. It makes us very happy to have found so many contributors and - with transcript Verlag - one of the few publishing houses who have a reputation in academic as well as artistic fields. Which leads us to this moment in time with you reading these lines. So what can you expect from the rest of this book?

We invited everyone contributing to the conference to send us articles for a conference proceedings. These are collected and printed in the same order as they were presented in the conference programme. If you are interested in watching the corresponding recorded livestream, the time of day and the respective venue is named with each contribution. The link to a playlist with all the live streams is to your right on page 13. All images and graphics are collected in an image block at the centre of the book (pp. 81-128). The presentations that were held at the conference, but are not accompanied by an article in this book are summarised on pages 174-177. Short biographies of the scholars can be found at pp. 178-190. Feel free to use our cover as an index. And that is pretty much it. We hope you enjoy diving into the imaginations and workings of everybody who made T2051MCC a reality.

Conference Website:
https://t2051mcc.com
⟨decorative script glyphs⟩

The digital conference centre
https://hubs.mozilla.com/6RGikPK/downright-enchanting-volume
⟨decorative script glyphs⟩

The VODs of all live streams
https://www.youtube.com/playlist?list=PLHlXwGhzeYJ6lFt0Mh9j9NEr_87Y11vwP
⟨decorative script glyphs⟩

Watch *Shroud for an Ancient Sea* by Sarah Nance.
Passcode: 2051
https://vimeo.com/783688390
⟨decorative script glyphs⟩

Report on the conference by Future Camp
Report on the conference by Rehab Republic
https://t2051mcc.com/downloads
⟨decorative script glyphs⟩

Essay on climate change narratives and T2051MCC in Foreign Policy Magazine: *The Tragedy of Stopping Climate Change* by Jessi Jezewska Stevens
https://foreignpolicy.com/2021/11/09/climate-change-narratives-sense-of-an-ending/#
⟨decorative script glyphs⟩

SEPTEMBER 18, 10 AM. VENUE: VIVARIUM AND MYCELIUM

Thank you very much for inviting me. It's a great pleasure for me to be here with you. So let me start with my vision of 2051, which will not have me in it because I'm not going to live till 2051. I'm not even sure my children will be able to live till then, but perhaps my grandchildren might be and I'm going to take a very rosy and optimistic view of that future of 2051 in which we have solved the climate change problem. And we did it in the period of 2021 to 2025, or up to 2030. This was the critical juncture at which the world was able to change. The world agreed to change, and the world did change. Now, how did it do that?

And what were the critical factors? I am going to name three that I feel were the biggest contributors to making that positive change. The first one is young people, and we just heard the voices of a couple of young people just now young people around the world. Around 2020, 2018, 2019, 2020, 2021 mobilised in a way that we had never seen before. All over the world. Every country had the Fridays For Future school children take going out of school, demonstrating, raising their voices. Advocating with their own leaders in their own countries. And then globally with global leaders and their voices got stronger and stronger, and they were able to make political differences as we just started in electoral processes, particularly in democratic countries where the electorate has a big, big say in changing policies and leaders. And I cite just one example that actually happened in that period where president Biden was able to defeat then president Trump in the United States election in 2020, a very large part of that success came from mobilising. The young people or mobilisation buy ad with the young people in the United States of America, for whom tackling climate change was a very high priority.

In fact, tackling climate change was not a high priority for then candidate Biden. He was not a convinced about the issue, but the young people that worked for him and voted for him and brought out the vote for him, convinced. And so when he came into the office, he understood that the magnitude of climate change was much bigger than he had realised before.

And in fact, he was able to take actions to do that. In fact, if you have just seen the last few days on the television screens, you will have seen that he's been visiting the affected areas in the United States that were hit by hurricane Ida just a few days ago that caused devastation. More than 50 Americans lost their lives. They lost it. So that's loss and damage from human induced climate change, and he accepts it. And now he is trying to pass a bill in the us Congress to tackle climate change along with other kinds of infrastructure in the United States of America. These are things that he originally was not convinced of, but the young people in the United States convinced him and they're pushing him and hopefully they will continue to do that. And in my scenario for 2051 they are successful or they were successful in changing the biggest economy in the world and putting it on a path towards development that is safe development and environmentally protective development. And a fossil fuel free development.

That is really the golden pathway that we need to develop for all countries going forward. Particularly the COP26 held in November 2021 was the pivotal moment in my view that shifted the rest of the world in that direction, in the positive direction, which eventually allowed us to solve the problem by 2051.

That's the first pillar, young people all over the world, everywhere, working at local level at national level and at global level. And. Inheriting and creating the world that they want to create and not just depending on their adult leaders to deliver who had up till then failed to do so. The second pillar of this success, I would say is amongst key leaders individual leaders matter a lot.

And having good leaders in some countries has been a very big factor in taking action, being a leader who does things and then persuades others to follow and join and do things. And I will say, that female heads of government have played a very, very key role in moving us forward. And I'll cite some examples from the past, and then some examples from the present, which I hope will be built on into the future.

In the original UN framework convention on climate change, a very key leader who brought the UN framework convention together was the then prime minister of the United Kingdom, Margaret Thatcher. Margaret Thatcher was a right-wing conservative politician. In general, her party is not a pro-climate-change-action party, but she herself had a science background.

She studied science in university. And when she saw the IPCC report, she understood the science. She understood what, you know, molecules of greenhouse gases, CO_2 and methane will do. She was a chemist herself. And she understood this was a global problem. And she was very instrumental in getting global leaders from around the world, including at that time, president Bush of the United States around the table to negotiate and agree the UN framework convention on climate change, which was a pivotal acceptance and action by global leaders.

Since then we also had chancellor Angela Merkel in Germany. She was the first president of COP1 in Berlin in Germany. I remember that many years ago. I was there myself. And since then she has been another leader again. She comes with a scientific background. She had an understanding of the science.

She didn't have to deny the science or have it explained to her. And she knew that this was a reality and she did what she could during her tenure, as a leader. First as the minister for environment. And then as the chancellor of Germany. Now, moving forward in this time of 2021 in the, the upcoming conference of parties.

I will name a few female leaders with whom I would ask everybody to keep in touch and keep an eye on. One of them is the prime minister of my country, Sheikh Hasina, who is currently leading a group of nearly 50 vulnerable countries called the climate vulnerable forum. And she will be going to Glasgow and representing them.

And she will be speaking on behalf of the vulnerable countries to keep 1.5 degrees in sight and to make sure that we also deliver on the a hundred billion dollars a year, which was promised. And we also deal with this new and upcoming problem of loss and damage from climate change, which unfortunately has become a reality.

At the same time, I would also like to ask you to keep an eye on the first minister of Scotland where the COP is going to be held. Not the prime minister of the UK, Boris Johnson. I don't really have much faith in him, but I do have faith in Nicola Sturgeon who is the first minister of Scotland. And Scotland actually has an independent policy on tackling climate change other than the United Kingdom. And it's much more progressive than the United Kingdom is. So keep an eye on Nicola Sturgeon. And then you have leaders like Jacinda Arden from New Zealand who has demonstrated in her leadership, particularly on dealing with COVID 19, that she is a leader head and shoulders above all the other leaders in every single country in the world.

She has been able to protect the citizens of New Zealand by taking scientific actions on time and with the consent of the people of her country. So female leaders, and there are many more to between between now and 2051, I think they will be pivotal. They will be the ones who will be able to change. They will make others change and they will persuade people to go along with them.

And then the third and final building block of this success in 2051 is my country Bangladesh. Bangladesh is perhaps the most vulnerable country to the impacts of climate change. It is now a country of 170 million people living in less than 150,000 square kilometres. One of the poorest countries in the world, one of the most vulnerable countries in the world, but at the same time becoming one of the most resilient countries in the world. And between now and 2051 Bangladesh will show the whole world how to tackle climate change. Not just deal with the impacts and manage the risk, but overcome the risk and overcome the impacts and become prosperous. And we are in the process of developing what we are calling our Mujib climate prosperity plan to deal with climate change. It's no longer just a resilience to climate change, but prosperity despite climate change. And I'll cite the example of Bangladesh, which is now in this year, 2021, celebrating 50 years of its existence as a country. 50 years ago, when we became a country, there were leading politicians like Mr. Henry Kissinger of the United States that predicted Bangladesh would die.

It would become a basket case. It would not survive. 50 years later. We are thriving. The whole country of Bangladesh is one of the leading developing countries in the whole world. And we will continue to do that. And a large part of that is investing in our young people, in our girls and in our boys. And they have already demonstrated their ability to lift the country up from a least developed country into a developing country over the next decades up to 2050.

We intend and plan to become a fully developed country based on our young girls and our young boys who are as bright and as energetic and as enthusiastic as any in the world. And we will not only help solve Bangladesh's problem, we will help solve the whole world's problems. Look to Bangladesh to be a world leader in the coming years and decades, and hopefully we will make that transition to 2051 and stay below 1.5 degrees and keep everybody safe. Thank you.

SEPTEMBER 18, 12 AM. VENUE: VIVARIUM

ABSTRACT
Early 21st century climate research and policy focused mainly on technological innovation to continue the status quo. Fundamental societal change remained absent and leaves us with the uncertainties of a world of 2.8°C warming. This article argues that we should have put more emphasis on the social and cultural aspects of transformation and thus paid more attention to sociological knowledge. By looking at the role of ideas and values, emotions and temporalities for climate inaction, I illustrate how thinking with the sociological imagination could have helped bridge the gaps between knowledge and action on climate change.

sociological imagination // climate change // socio-ecological transformation // techno-fix // value change

THE WORLD TODAY
The world we look at today is the world we have created upon pursuing a mainly technological path to transformation. It is a world of an average of 2.8°C of global warming. A world of many crises. Extreme weather events and novel diseases are no longer exceptional disasters but frequent events. Some places, such as small island states and those in hot climates, have become entirely uninhabitable for humans. Industrial production has decreased and supply with goods and services through the globalised economy has become increasingly difficult. Social inequalities have been amplified as the demand for energy to power modern technologies remains high, especially in countries of the so-called global North. Social inequalities across world regions, generations and social milieus have been amplified and, in part, escalated into social unrest, displacement, and armed conflict. In short, the future of humanity is as uncertain as ever.

To better understand how we got here and the path pursued, let me take you back to 1972 when the Club of Rome published its bestselling report "Limits to Growth". The research group around Dennis Meadows had used a dynamic systems model to calculate different models on the future of human civilisation. They identified five basic factors that determine – and thus limit – growth on Earth: Population, agricultural production, natural resources, industrial production and pollution. They came to the conclusion that if humanity kept pursuing economic

*   Rachel Carson Center for Environment and Society, Ludwig Maximilian University of Munich

growth without regard to environmental costs, global society would experience collapse, i.e. a sharp decline in both industrial production and human population within 50 years.

The study was met with controversy. Critics claimed the model had assumed too little natural resources and thus considered such a collapse unlikely. However, in the early 2020s when fires, floods and plagues unfolded at biblical extent, this confidence started to crumble. In an empirical comparison Dutch sustainability researcher Gaya Herrington (Herrington 2020) proved the projections by the Club of Rome were not only fairly accurate but even optimistic given historical data. Even doubling the resources assumed in the original report did not avoid collapse. On the contrary, with more resources available, incentives for change were reduced so business as usual could continue for longer, creating more pollution, and eventually agricultural out-put and human health deteriorated significantly (ibid.). However, even though scientists across disciplines (for many cf. IPCC 2018) called for fundamental change, we did not alter the deeper fabric of society. Instead, we put all our hopes in the innovative human spirit.

PATHS (NOT) TAKEN

The scenario pursued after the publication most closely resembles the "comprehensive technology" one. It represents the belief that humanity may simply innovate its way out of environmental constraints. It basically assumed that the transition to sustainable societies could be achieved entirely through technological innovation and that other societal changes would eventually follow. This idea was favoured by many stakeholders, because it did not require any fundamental shifts to the lifestyle of late modernity and the structure of neoliberal capitalism. This scenario did not show outright collapse, yet it harboured serious risks of decline, because the technology costs became so high that insufficient resource levels remained for agricultural production, health and education services. However, according to social scientists of the time, the idea that science could fix climate change was always inherently flawed.

To begin with, climate change is not a scientific but a social problem, and a "wicked" one at that (Grundmann 2016). When climate change first appeared on the political agenda, it was treated as a scientific problem akin to the ozone hole: a causal problem with an identifiable trigger that can simply be solved by addressing the trigger. However, in contrast to that, climate change is a multi-sectoral problem that reaches deep in the fabric of societies. It therefore also requires transformations of social systems, lifestyles and identities. Hence, the focus of early 21st century climate discourse on natural-scientific knowledge over social-scientific one was in itself part of the problem (Turnhout/Lahsen 2022). According to Mike Hulme (2014), technologies designed to control the climate (so-called "techno-fixes") are undesirable, ungovernable and unreliable due to their unpredictable dangerous side effects and the impossibility of a plausible and legitimate process to set up the world temperature. As such, the comprehensive technology path was always a risky one to pursue.

A more reliable path to a sustainable world would have been the "Stable World" scenario. In this scenario, humanity would have shifted priorities away from material consumption and industrial growth towards health and education services, pollution abatement and resource efficiency. Pursuing this path would have left humanity with the highest levels of welfare and best chances to avoid collapse. However, this would have required more fundamental changes of the values and ideas underlying social organisation (Meadows 1999, Göpel 2016) and was thus more readily dismissed by stakeholders at the time. To pursue that track, we should have tended more to questions about the good life and the values required for sustainable societies. This would have implied to broaden the scope of sustainability to cover the interrelated wellbeing of humans, nonhuman animals and nature and multispecies coexistence (Celermajer et al. 2021).

However, even though such a future would have been possible, we did not interrogate and readjust societal values and priorities accordingly and instead pursued a purely techno-scientific path to transformation. I argue that this was due to a lack of appreciation for sociological knowledge in climate research and policy at the time. In fact, the common understanding of the relationship between science and society at the time provided the legitimising grounds for that path. Research on climate-related transformation was predominantly based on the so-called information deficit model, i.e. the assumption of a causal relationship between information and action. It was presumed, once the public got more educated about climate change, behavioural and societal change would eventually follow. This idea is based on a rationalist model of human behaviour (Simis et al. 2016) and misrecognises the inherently political effects of knowledge production even when science seeks to take a neutral stance (Turnhout/Lahsen 2022). Based on such rationalist and positivist propositions, climate science and policy focussed largely on understanding human effects on biophysical systems of the earth while avoiding any engagement with the underlying social dynamics of climate change. We thus developed what Kari Norgaard (2018) calls "ecological imagination", while the environmentally damaging social structures and cultural norms underlying climate change remained unaddressed. Hence, sociological imagination would have been required to bridge that gap.

THINKING WITH SOCIOLOGICAL IMAGINATION

Indeed, sociological research shows that inaction on climate change was not due to a lack of knowledge or concern among the public, but a failure to connect this knowledge to everyday life (Norgaard 2011). The ability to connect individual troubles to larger societal structures can be described as "sociological imagination" (Mills 1959). Hence, it was not a lack of techno-scientific knowledge that slowed process on climate change, but a failure to translate this information into the "psychological, political, or moral implications that conventionally follow" (Cohen 2001, 8). Sociological thinking helps understand the social process behind this phenomenon, because keeping disturbing information at a distance is like "the elephant in the room" (Zerubavel 2006) – it takes a collective effort to ignore it. In the following sections, I sketch how thinking with the sociological imagination helps understand why fundamental change did not occur. I thereby focus on (1) an anthropocentric thought and value structure, (2) a particular emotional culture of hope and fear, and (3) a linear understanding of time dominant in Western societies.

IDEAS AND VALUES

Late modern societies were built on an anthropocentric worldview, i. e. one where humans are the central point of reference, and accordingly a value system that hierarchised other life forms according to their relevance to humans (cf. e.g. Nimmo 2011). This paradigm provided the grounds for all kinds of exclusion, exploitation and oppression of beings based on their otherness to the ideal of the human. It provided the legitimising framework for the exploitation of nature and nonhuman animals (cf. Bossert/Schlegel 2022) as well as for the Western imperial way of life that allowed to externalise the costs of a particular lifestyle from the global North into the global South and future generations (Brand/Wissen 2017, Lessenich 2019).

Thus, modern thought was inherently separating as it built on dualist distinctions between humans and nature, the material and the social, the body and the mind which were rendered essentially different. Hence, nature was considered a mere backdrop for human activity and other beings morally inferior (Braidotti 2019, Frost 2016). This thought structure is what allowed both extensive resource use without regard for environmental costs and the paradigm of control over nature underlying techno-fixes. Hence, sustainability was never to be achieved within this dualist thought structure and anthropocentric moral order. Thinking with sociological imagination would have allowed to untangle the interconnectedness of different power structures and modes of oppression and to work intersectionally towards socio-ecologically just societies.

EMOTIONS

The privilege of techno-scientific knowledge in climate discourse also represents a neglect for the role of emotions for societal change. Sociological research shows how emotions shape social order by motivating or inhibiting action (for many cf. Turner 1999). Social and cultural norms of emotion determine how people relate and respond to policy issues (Hochschild 1983). For example, a study on climate denial in Norway and the US showed that people were separating knowledge about climate change from their everyday lives in an effort to avoid troubling emotions (Norgaard 2011). We should have employed sociological imagination to better understand how emotions connect individual concerns with broader societal structures.

Emotions also affect societal structures by (re-)producing power structures, as research on emotions animating climate activist movements shows. While anger was more common among activists in the global South who thereby raised attention to inequalities and ascribed responsibility to the global North, hope and fear were more common in activist narratives in the global North (Kleres/Wettergren 2017). Fear has dominated Western environmental history from the early modern period when extreme weather was considered divine judgement, over colonialism where it reflected fear of unknown places to narratives of security evoked to bring climate change on the political agenda (cf. Dörries 2010). Narratives of fear, however, are problematic because they protect the status quo and generate distance and hostility rather than solidarity and community and openness for change (cf. Ahmed 2004). The second prominent narrative of hope is equally problematic in that it served the idea of the techno-fix (cf. Paterson 2017). The disposition to focus disproportionately on positive feelings common in Western culture and neoliberal capitalism (Head 2016) allowed to defer guilt and responsibility – in other world regions as well as in future generations.

TEMPORALITIES

Hence, my final argument addresses the role of temporalities for the failure to evoke fundamental change. The temporalities within which socio-ecological crises are perceived affect how we respond to them (cf. Fitz-Henry 2017). In late modern society, a linear understanding of history was dominant, which saw the future basically as a continuation of the past. Such understandings of time limit our ability to imagine alternative futures and lifestyles. We imagine our future lives as we have come to know it throughout our biography. Linear time conceptions evolved in line with the Christian orientation toward future redemption (cf. Ricoeur 1995). They thus deflect us from our moral presence in the here and now, which allows us to continue with harmful practices in the present without thinking about the consequences for the future (Rose 2004). The techno-scientific path to transformation was characterised by this kind of temporality. The conviction that humans could simply innovate out of this crisis served to legitimise the status quo while waiting for a technological deus ex machina to save us.

CONCLUSION

So, where does that leave the future of humanity? What can we hope for in a world where the ways we think, feel and value are in themselves part of the problem? Thinking with sociological imagination allows us to think beyond blind optimism in techno-fix and linear trajectories. It allows to tackle problematic power structures, question our cultural systems and imagine sustainable societies in terms of multispecies coexistence. Along these lines, we can think of hope as a transformative practice grounded in our relations (cf. Block 1959 in Anderson 2006). To unfold this transformative power, we need to culture an openness in our encounters with others, allow for the possibility to change our own ground and alter our sense of identity and belonging (ibid.). Ultimately, thinking with sociological imagination can help us to view socio-ecological change as a reconfiguration of human relationships with nature in a nonlinear fashion towards a world of multispecies coexistence. A stable world scenario was entirely possible, if only we had listened to all the sciences, as well as to the humanities. Today, even though the future is less clear upon the technological path we pursued, the sociological imagination is needed more than ever as the world around us is already changing rapidly.

REFERENCES

Ahmed, S. (2004). The Cultural Politics of Emotion. Edinburgh University Press.

Anderson, B. (2006). Becoming and Being Hopeful: Towards a New Theory of Affect. Environment and Planning D: Society and Space, 24(5), 733-752. https://doi/10.1068/d393t.

Bloch, E. (1959). Das Prinzip Hoffnung. Suhrkamp.

Brand, U., Wissen, M. (2017). Imperiale Lebensweise. Zur Ausbeutung von Mensch und Natur im globalen Kapitalismus. Oekom.

Bossert, L. N., Schlegel, L. M. (2022). Anthropocentrism in crisis. Why problems cannot be solved with the same mindset that created them. GAIA – Ecological Perspectives for Science and Society, 31(1), 14-18. https://doi.org/10.14512/gaia.31.1.5.

Braidotti, R. (2019). Posthuman knowledge. Polity Press.

Cohen, S. (2001). States of Denial: Knowing About Atrocities and Suffering. Polity Press.

Celermajer, D., Schlosberg, D., Rickards, L., Stewart-Harawira, M., Thaler, M., Tschakert, P., Verlie, B., Winter, C. (2021). Multispecies justice: theories, challenges, and a research agenda for environmental politics. Environmental Politics, 30(1-2), 119-140. https://doi.org/10.1080/09644016.2020.1827608.

Dörries, M. (2010). Climate catastrophes and fear. Wiley Interdisciplinary Reviews: Climate Change, 1(6), 885-890. https://doi.org/10.1002/wcc.79.

Fitz-Henry, E. (2017). Multiple temporalities and the nonhuman other. Environmental Humanities, 9(1), 1-17. https://doi.org/10.1215/22011919-3829109.

Frost, S. (2016). Biocultural creatures: Toward a new theory of the human. Duke University Press.

Göpel, M. (2016). The great mindshift: how a new economic paradigm and sustainability transformations go hand in hand (Vol. 2). Springer.

Grundmann, R. (2016). Climate change as a wicked social problem. Nature geoscience, 9(8), 562-563. https://doi.org/10.1038/ngeo2780.

Herrington, G. (2020). Update to limits to growth: Comparing the World3 model with empirical data. Journal of Industrial Ecology, 25(3), 614-626. https://doi.org/10.1111/jiec.13084.

Head, L. (2016). Hope and grief in the Anthropocene: Re-conceptualising human-nature relations. Routledge.

Hochschild, A.R. (1983). The Managed Heart: Commercialization of Human Feeling. University of California Pres.

Hulme, M. (2014). Can science fix climate change? A case against climate engineering. John Wiley & Sons.

Kleres, J., Wettergren, Å. (2017). Fear, hope, anger, and guilt in climate activism. Social Move-ment Studies, 16(5), 507-519. https://doi.org/10.1080/14742837.2017.1344546.

Lessenich, S. (2019). Living Well at Others' Expense: The Hidden Costs of Western Prosperity. Polity Press.

Meadows, D. H., Meadows, D. H., Randers, J., Behrens III, W. W. (1972). The limits to growth: a report to the club of Rome.

Meadows, D. (1999). Leverage points: Places to intervene in a system. The Sustainability Institute.

Mills, C. W. (1959). The sociological imagination. Oxford University Press.

Nimmo, R. (2011). The making of the human: Anthropocentrism in modern social thought. In R. Boddice (ed.), Anthropocentrism: Human, Animals, Environments (59-80). Brill.

Norgaard, K. M. (2011). Living in denial: Climate change, emotions, and everyday life. MIT Press.

Norgaard, K. M. (2018). The sociological imagination in a time of climate change. Global and Planetary Change, 163, 171-176. https://doi.org/10.1016/j.gloplacha.2017.09.018.

Norgaard, K. M., Reed, R. (2017). Emotional impacts of environmental decline: What can Native cosmologies teach sociology about emotions and environmental justice? Theory and Society, 46(6), 463-495, https://doi.org/10.1007/s11186-017-9302-6.

International Panel on Climate Change (2018): Special Report: Global Warming of 1.5°C.

Paterson, M. (2017). The sociological imagination of climate futures. In P. Wapner & Hilal Elver (eds.), Reimagining Climate Change (14-28). Routledge, 14-28.

Ricoeur, P. (1995). Figuring the sacred: Religion, narrative, and imagination. Fortress Press.

Rose, D. B. (2004). Reports from a wild country: Ethics for decolonisation. UNSW

Press.

Simis, M. J., Madden, H., Cacciatore, M. A., Yeo, S. K. (2016). The lure of rationality: Why does the deficit model persist in science communication? Public understanding of science, 25(4), 400-414. https://doi.org/10.1177%2F0963662516629749.

Turner, J. H. (1999). Toward a general sociological theory of emotions, Journal for the Theory of Social Behaviour, 29(2), 0021–8308

Turnhout, E., Lahsen, M. (2022). Transforming environmental research to avoid tragedy. Climate and Development. https://doi.org/10.1080/17565529.2022.2062287.

Willox, A. C. (2012). Climate change as the work of mourning. Ethics & the Environment, 17(2), 137-164. https://doi.org/10.2979/ethicsenviro.17.2.137.

Zerubavel, E. (2006). The elephant in the room: Silence and denial in everyday life. Oxford University Press.

SEPTEMBER 18, 3 PM. VENUE: MYCELIUM

Thank you for the invitation to T2051MCC. I am sending this message from my protective bubble – and, in keeping with the theme of the conference of 'looking back to 2021'– I have chosen to use a very out-of-date format [the zoom powerpoint] – I hope your technical systems can cope.

The focus of this conference is on the early 2020s and the years in which the Paris Agreement was meant to come into effect. This paper and visual presentation will give a brief review of geoengineering scenarios – before and after 2021– to learn what we might have anticipated better. It will do this via an archive of scenarios: models, patents, sketches, stories and micro-biospheres – miniature planet B's.

Looking back from 2051 – did we tell the right stories? Did we understand the dangers of a single story? Or the fallacies of narratives of scaling up and battening down? Did we mess everything up with speculative promises? Were we immersed in the wrong kind of speculative fiction?

> ...They still hung suspended between catastrophe and paradise, spinning bluely in space like some terrible telenovela. Scheherazade was Earth's muse, it seemed; it was just one damn thing after another, always one more cliffhanger, clinging to life and sanity by the skin of one's teeth...'[1]

SCHEHERAZADE IS EARTH'S MUSE.

In the run up to COP21 in Paris in 2015, the Intergovernmental Panel on Climate Change (IPCC) considered more than a thousand scenarios of future climate change, the majority of which led to potentially catastrophic increases beyond 2 degrees average global warming.[2] Following Paris, the IPCC produced a special report based on the 1.5 threshold. All of the scenarios modelling average global warming not exceeding 1.5°C relied on what were called at the time negative emissions (NETs) or carbon dioxide removal technologies (CDR). This brought them into the orbit of a whole range of planetary modification or geoengineering strategies that at the time were considered economically unviable, largely speculative, untested to scale,

1   Kim Stanley Robinson, 2312 (London: Orbit , 2013); p.305.
2   Prior to 2015, international climate policy under the United Nations Framework Convention on Climate Change focused on the goal of keeping the global-mean temperature increase below 2°C relative to pre-industrial levels. The Paris Agreement reset this long-term goal to holding the increase well below 2°C and pursuing efforts to limit it to 1.5 °C (Paris Agreement, 2015); see also Elizabeth Kolbert (2021) Under a White Sky. The Nature of the Future. The Bodley Head; p. 155.

COP21 // IPCC // Paris Agreement NETs // CDR
planetary modification // geoengineering
de-carbonisation // James Hansen // GISS climate models
Pinatubo scenarios // ozone hole

ungovernable and potentially devastating to ecosystems and climates. At the time it seemed futile to hope for radical de-carbonisation, and dangerous to depend on other grand-scale technofixes.

Taken together, geoengineering schemes proposed bringing experiments which had hitherto been confined to laboratories and computer models to a planetary scale – to actually transform the oceans, whiten the clouds, shield the Sun, bury the sky, and fix the Earth. While such projects veered between the sublime and the ridiculous, feasible and fantastic, – depending on one's point of view – they typically involved mundane ('of the Earth') materials and technologies: mirrors, pipes and pumps, iron dust, sulphate or diamond particles, pulverised rock. Yet pushed around a sandbox Earth, these materials could bring about massive changes – but would they save us, or destroy us – and was there any way to model this accurately before we locked ourselves into a planet–sized experiment with no off-switch?[3]

1991 'PINATUBO – P_N'

Sixty years ago, "On June 15, 1991, nature launched her own great climate experiment".[4] This is how climate scientist James Hansen described the eruption of Mt. Pinatubo in the Philippines. The volcanic explosion threw up an enormous cloud of ash, dust and gas, estimated as having injected 10 million tons of sulphur dioxide into the stratosphere at heights of over 25 km. The cloud drifted across the world and while the dust subsided the sulphur dioxide aerosol particles lingered, reflecting sunlight, and lowering average global temperatures by 0.5°C. This global cooling event suggested an accidental planetary thermostat – thus conspiring with and inspiring planetary modification schemes.

Hansen saw the eruption of Pinatubo as an opportunity to test GISS climate models, by running so-called 'Pinatubo scenarios'. These provided estimates of the likelihood of severe winter in Moscow, the delay to the date of cherry blossoming in Tokyo, and, predicted a return

3   See R. Tyszczuk, Provisional Cities: Cautionary Tales for the Anthropocene (Routledge, 2018); Chapter 6 'Monster Earth'.
4   James Hansen, Andrew Lacis, Reto Ruedy and Makiko Sato, "Potential Climate Impact of Mount Pinatubo Eruption" Geophysical Research Letters Vol 19. No. 2 Pp. 215–218, January 24 1992.

to record warm levels in the late 1990s. The stratospheric sulphate aerosols also caused excessive thinning of the ozone hole over Antarctica. Pinatubo's changing of the climate occurred in the context of increasing alarm – for the year that Pinatubo cooled the Earth was the year that the United Nations Framework Convention on Climate Change (UNFCCC) was introduced at the first Earth Summit, Rio de Janeiro, 1992.

As science journalist Oliver Morton observed, 'It's hardly surprising that some people wondered whether Pinatubo could be more than an experiment – whether it could, instead, be a *prototype*.'[5]

2001 'PLAN B'

In the first decade of the 21st century geoengineering – defined by the Royal Society as: 'the deliberate large-scale manipulation of the planetary environment in order to counteract anthropogenic climate change.'[6] – was established as a viable process of intentional Earth alteration even as – or precisely because – it reified the planet as an object of experimentation and control. It started to be commonly referred to as re-setting Earth's thermostat.[7] The model for averting the climate emergency was the Pinatubo eruption. Atmospheric chemist Paul Crutzen argued that it was possible to simulate the 'volcano loading effect' using balloons and artillery guns for stratospheric aerosol injections.[8] He pointed out that human activity was already putting more than 100 million tons of sulphur dioxide into the sky every year — the equivalent of 10 Pinatubos.

The 'largely speculative and unproven'[9] geoengineering technologies promised to either repair, or stabilise the Earth's climate, and get human societies out of the mess they had made. In part as a result of

5   Oliver Morton, The Planet Remade: How Geoengineering Could Change the World (London: Granta, 2015); p. 99.
6   John Shepherd et al. (Ken Caldeira, Joanna Haigh, David Keith, Brian Launder, Georgina Mace, Gordon MacKerron, John Pyle, Steve Rayner and Catherine Redgwell), "Geo-engineering the Climate. Science, Governance and Uncertainty," in The Royal Society, RS Policy document 10/09 Issued: September 2009 RS1636.
7   See R.Tyszczuk, 'Thermostat' in M. Grosskaufmanis (ed.) Together and Apart, Latvian Pavilion Catalogue Venice Biennale 2018.
8   Crutzen, Paul J., "Albedo Enhancement by Stratospheric Sulfur Injections: A Contribution to Resolve a Policy Dilemma? An Editorial Essay" in Climatic Change 2006 77 211–219.
9 ' 17. Geo-engineering options, such as ocean fertilisation to remove CO_2 directly from the atmosphere, or blocking sunlight by bringing material into the upper atmosphere, remain largely speculative and unproven, and with the risk of unknown side-effects. Reliable cost estimates for these options have not been published (medium agreement, limited evidence) [11.2].' IPCC (2007)'Contribution of Working Group III to the Fourth Assessment Report of the Intergovernmental Panel on Climate Change: Summary for Policymakers'; p. 15.

exasperation at the slow progress of the 'Plan A' of internationally coordinated emissions cuts, geoengineering started to be considered as 'Plan B'. Everyone knew that the stakes were high. As the familiar activist slogan asserted: *There is no Planet B.*There remained unease, misapprehension, and downright fear when it came to geoengineering. There was suspicion that societies would come to depend on it. Many doubted that the proposals would work, and were concerned about negative and unintended consequences, reconfiguring and de-stabilising regional and local climates in unprecedented ways. There was fear of hostile uses of climate control and the potential for new political and security emergencies. Deployment, it was argued, required a 'Manhattan Project scale of activity'.[10] Moreover, the task of convening appropriate and responsive modes of geoengineering governance on a fractious planet seemed impossible. In spite of all of this, some considered geoengineering as, 'a bad idea whose time ha[d] come'. [11]

2011 'LABORATORY EARTH'
In 2014 the IPCC's 5th Assessment Report had presented scenarios of up to 6 degrees of climate change by 2100: a world where most of the planetary surface was uninhabitable, the oceans had stratified, and mass species extinctions had taken place. At the same time, its 'Summary for Policymakers', had concluded with a terse warning about the real-world implementation of geoengineering schemes, and their side effects and long-term consequences on a global scale.[12]

Yet as commercial interests aligned with scenarios of a desperate world, many businesses, including oil companies Shell and ConocoPhillips, and individuals such as Bill Gates funded geoengineering research. The decade also saw a rush of private-led

10 See Geoengineering II: The Scientific Basis and Engineering Challenges' US Congress 111 (2010).
11 Eli Kintisch, Hack the Planet (John Wiley & Sons, 2010); see also Robock, Alan, "20 Reasons Why Geo-Engineering May Be a Bad Idea. Carbon Dioxide Emissions Are Rising so Fast That Some Scientists Are Seriously Considering Putting Earth on Life Support as a Last Resort. but Is This Cure Worse Than the Disease?" in Bulletin of the Atomic Scientists May/June 2008 Vol. 64 No. 2; pp. 14–18.
12 IPCC (2014) 'Climate Change 2014. Synthesis Report. Summary for Policymakers'; see also https://www.theguardian.com/environment/planet-oz/2014/aug/04/geoengineering-the-earths-climate-sends-policy-debate-down-a-curious-rabbit-hole'

patents for geoengineering technologies – which in itself indicated that the climate was no longer considered a commons, and even more, that climate instability could turn a profit. Many climate researchers expressed concern at such proposals to fix the Earth: "[A]s if we know enough to install and begin to operate a 'global thermostat.' Truly this qualifies as monstrous hubris."[13] Climate researcher Mike Hulme argued that "[t]he technology was ungovernable :... ' I find it hard to envisage any scenario in which the world's nations will agree to a thermostat in the sky."[14]

In her book, *This Changes Everything,* Naomi Klein warned that advocating geoengineering research would lead to implementation. She expressed horror at the prospect of a 'Monster Earth' — a toxic mix of geo-engineering projects gone awry: 'A grim picture emerges. Nothing on Earth would be outside the reach of humanity's fallible machines, or even fully outside at all. We would have a roof, not a sky — a milky, geoengineered ceiling gazing down on a dying acidifying sea.'[15] In other words, there was concern that we could not simply lock the door of *laboratory Earth,* and walk away — we would be the experiment.

2021 'UNDER THE DOME'
Across 2020 and 2021, the vast unplanned global experiment of the Covid-19 pandemic took place. Many climate commentators and researchers wondered if the time of the pandemic was a rehearsal for the greater challenges, not only of impending climate catastrophe, but also the far-reaching disruptions accompanying system transformation.

Even while 'pandemic politics' provided insights on human capacity for rapid and drastic action on a global scale[16], the record carbon dioxide levels in the atmosphere in 2021 reinforced the view that people power would never be enough to reduce emissions. Moreover, the extreme weather in this period – the heat domes, droughts, wildfires, floods, hurricanes and record wet bulb temperatures could not be ignored.

13 Clive Hamilton, Earth Masters: The Dawn of the Age of Climate Engineering (New Haven and London: Yale University Press, 2013).
14 David Keith and Mike Hulme, "Climate Science: Can Geo-engineering Save the World? Climate Professors Mike Hulme and David Keith go Head to Head over Whether Climate Engineering Could Provide a Solution to Climate Change" from The Guardian, 29 November 2013; http://www.theguardian.com/sustainable-business/blog/climate-science-geo-engineering-save-world.
15 Naomi Klein, This Changes Everything: Capitalism vs. the Climate (London: Allen Lane, 2014); p. 260.
16 H. Buck, O. Geden, M. Sugiyama and O. Corry 'Pandemic politics — lessons for solar geoengineering' Communications Earth and Environment 1, Article number: 16 (2020)

Covid-19 pandemic // heat domes // wet bulb //
COP26 // moral hazard // Earth systems
Mars mission // Climate Action Coalition

The delayed COP26 Climate conference in Glasgow in 2021 came in the wake of a decade of attempts at whole earth climate governance, characterised by global climate modelling, a focus on technological and market-led solutions, and aspirational, although not binding international agreements on reducing emissions. More drastic geoengineering approaches, those beyond carbon removal, were moved to the top of the agenda, framed both as an emergency measure and a stopgap approach[17] to buy time for mitigation.[18] Concerns of moral hazard were put aside. The signatories to the Glasgow Accord conceded that the risk of mitigation complacency and decreased emissions cuts did not outweigh the benefits of helping millions of people survive increasingly brutal temperatures. Scenario analysis combining climate science, impact and integrated assessment gained even more prominence.[19] However, the mechanism for holding politicians and states accountable to the goals established in multilateral UNFCCC processes– in any scenario – had yet to be developed. By 2030 emissions were supposed to have met the global targets – bending, flattening, even reversing the warming trajectories. Part of the issue with what happened next was the assumed fiction that we could somehow 'track the metrics'[20] of Earth systems, and 'manage the trajectories' of climate change, and that things would go to plan...

2031 'PLANET B'
2031 marked the move to Plan B – the beginning of 20 years of proliferating experiments: miniature eruptions, extractions, plantings and burials, in attempts to pause climate disruptions. Rather than a concerted effort, however – this was largely unregulated. The world was stuck in a fragile and volatile system of nation states – and no one knew – *and we still don't know* – exactly what the others were doing.

17 Buck, H. J., Martin, L. J. & Geden, O. et al. Evaluating the efficacy and equity of environmental stopgap measures. Nat. Sustain. 3, 499–504 (2020).
18 Talberg, A., Thomas, S., Christoff, P. & Karoly, D. How geoengineering scenarios frame assumptions and create expectations. Sustain. Sci. 13, 1093–1104 (2018).
19 Sugiyama, M., Arino, Y., Kosugi, T., Kurosawa, A. & Watanabe, S. Next steps in geoengineering scenario research: limited deployment scenarios and beyond. Climate Policy 18, 681–689 (2018).
20 H. Buck, O. Geden, M. Sugiyama and O. Corry 'Pandemic politics — lessons for solar geoengineering' Communications Earth and Environment 1, Article number: 16 (2020)

China's 2033 Mars mission was indefinitely postponed while it redirected state funds to geoengineering initiatives. The Climate Action Coalition, including, prominently, India, Bangladesh, Egypt and Nigeria, that shared both vulnerability to extreme climate disruption and high levels of adaptation know-how, initiated an incremental programme of hybrid geoengineering and ecosystem management. The Nordic nations took the lead in solar radiation management –considered the best chance of buying time, and embarked on a series of proxy-volcanic eruptions based on the Harvard ScopEx project.[21] Inevitably different states, corporations, and individuals had their own names for their various schemes – and the media toyed with the usual monikers to describe the global state of affairs: *Operation Earth; Mission Possible, Manhattan Projected* – but it was the more collective and colloquial Planet B that stuck. News headlines provoked the questions: *What on Earth? What is Planet B?*

In 2038, Alan Robock, former leader of the Geoengineering Model Intercomparison Project (GeoMIP), published a trenchant update to his seminal 2008 article, titled '20 reasons why geoengineering may be a bad idea'. This time it expanded to 40 entries. Numbers 1-20 were revisited, with number 1 being 'disruption to rainfall causing massive drought in Asia and Africa' – which had precipitated a colossal human tragedy. Number 24 indicated conflicts between countries; number 28 was, 'do humans have the right to do this?'[22] Number 30 noted the collapse of the Paris Agreement on account of the inability to deliver collective action[23], numbers 31 –35 listed a series of localised, regional and global physical effects, including disruptions to El Niño and El Niña, destruction of species habitats, and the disappearance of summer Arctic sea ice[24]; numbers 36–39 drew attention to industrial espionage, ensuing patent wars, financial catastrophe and insurance racketeering; finally, number 40 asked: *What if we got it wrong?*

2041 'GEOTINKERING'

The 2040s was a mess – a decade of climate interventions and interruptions that could be described, at best, as geotinkering... No-one

21 Stratospheric Controlled Perturbation or ScopEX project by Harvard scientists David Keith and Frank Keutsch: https://grist.org/science/who-gets-to-decide-if-we-study-solar-geoengineering-after-the-scopex-project-canceled/; see also Elizabeth Kolbert (2021) Under a White Sky. The Nature of the Future. The Bodley Head; p. 182
22 Elizabeth Kolbert (2021) Under a White Sky. The Nature of the Future. The Bodley Head; p. 181.
23 https://insideclimatenews.org/news/28072021/pairs-agreement-success-failure/
24 https://www.nationalgeographic.com/science/article/arctic-summer-sea-ice-could-be-gone-by-2035

ScopEx // GeoMIP // El Niño and El Niña // Arctic Sea Ice geotinkering // Precautionary Principle // termination shock Year without a Summer // SAILS // Climate Repair

wanted to talk about Paris, Pinatubo, or Precautionary Principles... it was way too late for that... Various experiments initiated in the 2030s were (and are) still ongoing – technofixes that needed to keep on fixing. No-one was prepared to risk the termination shock – or potentially catastrophic rebound effect– that climate models had predicted. Years without Winters were followed by Years with Strange Summers. As anticipated, the sky turned milky and sunsets glowed red, and the human catastrophe escalated.

If the previous decades of climate inaction had more or less guaranteed the emergency mandate and interventionist policies, it was quickly realised that commitment to any planetary modification schemes was irreversible. In other words, maintenance was required.[25] This also looked a lot like extending business as usual when it came to the generation of new market opportunities of carbon management and climate risk.

An immense infrastructure of power plants, capture facilities, and pipelines and wells was required for carbon removal at scale.[26] The fossil fuel industry doubled down on repurposing its technologies of extraction to try pumping out the meltwater from beneath glaciers in Greenland and Antarctica to stave off sea level rise. It was a simple equation – the less sea rise the better for its shareholders, surely. The aeronautical industry developed a fleet of high altitude craft, based on SAILS (or Stratospheric Aerosol Injection Lofter's) for the job of constantly replenishing sulphate or diamond particles sprayed into the sky.[27] The UK's Centre for Climate Repair, embarked in 2045 on its ambitious Gates Foundation project of 'marine cloud brightening' to 're-freeze' the Arctic. [28]

The question on everyone's lips: What did the future have in store?

25 Pak-Hang Wong (2014) 'Maintenance Required: The Ethics of Geoengineering and Post-Implementation Scenarios', Ethics, Policy & Environment, 17:2, 186-191.
26 See for example, Holly Jean Buck, (2020) ' How to decolonise the atmosphere' Progressive International 22.06.2020; https://progressive.international/blueprint/46253391-5b3d-4e68-bd3f-d53dc54180fd-holly-jean-buck-how-to-decolonize-the-atmosphere/en
27 See Wake Smith and Gernot Wagner (2018) 'Stratospheric aerosol injection tactics and costs in the first 15 years of deployment', Environmental Research Letters 13 124001; see also Elizabeth Kolbert (2021) Under a White Sky. The Nature of the Future. The Bodley Head; pp. 179–181.
28 See: https://www.theguardian.com/science/2021/jun/20/head-of-independent-sage-to-launch-international-climate-change-group

2051 '1001 SCENARIOS'

It's 2051. This is, and was, the future *now*.

It has taken us this long to acknowledge that the planet is not a machine that can be safely reconfigured. We have learnt the hard way that the Earth's systems cannot be controlled as if adjusting a planetary thermostat between threshold levels of 1.5 or 2 degrees of warming.[29]

One of the most worrying consequences of geoengineering and terraforming – or, 'fixing the Earth' – has proven to be the way the adoption of these ideas, tools and technologies threatens to alter much more than the physical parameters of a habitable planet. While changing climatic circumstances on Earth have driven many to consider ever more audacious acts of Earth shaping and recomposing, they have at the same time provoked a massive re-describing of human and non-human relations.

It was always the shaping of these relations that was at stake. And it was always the human communities, distant in space and time from the places where power was held, that suffered the burden of anthropogenic climate catastrophe. The challenge is not just about inventing or refining modes of whole earth intervention or governance, or of introducing more collaborative geoengineering.[30] It is about paying attention to the shifts in the human capacity for climate justice, cooperation, restraint, and respect in an increasingly precarious world.[31]

Living on planet Earth, or within our protective bubbles, calls for the kinds of improvised adjustments that recognise Earth's processes as always escaping human efforts to stabilise, restore or secure them. This is not about resisting change or future-proofing. It is about the collective imagination required for crafting more humble futures of coexistence, care and refuge. It is also about making room for acts of hospitality and generosity, among the infrastructuring practices that grapple with planetary turbulence and unsettlement. The challenge is both how to 'stay with the trouble' *and* 'change the story' (Haraway, 2016). And for this we still need myriad, multiple, scenarios that *rehearse the world otherwise*.

29 See R. Tyszczuk, 'Thermostat' in M. Grosskaufmanis (ed.) Together and Apart, Latvian Pavilion Catalogue Venice Biennale 2018.

30 See Holly Jean Buck,(2019) After Geoengineering; Climate Tragedy, Repair, and Restoration. Verso Books.

31 See R. Tyszczuk, 'Times of Urgencies: Speculative improvisations for the Anthropocene' in K. Facer, J. Siebers and B. Smith (eds.) Time as Method. Working with time in qualitative research: case studies, theory and practice (Routledge, 2022).

terraforming // climate catastrophe //
collaborative geoengineering // infrastructuring practices

1001 scenarios for a troubled Earth, is accompanied by a selection of micro-biospheres – miniature planet B's. These are artefacts made and unmade during research on scenarios of climate change. They are assemblies: shape-shifting between seemingly incompatible scales, ranging from models of Earth systems to the quirks of human domesticity. These micro-biospheres are redolent of emergency domes, spaceships, laboratories and proving grounds and the giant biospheric experiment that is Earth in the Anthropocene. They are analogues: serving as proxies for the terraforming themes that weave through the scenarios and at the same time old-school counterparts to a digital knowledge world. These little worlds speak to a sense of urgency and influence but also, paradoxically, a sense of insignificance.

p. 110, fig. 1: Planet B – micro-biosphere, Renata Tyszczuk, 2021

p. 110, fig. 2: Weather Chart – micro-biosphere, Renata Tyszczuk, 2018

p. 110, fig. 3: Pinatubo III – micro-biosphere, Renata Tyszczuk, 2018

p. 111, fig. 4: Nine Chairs to the Moon – micro-biosphere, Renata Tyszczuk, 2018

p. 112, fig. 5: Frigidaire – micro-biosphere, Renata Tyszczuk, 2018

p. 112, fig. 6: Toast – micro-biosphere, Renata Tyszczuk, 2018

p. 112, fig. 7: Mineshaft – micro-biosphere, Renata Tyszczuk, 2021

p. 113, fig. 8: Strange Weather – micro-biosphere, Renata Tyszczuk, 2021

p. 113, fig. 9: Carbon Capture – micro-biosphere, Renata Tyszczuk, 2021

p. 112, fig. 10: Smoky Fog – micro-biosphere, Renata Tyszczuk, 2018

p. 113, fig. 11: Pinatubo III & Nine Chairs to the Moon – micro-biosphere, Renata Tyszczuk, 2018

p. 113, fig. 12: Micro-Biospheres installation, Renata Tyszczuk, 2018, Royal Geographical Society (RGS) London

REFERENCES

Borunda, A. (2020) 'Arctic summer sea ice could disappear as early as 2035', National Geographic, 13 August. Available at: https://www.nationalgeographic.com/science/article/arctic-summer-sea-ice-could-be-gone-by-2035.

Buck, H. (2020) 'how to Decolonize the Atmosphere', Progressive Internationale, 22 June. Available at: https://progressive.international/blueprint/46253391-5b3d-4e68-bd3f-d53dc54180fd-holly-jean-buck-how-to-decolonize-the-atmosphere/en.

Buck, H. et al. (2020) 'Pandemic politics — lessons for solar geoengineering', Communications Earth & Environment, 1(1), p. 16. Available at: https://doi.org/10.1038/s43247-020-00018-1.

Buck, H.J. (2019) After geoengineering: climate tragedy, repair, and restoration. London; New York: Verso Books.

Buck, H.J. et al. (2020) 'Evaluating the efficacy and equity of environmental stopgap measures', Nature Sustainability, 3(7), pp. 499–504. Available at: https://doi.org/10.1038/s41893-020-0497-6.

Crutzen, P.J. (2006) 'Albedo Enhancement by Stratospheric Sulfur Injections: A Contribution to Resolve a Policy Dilemma?', Climatic Change, 77(3–4), p. 211. Available at: https://doi.org/10.1007/s10584-006-9101-y.

Facer, K., Siebers, J.I. and Smith, B. (eds) (2022) Working with time in qualitative research: case studies, theory and practice. London; New York, NY: Routledge, Taylor & Francis Group (Routledge research in anticipation and futures).

Hamilton, C. (2013) Earthmasters: the dawn of the age of climate engineering. New Haven and London: Yale University Press.

Hansen, J. et al. (1992) 'Potential climate impact of Mount Pinatubo eruption', Geophysical Research Letters, 19(2), pp. 215–218. Available at: https://doi.org/10.1029/91GL02788.

Hulme, M. and Keith, D. (2013) 'Climate Science: Can Geo-engineering Save the World? Climate Professors Mike Hulme and David Keith go Head to Head over Whether Climate Engineering Could Provide a Solution to Climate Change', The Guardian, 29 November. Available at: https://www.theguardian.com/sustainable-business/blog/climate-science-geo-engineering-save-world.

Kintisch, E. (2010) Hack the planet: science's best hope-- or worst nightmare-- for averting climate catastrophe. Hoboken, N.J: Wiley.

Klein, N. (2014) This changes everything: capitalism vs. the climate. London: Allen Lane.

Kolbert, E. (2021) Under a white sky: the nature of the future. First edition. New York: Crown.

Kusnetz, N. (2021) 'Why the Paris Climate Agreement Might be Doomed to Fail', Inside Climate News, 28 July. Available at: https://insideclimatenews.org/news/28072021/pairs-agreement-success-failure/.

Morton, O. (2015) The planet remade: how geoengineering could change the world. Princeton Oxford: Princeton University Press.

Pachauri, R.K. and IPCC (eds) (2008) Climate change 2007: contribution of ... to the fourth assessment report of the Intergovernmental Panel on Climate Change. 4: Synthesis report: [a report of the Intergovernmental Panel on Climate Change] / ed. by Rajendra K. Pachauri. Geneva: IPCC.

Pachauri, R.K., Mayer, L. and Intergovernmental Panel on Climate Change (eds) (2015) Climate change 2014: synthesis report. Geneva, Switzerland: Intergovernmental Panel on Climate Change.

Readfearn, G. (2014) 'Geoengineering the Earth's climate sends policy debate down a curious rabbit hole: Many of the world's major scientific establishments are discussing the concept of modifying the Earth's climate to offset global warming', The Guardian, 4 August. Available at: https://www.theguardian.com/environment/planet-oz/2014/aug/04/geoengineering-the-earths-climate-sends-policy-debate-down-a-curious-rabbit-hole.

Robinson, K.S. (2013) 2312. First oversize mass market edition. London: Orbit.

Robock, A., Jerch, K. and Bunzl, M. (2008) '20 reasons why geoengineering may be a bad idea', Bulletin of the Atomic Scientists, 64(2), pp. 14–59. Available at: https://doi.org/10.1080/00963402.2008.11461140.

Sheperd, J. et al. (2009) Geoengineering the climate: science, governance and uncertainty. London: Royal Society.

Smith, W. and Wagner, G. (2018) 'Stratospheric aerosol injection tactics and costs in the first 15 years of deployment', Environmental Research Letters, 13(12), p. 124001. Available at: https://doi.org/10.1088/1748-9326/aae98d.

Sugiyama, M. et al. (2018) 'Next steps in geoengineering scenario research: limited deployment scenarios and beyond', Climate Policy, 18(6), pp. 681–689. Available at: https://doi.org/10.1080/14693062.2017.1323721.

Talberg, A. et al. (2018) 'How geoengineering scenarios frame assumptions and create expectations', Sustainability Science, 13(4), pp. 1093–1104. Available at: https://doi.org/10.1007/s11625-018-0527-8.

Tyszczuk, R. (2018a) Provisional Cities: Cautionary Tales for the Anthropocene. 1st edn. First Edition. | New York: Routledge, [2018] | Series: Studies in architecture series: Routledge. Available at: https://doi.org/10.4324/9781315602769.

Tyszczuk, R. (2018b) 'Thermostat', Catalogue Venice Bienniale 2018 [Preprint]. Edited by M. Groskaufmanis.

Tyszczuk, R. (2021) 'Times of urgencies: Scenarios as speculative improvisations for the Anthropocene', in J.I. Siebers and B. Smith (eds) Working with Time in Qualitative Research: case studies, theory and practice. 1st edn. Routledge.

United States (ed.) (2010) Geoengineering, parts I, II, and III: hearing before the Committee on Science and Technology, House of Representatives, One Hundred Eleventh Congress, first session and second session, November 5, 2009, February 4, 2010, and March 18, 2010. Washington: U.S. G.P.O.

Watts, J. (2021) 'Head of Independent Sage to launch international climate change group', The Guardian, 20 June. Available at: https://www.theguardian.com/science/2021/jun/20/head-of-independent-sage-to-launch-international-climate-change-group.

Wong, P.-H. (2014) 'Maintenance Required: The Ethics of Geoengineering and Post-Implementation Scenarios', Ethics, Policy & Environment, 17(2), pp. 186–191. Available at: https://doi.org/10.1080/21550085.2014.926090.

SEPTEMBER 18, 3 PM. VENUE: VIVARIUM

PROLOGUE
In 2051, the world is an uncomfortable place to live in. Just as international institutions, NGOs and scientists have modelled and predicted around the 2020s, global temperatures have risen up to almost 3°C above the pre-industrialised average (Climate Action Tracker, 2021). What is interesting is the fact, that even when the data was unambiguously clear[2] and extreme weather events started to affect even the modern-capitalist countries of the global north, mankind couldn't agree on the large-scale transformation processes required to minimise the effects of the climate catastrophe – just as Ian Cook noted 30 years ago, "political institutions are by nature unable to initiate radical social transformations of the type required to divert from the trajectory toward humanity's final hundred years" (Cook, 2020, p. 4). Cook analysed political, institutional, societal, and economic factors that would prevent fundamental change to happen, thus keeping us on the path towards what he called the Final Hundred Years of Humanity.

For me, the 2051 Munich Climate Conference is therefore an interesting opportunity to investigate different politics and processes from around the 2020s which allowed the window of opportunity to close and bring us to the point where we are today. My contribution will analyse the visual climate discourse and how it helped normalising what should have rung all alarm bells – so, I'll connect to the conference hub now:

...connecting...initialising...
...connected...start transmission...

INTRODUCTION
We almost had it. The image that could have massively supported a global policy change in a time when humanity still would have had time to act. The image that made all the difference, standing out among the generic visual representations of industrial smokestacks, polar bears

1   I would like to thank Sebastian Schindler for his useful comments on the paper's underlying idea and his creative thought-provoking impulses. I would also like to thank the team of Büro Grandezza e.V. for their comments and input during the research phase.
2   The IPCC Report of 2021 for example stated that the world's "climate system is rapidly changing, overwhelmingly due to human influence" Masson-Delmotte, V., P. Zhai, A. Pirani, S. , L. Connors, C. P., S. Berger, N. Caud, Y. Chen, L. Goldfarb, M. I. Gomis, M. Huang, K. Leitzell, E. Lonnoy, J. B. , & R. Matthews, T. K. M., T. Waterfield, O. Yelekçi,

on drifting ice flows and people from developing countries affected or even displaced and killed by catastrophic weather events and other consequences of the climate catastrophe. It is the image that could have defined our collective memory in Susan Sontag's sense that it defined our understanding of what was important at this moment in time. The image that helped to "lock the story in our minds" (Sontag, 2003, p. 86) that we had to act now collectively before it is too late. I will show and contextualise this image at the end of my contribution.[3]

There is little dissent in the literature that images play a large role in shaping stories, ideas and narratives. Visual representations of politics and political events are a significant part of our collective memory including all types of events from 9/11 to catastrophic wildfires in Australia and California. Our world is of almost complete visual making. With the dramatic rise of digital communication and social media platforms shortly after the turn of the millennium, images became increasingly important to communicating any kind of information.[4] Hence, images of climate change where to be found all around the internet, on websites and social media.

As the visual discourse was as prominent as written or spoken discourse and with images often taking the lead in attracting and maintaining a reader's attention, one must wonder, why, in a time, when climate change was starting to eventually affect everyone's lives even in the most modern societies, images failed to serve the purpose and engage the public to act. I call this the *non-action paradox*, as humanity failed to act even when the looming catastrophe was evident and visible, scientifically backed, widely communicated and visually omnipresent.

I argue that the visualisation of climate change in the 2010-2020s[5] is mostly inadequate if not counterproductive. This is due to its depicted subjects as well the aesthetics that both lead to distancing the spectators from the topic of climate change and the need for urgent action. However, much emphasis and hope is put on photography and images not only for stipulation attention but also for triggering

R. Yu and B. Zhou. (2021). *Climate Change 2021: The Physical Science Basis. Contribution of Working Group I to the Sixth Assessment Report of the Intergovernmental Panel on Climate Change*. C. U. Press.

3   Thank you Sebastian Schindler for suggesting this dramaturgic spin.

4   The global marketing platform HubSpot found in 2021 that image-based content (pictures and video) largely outweighed text-based informational content in terms of attentiveness as well as in getting the consumer to remember the delivered content Mawhinney, J. (2021). 50 Visual Content Marketing Statistics You Should Know in 2021. HubSpot. Retrieved July 29 from https://blog.hubspot.com/marketing/visual-content-marketing-strategy.

5   I chose this period because it was the time when humanity had its last chance to

behavioural change and taking action. Activists, intellectuals, journalists and political actors believed that if you only depicted the horrific consequences, people would strongly oppose to continue the respective path of (in)action. Not only does this put too much emphasis on the visual discourse, it also triggers depictions that are inherently counterproductive to the activist agenda they are meant to support – such as catastrophic or fear-inducing photographs that grab the viewers' attention.

The idea that by means of photography or photojournalism one could "make a difference" had – as I will briefly discuss – its origin in early 20th century war photography when books like *War Against War!* by Ernst Friedrich were an integral part of the pacifist activist movement in the 1920s. The visual representations of conflicts as well as the climate catastrophe not only were mostly inadequate, I argue, to stipulate meaningful action, but could also foster inaction and contribute to the normalisation of a crisis.

In the end, and arguing with Susan Sontag, the climate catastrophe, its agony and ruin, became "ultra-familiar, ultra-celebrated images – unavoidable features of our camera-mediated knowledge" (Sontag, 2003, p. 24) – just like war. Neither ended, both killed.

My contribution will proceed in three steps. The next section looks at how the visual discourse shapes our understanding of the world followed by a brief analysis of how the climate crisis was depicted in news reports around the 2020s. This is followed by short section on the crisis of the image and the image in crisis which links the idea of change through images to the history of crisis (war!) photography.
Thus, I hope to clarify how the visual discourse contributed to the non-action paradox.

THE NON-ACTION PARADOX – IMAGES, CONFLICT AND THE CLIMATE CATASTROPHE

Images are one of the defining means of communication in our culture and you could argue, that the daily stream of journalistic photographs creates "a common spectatorship" that defines the public, as Frank Möller argues:

limit global warming to 1.5°C above the pre-industrial level by taking serious political, societal, and industrial action – which it failed to do. E.g. the UNFCC stated in its Sixth Assessment Report in 2022, that the risks presented by climate change were "becoming increasingly complex and more difficult to manage. Multiple climate hazards will occur simultaneously, and multiple climatic and non-climatic risks will interact, resulting in compounding overall risk and risks cascading across sectors and regions" IPCC. Intergovernmental Panel on Climate Change. (2022). Climate Change 2022. Impacts, Adaptation and Vulnerability. Summary for Policy Makers. S. PCC.

Thus, – most of the time individually but, as a member of the public, at the same time also collectively, the act of viewing constitutes the public as a part of which – and only as a part of which – the individual might exert political power (Möller, 2009, p. 783).

Without the appropriate cultural knowledge of iconic images, one cannot take part in meaningful political action. For the climate crisis, that means that knowing the visual discourse would be elemental to publicly engage in a meaningful manner. However, it is the images themselves that help drawing recipients' attention in the first place and "shape the possibilities for engagement" (O'Neill, 2013, p. 11).

In addition, photography can be seen as having globalised our conscience to a point where the claim of not having known has become impossible: "photographs have robbed us of the alibi of ignorance" (Linfield, 2010, p. 46). Regarding political violence, Linfield points out that the camera is the key tool to trigger empathy on a global scale and fostered the idea "that barbarous assaults are no longer the private property of the states that commit them" (2010, p. 47). The same is true for visual representations of climate change. The imagery showing how climate change looks like in its causes and effects, from smokestacks to polar bears, from floods and heat waves killing people to intensive livestock farming and burning fossil fuels for individual mobility is widespread. Neither on a personal nor a political level can anyone claim that they (we!) *"hadn't known"*. By the same token, can states, communities and even individuals no longer claim that their climate-hostile acts are matters of national interest, internal affairs, or private practice: not only through huge bodies of (scientific and news) texts but also through a comprehensive visual discourse (news photography, social media posts, etc.) does everyone know about the devastating effects that the climate crisis has on communities and individual humans.

This is the non-action paradox – from politics on all levels to the single individual: we knew what was going to happen, but we didn't take sufficient measures for transformation.[6]

The key problem with the visual discourse on communicating such topoi as war and climate crisis is that the causes of both are multifold and abstract, thus making it impossible to visualise them straight away. As the international news publication The Guardian has put it with

6 This paradox has been identified as early as 2009 by journalist Ian Katz Katz, I. (2009). The beauty of 10:10 is that it's both achievable and meaningful. The Guardian. Retrieved 03.01. from https://www.theguardian.com/environment/2009/sep/01/10-10-launch-ian-katz in The Guardian.

regard to the climate crisis: "It can also be difficult for photographers to capture images that reflect global heating, weather patterns and wildlife extinction, especially when trying to depict what cannot always be seen" (Shields, 2019). This is probably the main reason why photographs are usually reliant on depicting effects rather than causes. Even when there are certain causes that are tangible to visual representation they are necessarily *seen* (and thus perceived) as isolated. For example, there is no apparent visual connection between images of intensive livestock farming in Germany and the wildfires in the Amazonas rain forests which are mostly deliberately set to create farmland to grow animal feed. "Pigs confined to a barn in an intensive system, Midwestern United States" (p. 114, fig. 1) Burning fires in the Amazon rainforest (p. 114, fig. 2) The recipient will not make a meaningful connection between these two images unless caption or text will provide context for the inherent relationship between them. Moreover, each image alone represents a number of ethical, political and humanitarian problems that linking those images to one global issue such as the climate crisis almost renders the task futile.

The climate consulting agency and NGO Climate Outreach/Climate visuals has effectively summed up the dilemma that is inherent in the visual discourse of any crisis:

> Humans are visual animals: our understanding of the world is dominated by what we see, and how this makes us feel. But despite decades of public engagement (and the proliferation of research on the verbal and written communication of climate change), there is sparse evidence on which to base a choice that thousands of journalists, activists, bloggers and educators face on a daily basis: how to communicate climate change effectively using the visual medium. (Corner et al., 2015, p. 6)

In general, visual representations are a central means of the political communication of crises. At least since the First World War 1914-18 and the Spanish Civil War in the 1930s images have evolved from being merely decorative accessories for written text to being an independent element in the construction of reality (Sontag, 2003, p. 21). The image production has since increased dramatically to a point where they became not only part of the above-mentioned global conscience but also central to our collective memory or rather "collective instruction" as Sontag notes, because our memories of distant political events are not our own memories but often artefacts of produced images. "Photographs that everyone recognises are now a constituent part of what society chooses to think about, or declares that it has chosen to think about" (Sontag, 2003, p. 85). When we think of how climate change looks like, we probably think of icons such as smokestacks and polar bears. When thinking about World War I, most will probably see trenches with dead bodies and mutilated faces before their inner eye.

However, as much as (news and especially war or conflict) photographers might stress the mere documentary nature of their images, every photograph exists within an ontological paradox as Wilhelm Hofmann points out. On the one hand they are technically produced depictions of reality on the other hand they are framed (or even staged) and thus offer only one perspective and necessarily exclude every other possible view of a given situation making them subjective within objectivity (Hofmann, 2006, p. 162). One can safely assume, that news organisations as well as professional practitioners are aware of this tension, hence stressing the importance of credibility rather than objectivity (Campbell, 2014).

Nevertheless, if images play a central role in the construction of reality in shaping our collective memory, then subjectivity derived from Hofmann's ontological paradox plays an important role. It not only defines how we remember political events it also obscures the fact, that there could have been countless alternative perspectives. Through the claim to be depictions of (the) reality[7], the subjective dimensions of creation, statement and representation recede into the background. Images speak to us. But what they say and what political meaning(s) they have is not inherent in the image itself, be it a photograph or a moving image. An image does not stand on its own, it does not make a statement. The photographic or video-based documentation of war crimes for example is not a plea for an end to hostilities, writes Sontag. Images are screens and catalysts for existing worldviews, political positions, and ideologies (Sontag, 2003, p. 8). By the same token, the mere illustration of the consequences of climate change does not automatically demand for consequential action and public engagement.

In turn, by constituting what is a legitimate instance of depicting a subject in a certain genre of photography, the subjectivity can be rendered an intersubjective norm for the visual discourse in a certain field. "Imagery does not only impact how people engage with the media. The availability of compelling imagery also shapes the types of

7   The claim to be credible (rather than objective) stresses the point, that an image has not been manipulated which is in itself a contested concept Campbell, D. (2014). The integrity of the image. World Press Photo Foundation. Retrieved 15.08. from https://www.david-campbell.org/s/Campbell_Integrity_of_the_Image_2014.pdf. This however, implicitly brings back the notion of some sort of objectivity inherent in news photography reintroduces the tension between subjectivity within objectivity.

media narratives that are offered in the first place" (O'Neill, 2020, p. 11), thus, creating icons, that are endlessly cited and repeated, narrowing the *see-able* and therefore *think-able* to but a few options and perspectives:

> The repetition and normalisation of particular images or image types and the converse, i.e. the absence of particular images or image types — is therefore political, in that it empowers particular voices and promotes particular ways of conceptualising climate change, whilst disempowering others and marginalising others (O'Neill et al., 2013, p. 12)

THE VISUAL DISCOURSE OF THE CLIMATE CATASTROPHE

When looking at the visual discourse of the climate catastrophe one can find at least three types of images. The first type is what is called a cliché or synecdoche in the literature. These are generic or iconic images that are widely associated with the topic as they depict certain primary motifs like polar bears, smokestacks and melting glaciers.

The second type of image depicts victims of natural catastrophes that were associated with anthropogenic climate change while the third type shows either the disaster itself or some particular action contributing to climate change like the aforementioned slash-and-burn-farming or deforestation.[8]

The first type of images representing climate change were often weirdly similar and one-dimensional. The primary motifs could be categorised as non-specific, global, abstract or impersonal: smokestacks, melting arctic glaciers, wind turbines and polar bears. In a longitudinal study examining over 1000 photographs from US and UK newspaper outlets Saffron O'Neill (2020) could not only show that there was a widespread use of this iconic/generic imagery between 2001 and 2009, which is described as the pivotal decade for climate change engagement, but there are also two phases of the use of these images. While up to 2004 there is a "low level of visual coverage and little iconic imagery. Climate Change is only represented through the distancing frame [...], which portrays the issue as a risk distant in time and place to everyday. This is exemplified by the widespread use of awe-inspiring, vast, people-less polar ice imagery as a visual synecdoche" (O'Neill, 2020, p. 21).[9] "A typical 'ice imagery' visual (note this image is

8   See also Manzo Manzo, K. (2010). Beyond polar bears? Re-envisioning climate change. Meteorological Applications(17), 196-208.   for a slightly different categorisation.

9   Saffron O'Neill uses the term synecdoche to describe "a type of visual shorthand" that conveys cultural knowledge about a certain set of ideas that transcends the

(p. 114, fig. 3) O'Neill's study shows that the use of ice/glacier motifs decreases over time while images of polar bears and wind turbines are being used more frequently. However, the one thing they have in common is that they use what can be called a distancing frame. While being a "simple visual shorthand for the issue [...] it has also reinforced the impression that climate change is a distant problem and arguably 'closed down' the climate discourse around a concept that is remote from people's day-to-day lives" (Corner & Clarke, 2017, p. 18; Manzo, 2010; O'Neill et al., 2013). As Kate Manzo acknowledges that these images have their role to play in climate communication. But if the audience is only "wildlife-lovers" the images and their stories will have "little or no traction" in a wider society (Manzo, 2010, p. 198).

This 'remoteness from everyday-life' resembles the general political discourse which didn't convey the urgency needed with diplomats wrangling "over targets for 2020 and 2050. It all sounds like something we can afford to put off worrying about until next month or next year", as a newspaper article had put it in 2009 (Katz, 2009). From the Kyoto Protocol 1997 to the Paris Agreement 2015 and beyond, decision makers operated with large time frames for their nations' climate goals that spanned decades, distancing the urgency of action from the carbon dioxide emission goal.

Apart from the aspect of proximity and the lack of motifs of identification, the distancing frame appears in at least one additional form, the visual aesthetic of reports from regions hit by catastrophic weather events. Often, the framing of the photographs, the colour grading and the overall appearance resemble catastrophe or doomsday movies, citing a visual aesthetic that spectators connect to their pop-cultural knowledge of these films.

These images (and their accompanying texts) were often re-contextualised with pop-cultural signifiers of apocalyptic motifs on social media. They explicated what spectators might have seen only implicitly in the images from news reports.

The reporting on the massive droughts and wildfires of 2021 that hit regions across the globe and on every continent[10] are a typical example of the aesthetic of the visual discourse. Many of the photographs' framings resemble the aesthetic, style and framing that is used in doomsday movies. Alongside with dramatic often apocalyptic language like "Scientists warn time of reckoning has come for the planet" (McKie, 2021) many reports started to evoke a feeling of drama and draw on

immediate depiction O'Neill, S. (2020). More than meets the eye: a longitudinal analysis of climate change imagery in the print media. Climatic Change, 163, 9-26.
10 The free online encyclopaedia Wikipedia is offering an overview with links on the

Failing images. How the visual discourse on climate change changed nothing in the age of visual

well established pop-cultural themes. Moreover, the image that went with McKie's story in The Guardian showed a number of silhouettes of people standing against the blinding yellow-red light of a raging wildfire in Greece, a documentary image that could easily be taken to illustrate not volunteers supporting the firefighters tackling the wildfires nearby, as the caption reads, but a Judgment Day story.

The image going with the news story Scientists issue a climate code red is similar. The camera shoots from a low position upwards with a wide angle lens attached. The sky is fiery red with glimmering sparks flowing up in the sky. The picture must have been taken by night dramatising the scene even more through the contrast between the red-lit parts and the dark parts of the sky. The foreground consists of silhouettes of trees standing in half-circle, putting an emphasis on the extreme camera angle and two people – also silhouettes – standing small before the awe-inspiring scene. As the non-action paradox became increasingly visible through extreme weather events and other catastrophes, visual news reporting – especially the cover photos – often resembled this kind of aesthetic.[11] The Guardian, Aug 15, 2021 "It's now or never: Scientists warn time of reckoning has come for the planet. The IPCC is unequivocal: we must take urgent action to curb global heating and prevent catastrophe. Will our policymakers and the COP26 conference be up to the task?" (p. 114, fig. 4) The Guardian. Aug 11, 2021: "Scientists issue a climate code red. A major UN scientific report has concluded global heating is now irreversible and it is unequivocal that human influence has warmed the atmosphere" (p. 114, fig. 5) These kinds of images have a distancing effect on several levels. First, as they aesthetically resemble movie productions there is hardly room for identification between the viewers and the depicted scene. Second, as they depict huge disasters, individuals may feel that even though climate change is an important issue, their contribution "is akin to a 'drop in the ocean'" (O'Neill & Nicholson-Cole, 2009, p. 371). The authors have found that while fear/shock/catastrophe in news reports work well to trigger awareness, just as any journalist probably knows, but will likely have effects counter to what is often intended in the respective article. Using images like these are "likely to distance or disengage individuals from climate change, tending to render them feeling helpless and overwhelmed when they try to comprehend their own relationship with the issue" (O'Neill & Nicholson-Cole, 2009, p. 375) – meaningful engagement has to involve "some degree of connection with 'the everyday', in both spatial and temporal terms" (p.

regions affected by the wildfires in 2021 Wikipedia. (2021). Wildfires in 2021. https://en.wikipedia.org/wiki/Wildfires_in_2021.

11 For copyright and licensing reasons, the direct links to the news source is provided using QR Codes. Simply scan the code with your mobile device and you will be directed to the news stories with the respective images.

369), as O'Neill and Nicholson-Cole conclude. Images inducing fear and shock mostly led to one of two psychological functions: control the external danger or control the external fear. "If the external danger – in this case, the impacts of climate change – cannot be controlled (or is not perceived to be controllable), then individuals will attempt to control the internal fear. These internal fear controls, such as issue denial and apathy, can represent barriers to meaningful engagement" (O'Neill & Nicholson-Cole, 2009, p. 363).

These depictions create a tension between their fictional aesthetic, the urgency of action and the vastness of the present and prospected catastrophes that would possibly affect every human on the planet to a certain degree.

Screenshot taken from Twitter, original Tweet see https://twitter.com/elhotzo/status/1430070919628795904?s=20 (p. 114, fig. 6)

A tweet by the German artist and journalist Sebastian Hotz @elhotzo from August 2021 saying "2012 extreme movie", illustrates this point. The user had put together a montage with the title cover of Roland Emmerich's apocalypse movie 2012[12] (upper left corner) with real scenes from 2021s events of the climate catastrophe. The idea is of course that the real images hardly differ in content and style from the blockbuster's imaginative end-of-the-world story.

The depicted events in the tweet are the following:

The extended wildfires in Greece and Turkey from July/August 2021 (upper right corner) have burnt more than 125.000 hectares of forests in Greece and more than 160.000 hectares in Mediterranean Turkey and were fuelled by extreme heatwaves with temperatures of 37 degrees Celsius and above lasting for around two weeks.

The burst pipeline in the Gulf of Mexico (lower left corner) caused a fire on the ocean surface that took more than five hours to take out. According to news outlets, 10.000 barrels of gasoline (ca. 1.6 million litres) were going through the pipeline when it ruptured. CBS News introduced the news story with stating that these pictures looked like a movie, but were reality (Cohen, 2021).

Finally, the last image (lower right corner) depicts a huge sinkhole that opened up in Erftstadt-Blessem, Germany after a devastating heavy rain event in August 2021.

On a certain level, this tweet works really well, as most of the audience is familiar both with the iconography of American blockbuster doomsday movies and news reporting (imagery and text) on catastrophic weather events in 2021. Both are part of the public visual literacy that allows spectators to understand, link and contextualise

12 For an overview of plot and context see https://en.wikipedia.org/wiki/2012_(film)

these four images. One of the commentators even stated, that the Maya had accidentally transposed digits, showing that relating the real consequences of the climate crisis with the fictional apocalypse story had been understood.

This is a special type of distancing imagery that consist of artistic combinations of images that re-contextualise different images with different cultural meaning. This type is found especially on social media and often with activist implications. They often draw on the pop-cultural knowledge about films, photographs or texts that are about end-of-the-world topics. However, linking the real world scenarios with fiction stories of one or another apocalypse either re-contextualises them, making them transcend from real-life into fiction or rendering the problem so huge, that the individual will refrain from taking action because the problem is too big to be handled on an individual scale, as discussed above.

IMAGES OF CRISIS AND THE CRISIS OF THE IMAGE

The visual representation of the climate catastrophe comes with serious limitations to its intended effects.[13] This stands in contrast to the expectations practitioners in the news and documentary photography industry have. Especially photographers documenting crisis like war/conflict or climate change as well as institutions in either conflict resolution or climate change politics[14] often stress the importance of the image to help furthering their cause. It is true that photo journalism has helped to visualise the benefits and costs of political decisions and "stimulates public opinion and gives impetus to public debate, thereby preventing the interested parties from totally controlling the agenda as much as they would like to", as famous war photographer James Nachtwey (2007) has put it. Photojournalists often see themselves as witness-bearers of the world's atrocities, violence and suffering, making sure that evidence that events happened in a certain way and not another are not lost (Lowe, 2014, p. 211; Nachtwey, 2007). The underlying notion of course is the belief that news or documentary photography are items or artefacts of truth and as such are objective devices of telling a story "accurately and appropriately" (Shields, 2019)[15], a narrative upon which not only photographers and news outlets rely but also human rights campaigns from the earliest days of photography. When mechanically produced images became

13 See Susie Linfield Linfield, S. (2010). The Cruel Radiance. Photography and Political Violence. University of Chicago Press. "A Little History of Photography Criticism" from her book The Cruel Radiance for not only a comprehensive overview of criticism but also a declaration of love for the art and the craft of photography.
14 That is probably true for any agenda in any field or sector.

such items or artefacts of representation of truth it was war and its atrocities that were in focus. And, indeed, early image-driven campaigns could achieve successes. For example, the distribution of photographs of mutilations and other atrocities in Congo from around 1903 can be seen as a significant factor for the success of the humanitarian campaign (Twomey, 2014, p. 11). Mark Twain who among other prominent writers, supported the campaign, coined the phrase of the "incorruptible Kodak" as the only witness that cannot be bribed (Twomey, 2014, p. 11). And indeed, the truth of the claim that atrocities – and by this token any other form of violence or catastrophe – have really happened or are real is inseparably linked to pictorial evidence, as Judith Butler notes. This means that "photography is built into the case made for truth, or that there can be no truth without photography" (Butler, 2010, p. 70). The idea behind Twains statement, however, goes beyond. It is not only the truth in the sense of an objective reality that is depicted. There is an implied moral obligation for the viewer to act or at least support the objective of the campaign or group by simply looking at and recognising the respective photography/ies of violence. As Susan Sontag points out by discussing Virginia Woolfs Three Gunieas, "Not to be pained by these pictures, [...] not to strive to abolish what causes this havoc, this carnage – these, for Woolf, would be the reactions of a moral monster" (Sontag, 2003, p. 8). This is also reflected in a statement of one of the world's most prominent war photographers, James Nachtwey, when he contends that "a picture that revealed the true face of war would almost by definition be an anti-war photograph" (Nachtwey, 2007). This narrative inscribes a metaphysical level into photography, stating that an image in and of itself can evoke ethical power beyond the scope of its content. As one photographer associated with the International League of Conservation Photographers stated, "you ascribe the public to your point of view by the appeal of your pictures" (International League of Conservation Photographers, 2005). Most photojournalists and editors would agree and emphasise their role in "making a difference" (Newton, 2012 [2000], p. 11).

It remains unclear, though, if and how the presumed ethical power of a photograph could and would translate into a moral imperative to act a certain way. I have cited Susan Sontag who doubts that images of war could be a plea to end hostilities. Similarly, Judith Butler regarding images of torture at Abu Ghraib emphasises that although we might expect the photo to alert us to the depicted human suffering, "it has no magical moral agency of this kind" (Butler, 2010, p. 91); every photograph is, as Roland Barthes put it, ignorant towards any mediation (Barthes, 2016 [1985], p. 96).

The ideas about both the self-explaining moral imperative and the potential impact of the image can be traced back to the very beginning of photojournalism, from Mark Twain's incorruptible Kodak to Ernst Friedrich's War Against War! from 1924.

In the 1920s/1930s the idea that photography can rid societies of the atrocities of war to evoke resistance by showing the ordinary man the truth behind the propaganda was widely spread. It was vibrant in the leftist peace movement that formed itself across Europe in the wake of World War I and its aftermath. Friedrich's War against War! is the only comprehensive photography book and almost the only reference there is about the resistance of the peace movement against the looming war in the Weimar Republic (Krumeich, 2017, p. X). Even by today's standards with images of atrocities from around the world being ubiquitous, this book and its images mark a tremendous transgression on multiple levels. Aside from the obvious fact that it challenged authorities and (often violent) political groups at the time of its publishing, it shows some of the most brutal and horrifying images of war that exist.[15]

High hopes were pinned on this collection of almost 200 war photographs. Writing under the pseudonym Ignaz Wrobel German journalist and writer Kurt Tucholsky urged the readers of the weekly magazine Die Weltbühne (The World Stage) to buy this book and use it as a counter-weapon against the war propaganda in various societal groups as well as within the government. "Here's the weapon", he writes, "anyone who sees this and does not shudder, cannot be called a human being" (Wrobel, 2017 [1926], p. LXXV). "No artist of the word, not even the best, can cope with the weapon of the image"(p. LXXIV).[16] Friedrich emphasises that the words of all languages fail to describe this human slaughter. For him, the photographs present war in a way that is "objectively true and faithful to nature, [...], obtained by the inexorable, incorruptible photographic lens" (Friedrich, 2017 [1924], pp. 20-21).

However explicitly photographs depict the consequences of a crisis – be it war or the climate catastrophe – their impacts and effects are always bound to context, caption and the visual literacy of the viewer, the "photographer's intentions do not determine the meaning of the photograph" (Sontag, 2003, p. 39). Thus, under no circumstance can they exert an agency of their own, trigger a pre-determined action or

15 The fact that the technical ability to capture detail was primitive by today's standards helps mitigate the immediate effect on the modern-day viewer. This, however, does not compensate from the sheer horror that is depicted by the photographs.

16 Citations of Ignaz Wrobel aka Kurt Tucholsky were translated by the author.

even serve as a backplane for a universal kind of ethics or moral conviction. The idea that photography could do otherwise is a historical artefact that has been reproduced and re-contextualised over these almost 150 years in which photojournalism exists.

CONCLUSIONS ON THE VISUAL DISCOURSE ON THE CLIMATE CRISIS

How did the visual discourse on climate change contribute to the non-action paradox? Why didn't photography and photojournalism live up to the expectations that were put in them at a time when images had become an integral part of the collective understanding of the world?

Probably, and with the previous chapters in mind, it all comes down to the somewhat trivial question of what images really can and cannot depict. Capturing "complexity, invisibility and change is inherently difficult [...] – especially at a single moment in time" (Manzo, 2010, p. 207). Moreover, by nature crisis like climate change and or conflict are complex and derive from causes on multiple levels. Climate change is in and of itself a genuinely abstract process of events, hardly tangible by individual human experience. Surely, extreme weather events are felt by whole populations but the unambiguous connection of a single event to climate change is hard to be established, as any extreme weather event could be just a deviation from the norm just as – in common sense and knowledge – it has always been before. It is only by means of statistics, long term observation data and computer-based projection models that the cumulations of these events and the underlying causes reveal the accelerating dynamics of the climate catastrophe.

It is a fact, and at the same time highly abstract and heavily reliant on data rather than general human experience, that in the early 2020s, humanity has reached several tipping points (IPCC. Intergovernmental Panel on Climate Change, 2022) because concerted planetary action could not be reached. Its abstract nature renders climate change a communication problem rather than a problem arising from lack of (wide public) knowledge. First of all, it requires "expertise and understanding that cuts across disciplines, sectors and cultures" (Corner & Clarke, 2017, p. 2) as it is not a "'single issue' or even a related set of related issues" (ibid.). Second, the problem with climate change and its consequences is linked to exponential growth of both the rate at which human industrial activity contributes to climate change and the problem of tipping points to the climate as well. "For a long time the growth looks insignificant. [...] Still that exponential growth accumulates suddenly to produce a problem that is unmanageable" (Meadows et al., 2004, p. 22). It is obvious that communicating a multi-faceted, multi-level, multi-sector crisis that on the one hand relates to almost everything humans do daily and on the other is represented in distancing frames is problematic. Add to this the mathematical factor of exponential growth that is often poorly understood publicly and you have a serious problem reaching people to sustainably changing their behaviour in a meaningful way at a time when the crisis is hardly seen or felt by most of the people.

All of this creates an obvious tension between the complexity of the problem and the simplicity of depiction, which makes it almost impossible to properly categorise images from very different locations and topics (e.g. livestock farming and burning the rainforest) under the same category of climate crisis. Moreover, as we have seen, the images that were used often proved to be counterproductive to trigger engagement, even to a point where they would induce the very opposite behaviour (apathy, agony, denial) or distanced spectators from the impacts and consequences. Probably out of a historically developed conviction, that photography could make a difference in crisis, news editors rarely used alternative imagery or even evaluated what kind of image or depiction (photograph, statistics/graphs, artistic images, etc.) would be best to visually support and further the message of the respective story. Kate Manzo (2010, p. 203) found that even when images were more suitable to help the cause of the reporting, they were often found to be less newsworthy by the editors, resulting in lesser circulation and thus reaching a smaller audience.

But how could a perfect picture look like? As I said at the beginning of this paper, we almost had it, so I conclude this contribution with the iconic image that could have triggered the necessary policy change. It w%s p$§blish3d i.. t-...

...re-connceting...

had it 3v38(

...re-connecting...

...

...connection failure...

...end transmission...

...end transmission...

REFERENCES

p. 114, fig. 1: Hog confinement barn interior, Source: https://commons.wikimedia.org/wiki/File:Hog_confinement_barn_interior.jpg, This work is in the public domain in the United States because it is a work prepared by an officer or employee of the United States Government as part of that person's official duties under the terms of Title 17, Chapter 1, Section 105 of the US Code.

p. 114, fig. 2: Burning fires in the Amazon rainforest, source: Shutterstock, Standard License. The use of this image is due to copyright and license issues. It is very similar to the actual image that was analysed, entitled: Amazon rainforest now emitting more CO2 than it absorbs, source: The Guardian https://www.theguardian.com/environment/2021/jul/14/amazon-rainforest-now-emitting-more-co2-than-it-absorbs, original caption: "The study found fires produced about 1.5bn tonnes of CO2 a year, with forest growth removing 0.5bn tonnes. The 1bn tonnes left in the atmosphere is equivalent to the annual emissions of Japan."

p. 114, fig. 3: "The crystal desert" by Christopher Michel, licenced under CC BY 2.0", source: https://www.flickr.com/photos/cmichel67/8381965560/in/photostream/, cited from O'Neill (2020, p. 17).

p. 114, fig. 4–5: These images are represented as QR-Codes linking their original source.

p. 114, fig. 6: Tweet by @elhotzo, source: https://twitter.com/elhotzo/status/1430070919628795904?s=20Tweet by @elhotzo, source: https://twitter.com/elhotzo/status/1430070919628795904?s=20

Barthes, R. (2016 [1985]). Die helle Kammer. Bemerkungen zur Photographie. Suhrkamp.

Butler, J. (2010). Torture and the Ethics of Photography: Thinking with Sontag. In J. Butler (Ed.), Frames of War. When is Life Grievable? (pp. 63-100). Verso.

Campbell, D. (2014). The integrity of the image. World Press Photo Foundation. Retrieved 15.08. from https://www.david-campbell.org/s/Campbell_Integrity_of_the_Image_2014.pdf

Climate Action Tracker. (2021). Temperatures. Addressing global warming. Retrieved 26.05. from https://climateactiontracker.org/global/temperatures/

Cohen, L. (2021). Burst pipeline causes bubbling, steaming „eye of fire" to emerge in the Gulf of Mexico. Retrieved 07.07. from https://www.cbsnews.com/news/gulf-of-mexico-fire-ocean-burst-pipeline/

Cook, I. (2020). The Politics of the Final Hundred Years of Humanity (2030-2130). Springer Nature.

Corner, A., & Clarke, J. (2017). Talking Climate. From Research to Practice in Public Engagement. Palgrave Macmillan.

Corner, A., Webster, R., & Teriete, C. (2015). Climate Visuals: Seven principles for visual climate change communication (based on international social research). Climate Outreach. Retrieved 02. April 2021 from https://climateoutreach.org/reports/climate-visuals-seven-principles-for-visual-climate-change-communication/

Friedrich, E. (2017 [1924]). Krieg dem Kriege. Neu herausgegeben vom Anti-Kriegs-Museum Berlin. Mit einer Einführung von Gerd Krumeich und einem Lebensbild Ernst Friedrichs von Tommy Spree und Patrick Oelze. Ch. Links Verlag.

Hofmann, W. (2006). Die Politik der Bilder und der Worte. Anmerkungen zum Verhältnis von sprachlicher und visueller Kommunikation bei Susan Sontag und Roland Barthes. In W. Hofmann (Ed.), Bildpolitik, Sprachpolitik: Untersuchungen zur politischen Kommunikation in der entwickelten Demokratie (pp. 157-179). LIT-Verlag.

International League of Conservation Photographers. (2005). Supporting environmental and cultural conservation through ethical photography and filmmaking. Retrieved 18.8. from https://conservationphotographers.org/about-us/

IPCC. Intergovernmental Panel on Climate Change. (2022). Climate Change 2022. Impacts, Adaptation and Vulnerability. Summary for Policy Makers. S. PCC.

Katz, I. (2009). The beauty of 10:10 is that it's both achievable and meaningful. The Guardian. Retrieved 03.01. from https://www.theguardian.com/environment/2009/sep/01/10-10-launch-ian-katz

Krumeich, G. (2017). Ein einzigartiges Werk. Einführung zur Neuausgabe von „Krieg dem Kriege". In Anti-Kriegs-Museum-Berlin (Ed.), Krieg dem Kriege (pp. VII-XXXVII). Ch Links Verlag.

Linfield, S. (2010). The Cruel Radiance. Photography and Political Violence. University of Chicago Press.

Lowe, P. (2014). The Forensic Turn. Bearing Witness and the 'Thingness' of the Photograph. In L. Kennedy & C. Patrick (Eds.), The Violence of the Image. Photography and International Conflict (pp. 211-234). I.B. Tauris & Co Ltd.

Manzo, K. (2010). Beyond polar bears? Re-envisioning climate change. Meteorological Applications(17), 196-208.

Masson-Delmotte, V., P. Zhai, A. Pirani, S. , L. Connors, C. P., S. Berger, N. Caud, Y. Chen, L. Goldfarb, M. I. Gomis, M. Huang, K. Leitzell, E. Lonnoy, J. B. , & R. Matthews, T. K. M., T. Waterfield, O. Yelekçi, R. Yu and B. Zhou. (2021). Climate Change 2021: The Physical Science Basis. Contribution of Working Group I to the Sixth Assessment Report of the Intergovernmental Panel on Climate Change. C. U. Press.

Mawhinney, J. (2021). 50 Visual Content Marketing Statistics You Should Know in 2021. HubsSpot. Retrieved July 29 from https://blog.hubspot.com/marketing/visual-content-marketing-strategy

McKie, R. (2021). It's now or never: Scientists warn time of reckoning has come for the planet. The Guardian. Retrieved 29.08. from https://www.theguardian.com/environment/2021/aug/15/its-now-or-never-scientists-warn-time-of-reckoning-has-come-for-the-planet

Meadows, D., Randers, J., & Meadows, D. (2004). Limits to Growth. The 30-Year Update. Chelsea Green Publishing.

Möller, F. (2009). The looking/not looking Dilemma. Review of International Studies, 35(2), 781-794.

Nachtwey, J. (2007). My photographs bear witness - TED Talk. Retrieved 18.08. from https://youtu.be/AGKZhNK_pHw

Newton, J. H. (2012 [2000]). The Burden of Visual Truth. The Role of Photojournalism in Mediating Reality. Routledge.

O'Neill, S. (2020). More than meets the eye: a longitudinal analysis of climate change imagery in the print media. Climatic Change, 163, 9-26.

O'Neill, S., Boykoff, M., Niemeyer, S., & Day, S. A. (2013). On the use of imagery for climate change engagement. Global Environmental Change, 23(2), 413-421.

O'Neill, S., & Nicholson-Cole, S. (2009). "Fear Won't Do It". Promoting Positive Engagement With Climate Change Through Visual and Iconic Representations. Science Communication, 30(3), 355-379.

O'Neill, S. J. (2013). Image matters: Climate change imagery in US, UK and Australian newspapers. Geoforum, 49.

Shields, F. (2019). Why we're rethinking the images we use for our climate journalism. The Guardian. Retrieved March 12 from https://www.theguardian.com/environment/2019/oct/18/guardian-climate-pledge-2019-images-pictures-guidelines

Sontag, S. (2003). Regarding the Pain of Others. Picador.

Twomey, C. (2014). The Incorruptible Kodak. Photography, Human Rights and the Congo Campaign. In L. Kennedy & C. Patrick (Eds.), The Violence of the Image. Photography and International Conflict (pp. 9-33). I.B. Tauris & Co Ldt.

Wikipedia. (2021). Wildfires in 2021. https://en.wikipedia.org/wiki/Wildfires_in_2021

Wrobel, I. (2017 [1926]). Waffe gegen den Krieg. In Anti-Kriegs-Museum-Berlin (Ed.), Krieg dem Kriege (pp. LXXIII-LXXV). Ch Links Verlag.

SEPTEMBER 18, 5:30 PM. VENUE: MYCELIUM

Subsurface meteor craters, fossilized coral reefs, exhumed mountain ranges. These "archived" landscapes are often observable only through fossil records, artifacts, or recorded data. Yet, they are inextricably layered within contemporary land- and cityscapes, creating entangled strata of geologic and human histories. As an artist, I create handworked textiles, prints, and performances that highlight the resonances between geologic processes and human experience, exploring a de-centered perception of place. My current research, *shroud for an ancient sea*, is composed of site-responsive shrouds which vary from expansive textiles to experimental vocal performances, acting as momentary surface layers that point to the complex records of deep time within the geo-anthropic landscape.

One of these works, *marseille tidal gauge aria*, is a vocal shroud composed from tide level data collected over 130 years (1884-2014) from a tidal gauge in the bay of Marseille, France. I translated each yearly average tide level into an individual note within my vocal range and set the resulting atonal composition to a poem from Rasu-Yong Tugen's book, *Songs from the Black Moon*. I perform the piece operatically, drawing on the genre's propensity for magnified human emotion; the rising sea levels in the bay can be heard in the increasingly higher pitches of the aria. As a performer of this work, I embody the data records of this ancient sea in a way that precludes the separation of the human and the geologic, and that mourns the products of this entanglement. I recorded a performance of this piece at the fossilized Capitan Reef in Texas's Permian Basin, locating the work inside another ancient sea.

For the composition *skagway tidal aria*, written for The 2051 Munich Climate Conference, I sourced not only recorded but predictive tidal data, sonifying tide levels from 1941-2081. I was drawn to the tides in Skagway, Alaska for their deceptive nature. In contrast to the global trend of rising ocean levels, Skagway's waters appear to be retreating. In reality the land itself is rising, buoyed by the releasing pressure of melted glaciers as they dissolve into the sea. Still, in a few short decades, the ocean level's rate of increase will eclipse that of Skagway's landmass, and the tides will join the overarching trend of the rest of the world. As Tugen (2014, p. 28) writes, "and what is up is what is down."

Skagway, AK (1945-2081) sonified as a vocal composition & performed by the artist. Text from Songs From the Black Moon by Rasu-Yong Tugen. Audio recording by Burke Jam. Filmed at Mineral Wells Fossil Park, TX. Premiered 18 Sept 2021 at T2051MCC. (p. 115, fig. 2)

Sarah Nance. Score for skagway tidal aria, 2021. Recorded & speculative tidal data from Skagway, AK (1945-2081) sonified as a vocal composition & performed by the artist. Text from Songs From the Black Moon by Rasu-Yong Tugen. (p. 115, fig. 3)

REFERENCES

NOAA (2021) Relative Sea Level Trend 9452400 Skagway, Alaska. Available at: https://tidesandcurrents.noaa.gov/sltrends/sltrends_station.shtml?id=9452400 (Accessed: 1 July 2021).

Permanent Service for Mean Sea Level (2021) Skagway. Available at: https://www.psmsl.org/data/obtaining/stations/495.php (Accessed 1 July 2021).

Sea Level Rise (2021) As Lands Rise, Alaska's Sea Level is Sinking. Available at: https://sealevelrise.org/states/alaska/ (Accessed: 1 July 2021).

Tugen, R. (2014) Songs From the Black Moon. gnOme books.

Wöppelmann, G., Marcos, M., Coulomb, A., Martín Míguez, B., Bonnetain, P., Boucher, C., Gravelle, M., Simon, B. and Tiphaneau, P. (2014) 'Rescue of the historical sea level record of Marseille (France) from 1885 to 1988 and its extension back to 1849-1851', Journal of Geodesy, 88, pp. 869-885. doi:10.1007/s00190-014-0728-6.

WWW Tide and Current Predictor (2021) Skagway, Taiya Inlet, Lynn Canal, Alaska. Available at: http://tbone.biol.sc.edu/tide/tideshow.cgi?site=Skagway,+Taiya+Inlet,+Lynn+Canal,+Alaska (Accessed 1 July 2021).

SEPTEMBER 18, 5:30 PM. VENUE: VIVARIUM

The museum to be known as FOSSIL was commissioned by the Swedish government in early 2049, in recognition of the nation meeting decarbonisation goals established three decades previously. As members of the directorial committee of the museum — scheduled to open in the next few years — we will use this essay to discuss the ethical challenges attendant on the museum's founding, and on the curation of its inaugural exhibition, Carbon Ruins, which aims to explore the material-cultural legacy of the "fossil era" which Sweden has now left behind.

As academics and decarbonisation activists from the 2010s to the present day, we are painfully aware of the vexatious questions hanging over this endeavour. Foremost, sociologically speaking, is the implicit periodisation of the commission: when exactly was this "fossil era"? What are the criteria that define its beginning and end? In popular Swedish discourse, it is defined by the unrestrained emission — by Swedish consumers and firms, and in some cases also by firms from which Swedish firms acquire raw materials or components for their products — of "greenhouse gases" (itself a vexed category, whose membership has fluctuated considerably over the years). Like the related concept of the Anthropocene, dating the beginning of the "fossil era" remains contentious, but its ending — at least for the majority of Swedes — is pegged somewhere between 2045 and 2048, within which period various models (academic, commercial and governmental) judge the nation to have achieved a net-zero balance in its carbon budget.

For those of us trained to critical interpretation, this periodisation raises more questions than it answers, many of which we asked when offered the roles we now occupy. We are of course privileged to have been told by the Swedish government, the institution's funder and commissioning body that these questions are ours to answer — but fellow travellers in the critical disciplines will surely detect the poison in this particular chalice. However, we also recall the difficult years of the 2020s and 2030s, when we craved exactly the political voice on these issues which this commission offers us; it is on this basis that we accepted our roles, and the risks that are attendant upon them.

Those challenges are best explored through the work of our curatorial team, as they develop the narrative of the Carbon Ruins exhibition, and acquire the artefacts and media which will form its

*   Lund University, Sweden
**   Muséet FOSSIL, Sweden
*** Institute for Atemporal Studies

backbone. Curation is a narrative act, and narrative implies a narratorial voice or positionality - though this may be obscured or effaced in various ways, intentional or otherwise. Here our intention is to expose that positionality, which is held collectively by the curatorial and directorial staff, but for which we (as the latter) accept full authorial responsibility. Or, more plainly: we want to illustrate the thinking that goes into the selection and framing of the objects, which will comprise the exhibition, and the framing of the museum itself. This in turn should shed some light on the enduring ethical controversies attendant on the era with which the commission is concerned.

Our first example is as Scandinavian as they come, recognisable to almost anyone under the age of 80: Lego. This Danish brand—enduringly popular with all age-groups—provides a synecdoche for the fossil era: Lego is still very much a thriving business, a position secured through successful efforts at cross-marketing with major media properties throughout the C21st. Furthermore, Lego began to make use of bioplastics (rather than petroleum derivatives) long before retaxation and regulation required them to; indeed, their efforts to identify replacement feedstocks resulted in a significant secondary revenue stream from intellectual property related to bioplastic recipes.

Lego was never cheap compared to its competitors, and became less so as they transitioned to bioplastics. As such, Lego—and 'legacy Lego', made from petroleum derivatives (PD), in particular—serves as a gateway to the political economy of fossil-based toys. The era of cheap oil put PD plastics into the toyboxes of countless children (not to mention the pockets and homes of almost every adult) but such things are now prohibitively expensive for all but the wealthiest; as such, Lego's enduring premium brand status echoes the present premium on plastics more broadly. Of course, PD plastics are also notoriously durable, and a lively heritage market exists for collectors, wherein the increasing rarity (and, for some, the ecopolitical symbolism) of legacy Lego commands high prices.

Meanwhile, toy libraries in Scandinavian countries ensure that children from a wide range of socioeconomic backgrounds have access to these toys - whose value as toys should not be underestimated! But in the context of a net-zero-carbon nation, their materiality serves to trouble that innocent use-value: some parents have campaigned for warning labels on heritage toys made from PD plastics, due to concerns about toxicity whose origins are more sociopolitical than medical. Furthermore, our curatorial research shows that adults with fond recollections of Lego from their childhoods can be coaxed into revelatory reflection through a simple reminder of the source of the material from which they were made. Even now, many adult Swedes are

Paul Graham Raven[*, **, ***]

A museum of carbon ruins? Reflections on the ethics of memorialising decarbonisation

shocked to be reminded that PD plastics were ubiquitous in the ludic life of children and adults alike. Many objects might exemplify this legacy but Lego's international ubiquity and desirability makes it perhaps the most powerful example we have yet identified — hence its early accession to the Carbon Ruins collection.

Our second example, the steel water bottle, is less playful — and perhaps less obvious, at least at first. Through the 2020s and into the 2030s, the Swedish steel industry decarbonised rapidly through the roll-out of hydrogen furnaces. Given steel's centrality to Swedish exports, this meant steel became expensive for use within Sweden. This phenomenon became the basis of a popular movement for steel recycling which has frequently been compared to the British campaign for scrap iron during the second world war — in terms of its expression of national camaraderie, but also in terms of its minimal economic impact. The camaraderie, however, should not be discounted: while there had already been fashions for abjuring products with direct links to fossil fuels, the Stålåtervinningsrörelsen was unique for its focus on a material whose reliance on coal was less obvious. Items such as these bottles — fairly commonplace during the 2010s, as an alternative to buying water bottled in plastic — became scarce, as did antique bicycle frames and other items, which had been part of Swedish domestic materiality for many years.

Scarcity and sacrifice is only half the story. Sweden's efforts at fully re-nationalising decarbonising its steel industry paid off, maintaining its position as a major player in the global market for this crucial metal, in both its 'virgin' and recycled forms. But there were other costs, largely concealed from the public, but painfully obvious to the Sami people of the far north: their ancestral lands, already changing rapidly due to global warming, had long been expropriated as sites of iron ore extraction, in injury compounded by the construction of immense windfarms to power the production of hydrogen for the new steelmaking foundries, as well as for domestic fertiliser security.

The importance of steel to Swedish exports highlights the still-ongoing debate over what "decarbonisation" actually means: as noted above, numerous models rate the Swedish economy as "net zero" with regard to carbon, but the proprietary nature of the data (and, in some cases, of the models themselves) makes it hard to assess whether "net zero" represents something close to zero emissions measured across domestic and imported production, or rather represents continued emissions in some sectors which are "paid off" by the export of zero-carbon steel. Factoring in the necessity of estimates in constructing these datasets there exists an enduring controversy: while the majority of Swedes accept the government's claim of carbon neutrality at face value, a significant chunk of the population argues it is a sham. This position has considerable overlap with the post-carbon anti-extractivism movement, which focusses in particular on the destruction and dispossession of Samí lands, not only for steel production but also, more recently, lithium extraction as the base of the country's battery industry.

As such, these two items — familiar, almost banal in the context of their time — serve to illustrate and trouble the definition of the "fossil era" whose passing our institution is meant to memorialise. This poses ethical questions regarding the founding of such an institution: has the transition it celebrates actually occurred? If so, was that transition sufficient, and are the alternatives now in play themselves sustainable, ecologically and ethically? Is it an act of arrogance or hubris to celebrate that transition when the planetary average temperature has nonetheless increased further than the level the transition was intended to avoid, or is it an act of encouragement for nations still struggling to meet similar targets? Is such a celebration just, when we consider the positionality of those (such as the Samí) dispossessed by the infrastructures of the transition, or those who have fled to Sweden in order to escape the effects of inadequate decarbonisation elsewhere?

Neither we nor our team have the authority or expertise to answer these questions definitively — and, we suspect, nor does anyone else. As such, we invoke the memory of Donna Haraway by expressing our obligation to "stay with the trouble", both in the course of executing the commission entrusted to us, and in the course of our own lives. Decarbonisation was never going to be the end of the story; meanwhile, the extent to which it should stand as an important waypoint on our planetary journey is an open debate, in which we can only be one voice among many.

Paul Graham Raven
Alexandra Nikoleris

SEPTEMBER 18, 6:30 PM. VENUE: MYCELIUM

ABSTRACT

This paper assumes it is the year 2051, and we look back to how a new science, Earth Operations Management (EOM), has started and developed since the beginning of the 2020s. EOM was triggered by the idea to regard planet Earth as a business (PEaaB). Millions of business managers were enthused by this idea and have utilised their knowledge and power to achieve PEaaB´s vision: "Humans live their lives with dignity – now and for all generations to come." The paper reminds of the reasons for PEaaB, its basic characteristics, and key issues from a business management perspective. Then it gives a brief insight into the startup phase of PEaaB and illustrates how it has contributed to climate protection until 2051.

1 30 YEARS AGO, 2021: INITIAL SITUATION AND TRIGGERING QUESTIONS

By 2021, the world had seen two tremendous developments starting in the 19th century (p. 116, fig. 1: Gross Domestic Product per capita (real prices as of 2011; above), atmospheric CO_2 concentration (below)). Gross domestic product per capita, a measure for economic output, had grown exponentially in all world regions [1], bringing wealth and prosperity to billions of people. At the same time the atmospheric CO_2 concentration had increased by half, roughly [2], causing the well-known climate catastrophe, and other planetary boundaries had been crossed, too [3].

There are several reasons for these developments, e.g. technical inventions, the use of natural resources, the division of labor and specialisation, market economy, and international value chains. However, to bring all these into effect, one specific human factor was needed: business management [4].

In 2021, there were around 400 million business managers globally. As the two mentioned developments illustrate, business managers collectively were powerful on a global scale – regarding not only their individual business and the economy as a whole but also with respect to planetary developments such as climate change [e.g. 5].

Therefore, the following questions became obvious:

· Why not utilise the power of business management for the best purpose that humans share?

· What is the right business for managers in order to let all human

*   Landshut University of Applied Sciences, Department of Electrical and Industrial Engineering, Am Lurzenhof 1, 84036 Landshut, markus.schmitt@haw-landshut.de

** Rosenheim Technical University of Applied Sciences, Faculty of Management and Engineering, Hochschulstraße 1, 83024 Rosenheim, Klaus.wallner@th-rosenheim.de

beings live with dignity, preserve the natural foundations of life as long as possible, and keep climate under control?

The simple and striking answer was: Let planet Earth be the business that managers take care of!

The following is a condensed review of the "Planet Earth as a Business" (PEaaB) idea and the related Earth Operations Management. For a more detailed review see [6].

2 BASIC CHARACTERISTICS OF PLANET EARTH AS A BUSINESS

To conceive planet Earth as a business several terms needed to be clarified (p. 117, fig. 2: Basic characteristics of planet Earth as a business).

In particular, three major stakeholder groups had to be redefined: owners, customers, and managers. It took several years in the 2020s until a majority of PEaaB scholars and practitioners agreed on a definition of the owners of PEaaB. There was broad accordance from the beginning that humans and all kinds of legal entities established by humans are co-owners of PEaaB in order to enable freedom, responsibility, and ethical development of the individual [7]. But more and more other aspects were taken into consideration, too: the necessity to preserve the natural foundations of life, the dependence of humans on their relationships with other living organisms [8], the increasing loss of biodiversity during past decades [9], the incompetence of humanity to stop this loss [10], and the bundle of rights related to ownership. These aspects lead to the conviction that, in a holistic view, all other living things, not only humans, should be regarded as PEaaB owners, too [cf. 11]. To be precise, the PEaaB owners are the living things of all species, from plants to invertebrate animals (insects, molluscs, corals) and vertebrate animals (fish, amphibians, reptiles, mammals including humans, birds), to fungi and protists [10]. All of these have their own space on planet Earth, they have their own right of living, and they have their own needs to be satisfied – just as the humans do. And many of the species had existed before humans [12].

The implementation of the new ownership concept required, among others, a globally accepted typology of property. For PEaaB, a typology that had been widely used in ecological economics has proven actionable. It distinguishes four types of "capital", or "assets" [13]: natural, human, social, and built.

PEaaB uses assets of these four types as resources to produce goods[1] and perform services for achieving the three common goals: maintenance of the natural foundations of life, long-term survival of humankind, and human well-being. These goods[1] can, in line with traditional economics, be grouped: excludable goods, i.e. private goods like the smartphones purchased from traditional business and club

Earth operations management – How managers found their right business
A fictional science development review

Markus Schmitt[*]

Klaus Well... [**]

goods like flat-rate online-streaming services, and non-excludable goods, i.e. common-pool resources like fish stocks in open waters and public goods like air. In this sense, for example, stable global climate is a public good; it contributes to achieving maintenance, survival, and well-being; and, in the Anthropocene, it is provided by the interaction of natural, human, social, and built capital [cf. 14].

The PEaaB components introduced so far – goals, types of capital, goods and services – have frequently been used to describe, at least roughly, the business process of PEaaB (p.117, fig. 3: Business process) i.e. the way inputs are used in order to generate outputs which help achieving the goals. In part, the business process of PEaaB includes the "empty world" model [15] of traditional economical theory: the four types of capital are utilised in the economic process, which is organised by humans, to produce goods and perform services which are consumed or used as investments by humans. Thereby, consumption is regarded as the key to individual survival and well-being. However, traditional economical theory had almost entirely neglected three essential elements, as ecological economists had pointed out [e.g. 13]: natural capital plays a much bigger role to the economic process than assumed; natural capital provides ecological services which substantially contribute to the PEaaB goals; and humans cause waste, pollution, and depreciation, which deteriorate the ecological services and the four types of capital. Further aspects can be added to the process model, e.g. the modes of individual human engagement (being, having, doing, relating; [16]) that depend on, among others, the way the economic process is organised [cf. 17].

The above definition of "business" includes "while operating at a profit". For PEaaB a new profit calculation method had to be developed which is in line with the vision and goals (p.118, fig. 4: Accounting, profit and loss) [2]. Traditional economic accounting did not provide a proper solution, because it neglected a large part of the natural capital and had been obsessed with value creation based on market activities as measured by Gross Domestic Product (GDP) [cf. 18]. As a result, for decades human society had misguided themselves with the illusion of a profitable economy and concluded that their traditional way of doing business was alright and should be continued as usual [cf. 19].

The new profit calculation method is more comprehensive. It values

1   In the following, for convenience, the term "goods" is used instead of "goods provided or services performed".
2   Values for t_1 are net present values for 80 years into the future, based on estimates for GDP and ecosystem services for 2011, adapted from [20] with discount rate option 1, rounded to 1014 2007 USD. Values for t_2 are illustrative; for natural capital deviation see [21].

the various ecosystem goods and services based on natural capital and the combination of the four capital types [20]. In particular, the value of many public goods and common-pool resources are taken into account; before, these had been widely neglected by GDP because they are not traded on markets. With this new perspective, economists disclosed the huge value of natural capital – but also its ongoing decline [21, 10]. They revealed the real losses of capital and made clear that PEaaB needed a strict business turnaround to get back to "operating at a profit".

According to the definition above, a business seeks to provide goods and services "to others". In traditional business, "others" are external people or organisations that usually are called "customers". In the case of PEaaB there are no external people, organisations, or any other living things. Rather, PEaaB provides its goods and services to all its Earth-based living things, including humans, and to legal entities of the latter. All of these, therefore, can be regarded not only as co-owners of PEaaB but also as internal customers.

The next question to be answered was: who are the managers of PEaaB, i.e. the conscious, authorised, and responsible subjects that, in a continuing and systemic process, exert meaningful and purposeful influence on the behaviour of PEaaB [22]? In traditional business the managers are either the owners of the business, or people or organisations acting on behalf of the owners. At PEaaB this was not possible: there was too much uncertainty among humans about which of the non-human owners are conscious [23] and, if so, how to interact with them as managers; and the human owners did not agree on common authorised managers [cf. 24], even though the United Nations had established a continuing and systemic process in which more than 190 member states showed mutual recognition [25]. Therefore, the initial conceptualisation of PEaaB was still largely anthropocentric and the managers taken into consideration were all kinds of anthropogenic forces in the private, the public, and the plural sector of society [cf. 26], i.e. all people, groups, or organisations that continually and systemically exert influence on planet Earth or parts thereof. Among them were individuals, business managers in particular, for-profit and nonprofit organisations, civil society initiatives, as well as governmental or non-governmental organisations. So, again, PEaaB has hundreds of millions of managers.

From a systems perspective, PEaaB is autonomous and relies on self-organisation. This maybe was the biggest challenge for all managers of planet Earth: there is no one from the outside who executes or delegates command over this business. Therefore, the management of PEaaB, later on called "Earth Operations Management" (EOM), has

Markus Schmitt
Klaus Wellner

65

turned out to be a new and demanding field of expertise which needed a sound theoretical foundation.

3 KEY MANAGEMENT ISSUES AND FIRST ANSWERS

In the 2020s, there were basic research approaches, e. g. Earth System Governance [27], to build theory on how to manage global transformations. Parts of this theory have become rigorous and actionable for PEaaB. However, another and more pragmatic stream of research has contributed most to PEaaB management theory so far: the transfer and adaptation of proven concepts, methods, and tools from other academic disciplines. In particular, traditional management theory and economics had provided a rich repository, even though it

Issues	Concepts from management theory or economics	Major findings from transfer and adaptation to PEaaB	Implications for PEaaB managers
Business model	Business model typology [30], managing a hub economy [31]	Platform business, out of balance, humankind as destabilising superpower	Reduce humankind's value capture and cupport the other species as ecosystem partners
Generic strategies	Cost leadership – differentiation – focus [32], efficiency – consistency – sufficiency [33], green groth – post-growth – degrowth [34]	Hybrid strategy possible (sequential or simultaneous), right-mix debate	Facilitate the right-mix debate
Organisational structure	Line(-and-staff), matrix, project, organisation by business functions, product groups, customer industries, projects etc. [35]	If design authority existed: multi-dimensional matrix by economic ecosystems, types of capital, place, forms of life etc.	Cope with PEaaB as a wicked system with unstable structure in a seamless web
Organisational culture	Interrelated set of assumptions, values, levers, and evident phenomena [36], global economic ethic [37]	Strongly needed, but still too big differences among too many agents	Emphasise the few common culture elements, seize discontinuities as culture development opportunites
Behavioural innovation	Principles: rhythm, system levers, internal compass, reframing, impulse [38]	Applicable in line with wicked-systems theory	Pursue behavioural, harnessed innovation on sub-wicked system level

mainly represents a "Western" and less so an "Eastern" or Indigenous perspective [cf. 28, 29]. Several concepts of this repository have, after adaptation, provided guidance to new PEaaB (or Earth operations) managers (p. 118, fig. 5: Key PEaaB management issues and first answers).

PEaaB benefited from management theory and economics to some extent, but it needed to become an own specific field of expertise. Consequentially, in the following years further management issues have been worked on, based on concepts from management theory, economics, or other areas of knowledge, for example:

• Core processes: the biogeochemical cycles for carbon, nitrogen, phosphorus, and water [39];
• Core competences [40]: life, evolution, regeneration;
• Lean production [41] for the reduction of waste, pollution, and depreciation;
• Organisational learning [42] for exchanging knowledge in all its forms among PEaaB members;
• Operationalised goals: the United Nations´ 17 Sustainable Development Goals [43].

The successful application of management theory and economics to PEaaB issues enthused millions of people, traditional business managers particularly, and kick-started an era of inter- and transdisciplinary work with valuable answers from other fields of expertise: from the humanities, including art and philosophy, from social, natural and health sciences, from engineering and technology.

4 STARTING THE NEW BUSINESS: EXAMPLES

4.1 ALL-INCLUSIVE PRICING

One example of an operational PEaaB goal is the Sustainable Development Goal no. 12: "Responsible consumption and production". There are so many consumers and producers on the PEaaB platform that market mechanisms had to be utilised for coordination. And complexity gets even higher if we consider that each agent could be a consumer and a producer at the same time. However, they needed to be coordinated in a more intelligent way than through completely free markets. Rather, for these internal markets rules had to be designed to secure sustainability.

As an example, consider a traditional business company that builds a windmill, and the produced electric energy is sold to customers (p. 118, fig. 6: All-inclusive pricing model (left) and resulting prices (right) for a windmill and its produced energy). The company uses different resources to build the windmill: components based on non-renewable resources, like concrete or steel;

knowledge of its employees; existing equipment like buildings. The used resources are valued directly via prices, wages and so on. In general, all these aspects belong to what traditionally was regarded as the "company sphere".

But paying only for the specific component or service is not sufficient for PEaaB. For an all-inclusive pricing it is necessary to take into account the "earth sphere" based on the use of all mentioned types of capital: natural, human, social, and built.

In the example, the construction of the windmill has a certain all-inclusive price. The pricing based on the earth sphere is much higher than the conventional pricing based on the company sphere. But the consumers of the produced electric energy have a big advantage: The charged all-inclusive price for consumption is significantly lower than for conventional electric energy.

Recent years have shown that the trigger to produce goods or offer services with a low all-inclusive price was a huge step forward. As a result, companies producing goods and services based on renewable resources have been ahead.

4.2 GRASSROOTS RECRUITING

All-inclusive pricing was only one of the practices of Earth Operations Management. Before, PEaaB, just as every startup business, needed to find enough committed people. Therefore, a grassroots movement all around the globe was initiated in order to find hundreds of millions of "Earth Operations Managers". Fortunately, early in the 2020s, one job advertisement went viral on social media (p. 119, fig. 7: Job advertisement) Within a short time more and more people joined the new business, planet Earth, as Earth Operations Managers, besides their current positions.

5 THE CONTRIBUTION OF PEAAB AND EOM TO CLIMATE PROTECTION UNTIL 2051

Regarding climate protection, since the 1990s the world has experienced ups and downs until today. This is particularly true for the level of climate control that has been gained in the last 30 years; only in the last decade real progress has been achieved (p. 119, fig. 8: Perceived and actual level of climate control) Initially, in the 2020s, humans fooled themselves into thinking they were protecting the climate: they were strong at setting ambitious climate targets while continuing business as usual, which historians today construe as a subtle anti-transformation movement. Accordingly, society pushed non-transformative solutions based on technological optimism, fossil fuel solutionism etc. The 2030 climate targets were widely missed, thus people became aware that humans cannot cope with the Anthropocene approach to running planet Earth. As a reaction, the political leaders of the US, China, and Russia enforced a new kind of global climate governance that many other countries joined ("G3+n"). Together they implemented Earth Operations Management, which finally led to "smart humility" as the guiding EOM paradigm and, thanks to its inter- and transdisciplinary approach, to climate control.

6 FROM PEAAB TO PEAAX

The success of PEaaB and EOM suggested other PEaaX experiments, i.e. thought experiments with planet Earth as the frame but with a different perspective (X) than business and management. Thus, many people with their specific perspective (X) have been attracted to the sustainability debate, too. So far, and building on previous research [e.g. 44–46], planet Earth has been regarded as, for example, an artwork, a single state, a story, a biotope, a game, or a patient. Overall, these experiments have contributed to a much better science-based understanding of climate change and protection, sustainable development, and the Anthropocene.

REFERENCES

1.   Roser M (2013): Economic Growth. Our World in Data. https://ourworldindata.org/economic-growth (01/15/2022)

2.   Ritchie H, Roser M (2020): CO₂ and Greenhouse Gas Emissions. Our World in Data. https://ourworldindata.org/atmospheric-concentrations (01/15/2022)

3.   Steffen W, Richardson K, Rockström J, Cornell SE, Fetzer I, Bennett EM, … Sörlin S (2015): Planetary boundaries: Guiding human development on a changing planet. Science, 347(6223), 1259855. doi.org/10.1126/science.1259855

4.   Kiechel W (2012): The Management Century. Harvard Business Review, 90(11), 62–75.

5.   Griffin P (2017): CDP Carbon Majors Report 2017. CDP Worldwide.

6.   Schmitt M, Wallner K (2022): Earth Operations Management – How managers found their right business. doi.org/10.57688/315

7.   Waldron J (2020): Property and Ownership. In E. N. Zalta (Ed.), The Stanford Encyclopedia of Philosophy (Summer 2020.). Metaphysics Research Lab, Stanford University. https://plato.stanford.edu/archives/sum2020/entries/property/

8.   Reyers B, Folke C, Moore M-L, Biggs R, Galaz V (2018): Social-Ecological Systems Insights for Navigating the Dynamics of the Anthropocene. Annual Review of Environment and Resources, 43(1), 267–289. doi.org/10.1146/annurev-environ-110615-085349

9.   IPBES (2020): Global assessment report of the Intergovernmental Science-Policy Platform on Biodiversity and Ecosystem Services.

10. NABU (Naturschutzbund Deutschland) e. V., BCG (Boston Consulting Group) (2020): The Biodiversity Imperative for Business - Preserving the Foundations of Our Well-Being.

11. Hickey C, Robeyns I (2020): Planetary justice: What can we learn from ethics and political philosophy?. Earth System Governance, 6, 100045. doi.org/10.1016/j.

12. Christian D, Brown CS, Benjamin C (2014): Big history: between nothing and everything. New York, NY: McGraw Hill Education.

13. Costanza R, Cumberland JH, Daly H, Goodland R, Norgaard RB, Kubiszewski I, Franco C (2014): An Introduction to Ecological Economics (2nd ed.). Boca Raton: CRC Press. doi.org/10.1201/b17829

14. Steffen W, Richardson K, Rockström J, Schellnhuber HJ, Dube OP, Dutreuil S, ... Lubchenco J (2020): The emergence and evolution of Earth System Science. Nature Reviews Earth & Environment, 1(1), 54–63. doi.org/10.1038/s43017-019-0005-6

15. Ekins P (1992): A four-capital model of wealth creation. In P. Ekins, M. Max-Neef (Eds.), Real-life economics: Understanding wealth creation. (pp. 147–155). Routledge.

16. Max-Neef M (1992): Development and human needs. In P. Ekins, M. Max-Neef (Eds.), Real-life economics: Understanding wealth creation. (pp. 197–213). Routledge.

17. Göpel M (2016): The great mindshift. New York, NY: Springer Berlin Heidelberg.

18. Dasgupta P (2021): The economics of biodiversity: the Dasgupta review: full report (Updated: 18 February 2021.). London: HM Treasury.

19. Raworth K (2018): Doughnut economics: seven ways to think like a 21st-century economist (Paperback edition.). London: Random House Business Books.

20. Costanza R, Kubiszewski I, Stoeckl N, Kompas T (2021): Pluralistic discounting recognizing different capital contributions: An example estimating the net present value of global ecosystem services. Ecological Economics, 183, 106961. doi.org/10.1016/j.ecolecon.2021.106961

21. Costanza R, de Groot R, Sutton P, van der Ploeg S, Anderson SJ, Kubiszewski I, ... Turner RK (2014): Changes in the global value of ecosystem services. Global Environmental Change, 26, 152–158. doi.org/10.1016/j.gloenvcha.2014.04.002

22. Marshev VI (2021): History of management thought: genesis and development from ancient origins to the present day. Cham, Switzerland: Springer. doi.org/10.1007/978-3-030-62337-1

23. Allen C, Trestman M (2020): Animal Consciousness. In E. N. Zalta (Ed.), The Stanford Encyclopedia of Philosophy (Winter 2020.). Metaphysics Research Lab, Stanford University. https://plato.stanford.edu/archives/win2020/entries/consciousness-animal/

24. ACLED (2022): The Armed Conflict Location & Event Data Project. https://acleddata.com/ (02/02/2022)

25. United Nations (2022): United Nations Charter (full text). United Nations. United Nations. https://www.un.org/en/about-us/un-charter/full-text (02/02/2022)

26. Mintzberg H (2015): Rebalancing society: radical renewal beyond left, right, and center (1st ed.). San Francisco: Berrett-Koehler Publishers, Inc.

27. Earth System Governance Project (2018): Earth System Governance. Science and Implementation Plan of the Earth System Governance Project. Utrecht.

28. O'Loughlin E (2012): Decades of Influence. Harvard Business Review, 90(11), 30–31.

29. Härtel CEJ (2015): Indigenous Management Styles. In International Encyclopedia of the Social & Behavioral Sciences (pp. 784–787). Elsevier. doi.org/10.1016/B978-0-08-097086-8.22026-6

30. Linz C, Müller-Stewens G, Zimmermann A (2021): Radical business model transformation: how leading organizations have successfully adapted to disruption (2nd ed.). London, United Kingdom; New York, NY: Kogan Page.

31. Iansiti M, Lakhani KR (2017): Managing Our Hub Economy: Strategy, Ethics, and Network Competition in the Age of Digital Superpowers. Harvard Business Review, 95(5), 84–92.

32. Porter ME (1985): Competitive advantage: creating and sustaining superior

performance. New York: London: Free Press; Collier Macmillan.

33. Huber J (2000): Towards industrial ecology: sustainable development as a concept of ecological modernization. Journal of Environmental Policy & Planning, 2(4), 269–285. doi.org/10.1080/714038561

34. Petschow U, Lange DS, Hofmann D, Pissarskoi DE (2020): Social Well-Being Within Planetary Boundaries: the Precautionary Post-Growth Approach (No. TEXTE 234/2020). German Environment Agency.

35. Nickels WG, McHugh JM, McHugh SM (2021): Understanding business (13th ed.). New York, NY: McGraw Hill Education.

36. Whittington R, Regnér P, Angwin D, Johnson G, Scholes K (2019): Exploring Strategy: Text and Cases (12th ed.). Hoboken: Pearson Education.

37. Global Ethic Foundation (2009): Global Economic Ethic. Consequences for Global Business. A Manifesto.

38. Wördenweber B, Eggert M, Schmitt M, Wördenweber B (2012): Verhaltensorientiertes Innovationsmanagement: unternehmerisches Potenzial aktivieren. Berlin Heidelberg: Springer.

39. Rockström J, Steffen W, Noone K, Persson Å, Chapin FSI, Lambin E, … Foley J (2009): Planetary Boundaries: Exploring the Safe Operating Space for Humanity. Ecology and Society, 14(2). doi.org/10.5751/ES-03180-140232

40. Prahalad CK, Hamel G (1990): The Core Competence of the Corporation. Harvard Business Review, 68(3), 79–91.

41. Ohno T (1988): Toyota production system: beyond large-scale production. Cambridge, Mass: Productivity Press.

42. Nonaka I, Takeuchi H (1995): The knowledge-creating company: how Japanese companies create the dynamics of innovation. New York: Oxford University Press.

43. United Nations (2015): Sustainable Development Goals. https://sdgs.un.org/goals (01/26/2022)

44. Burch S, Gupta A, Inoue CYA, Kalfagianni A, Persson Å, Gerlak AK, … Zondervan R (2019): New directions in earth system governance research. Earth System Governance, 1, 100006. doi.org/10.1016/j.esg.2019.100006

45. Lovelock J (1979): Gaia, a new look at life on earth. Oxford; New York: Oxford University Press.

46. Schramski JR, Gattie DK, Brown JH (2015): Human domination of the biosphere: Rapid discharge of the earth-space battery foretells the future of humankind. Proceedings of the National Academy of Sciences, 112(31), 9511–9517. doi.org/10.1073/pnas.1508353112

SEPTEMBER 18, 6:30 PM. VENUE: VIVARIUM

When gathered for global Climate Conferences we have been known to picture the entire globe, floating defencelessly in the vast universe. Our total visions can become abstracted by the sheer magnitude of the issues we face. My contribution to this conference attempts to place us more solidly in 2051: to use speculative fabulation to imagine the daily frustrations of the individual and the community they inhabit; their perception of the realities around them and the fictions they've clung on to for answers.

My contribution is written in the form of "Agony Aunt" letters. In Britain (though similar incarnations exist almost everywhere) this is a traditional epistolary style where people send letters to a newspaper or tabloid columnist who replies with advice or a witty comment. The columnists came to be known as Agony Aunts, people who you can go to for support or guidance, or simply to express your grievances.

Using this method we can imagine the implications of climate change on the everyday lives of people in 2051. In this case the letters are written by the same person, from the same address in Bristol, UK. Letter 1 is written from a world facing the consequences of a more than 2°C rise. Letter 2 from a world where global temperatures have risen less than 1.5°C (p. 145). They are very different places.

The letters offer their respective histories, tracking the actions that led to their situation. The point of departure, where the two versions start to separate, is the issue of reparations. In March 2021 the Bristol City Council approved a motion that committed them to recommend the cause of reparations to the UK Government. The reactions are different and unleash a chain of events that lead to very different climate outcomes.

Dear Agony Aunt,

I thought I'd tidy up my room this morning. I've been 3 days deep into the Marvel Marathon. Its mad. It's a "holistic" experience, really sensorial and it comes with food and energy drinks to keep you going. The camera shows it when I'm falling asleep and the volume comes up or they cut to an explosion. It links up with the auto-SAD and the lighting in your room. Super immersive. You know I liked the first 7 guys that played Spiderman but I think the latest ones are getting kind of sloppy. Anyway, my room is a mess. Too much for the Roomba and even the SweepSweep. I get to work.

I pick a playlist, sync the big speakers, switch on the air enhancer, plug in all the candles and incense-bots and I start cleaning. But my SAD windows were far too bright. I switched from Spring morning to sunset. The new SADs can sync with your Spotify and adapt to the music, but you need to buy new hardware apparently, even though mine's only 3 years old. There's been some controversy.

Cleaning up – tidying - always makes me feel melancholic. I finished chucking all the food packaging down the waste hole in the corner of my room but I was in good spirits and felt like exercising a little bit so I decided to keep going. I attacked the depths of my wardrobe, getting at the dust that the robots miss. I came across my old boxes. There were my old degree certificates, my love letters and photographs, the folded up posters that used to hang from the walls of the different rooms I've had. There was festival promo flyers and protest signs. A t-shirt where Bruno and I had written "Make America Gay Again" back when we thought we were witty. Back when we cared.

Underneath all this I found a grenade. It was made of paper, and still had its promotional card clipped on: "SEEDBOMB. Throw it. Grow it." I was taken aback. I'd bought this as a present for my neighbour Judit, 30 years ago. Our neighbour Judit. I haven't always lived alone like this. I used to share this room with my partner, but she left ages ago, saying she could no longer face the inaction all around her, saying she couldn't just watch the city she loves dissolve into… into what it is now I guess. She went up North when Scotland finally became independent, moving into one of those communal land associations that were being promoted. When she was still here the house felt like a family. There were 8 of us, at first complete strangers but then bonded together by the love of place. We shared dinners, parties and in general lived in convivial spirit, celebrating each other as much as possible.

The house is an old Georgian build, on the corner where Montpellier meets St Pauls. These names, these neighbourhoods, used to mean something. Montpellier always quirky (which was white middle class speak for wealthy but open-minded), St Pauls always... harder to define, a world onto itself. When we moved in many of the similar houses had already been divided up into flats. We were a proud exception. Housemates came and went, and we would carefully select the future people, inviting them over for tea and assessing their compatibility in a kind and caring way. The letting agency let us do this – they wouldn't interfere so long as rent was paid. So we painted the walls, built beautiful garden furniture and nurtured the plants that covered every corner of the house. Most nights we would all meet down in "the pit" (the room downstairs) to listen to music, have a boogie, talk over our day, laugh.

But things were always changing. Every summer the reality of the climate crisis seemed closer, more invasive. Some mornings I woke up feeling choked by fear. We celebrated all the little victories. Beavers were recognised legally and were being helped to spread along the UK's waterways. Streets across town were being pedestrianised, community garden projects were gaining momentum and impact – in St Pauls we were producing enough vegetables to feed 40 families, and enough compost to give away and encourage people to start growing in their own front gardens. The biodegradable grenade in my hand was meant for Judit, who had started much of this. I find another flyer: it's an invitation to an inauguration party for Judit's portrait, painted on the wall of the Malcolm X Garden, where her movement had started. It was dated 2025. I faintly remember it: dub music blasting off a big rig, Red Stripe beers. The Mayor was there. Judit spoke about our power to change things, about hope.

The 20s were all about hope. I lost count of the number of times I laid down in the middle of the street to stop the traffic, making time for one rebellious stunt or another. We built barricades and sang and danced and chained ourselves to things – my voice grew grainy from all the shouting. But we weren't really winning.

It became harder and harder to convince people to come out. Working from home became basically fixed after the 2020 pandemic. My friend Luke had been a carpenter, but his company went bust once robotics and AI became sophisticated and cheap enough to replace him. All the people we knew who were waiters, care workers, delivery drivers...those who actually needed to leave

Nina B...well

the house every day and brought news from the Outside were soon replaced. The lucky ones were retrained as office support workers, managing the AIs that were now doing their jobs, the rest were put on benefits, given no reason to ever go Outside again. VR, which had been a sort of exciting and expensive joke when it first came out, started dominating our everyday. Children didn't have to go to school and simply logged into their lessons every morning. Social media merged with videogame technology – the new platform Forum allowed you to embody your Avatar and travel around the entire world, meeting new people, hanging out with whoever you wanted. It was great you know, better than what real life was becoming. I had always dreamt of doing the Camino de Santiago, of surfing in Tahiti. In Forum I didn't have to be afraid all the time. My lungs were not being attacked by pollution, I didn't have to worry about the constant flooding, I didn't have to take care of everything around me – always working towards resilience, always fighting impossible odds.

My partner had fought the Forum. I told her I was so tired. She worked with children and saw how so many of them just took to Forum so naturally. The youngest ones had never seen much worth fighting for, not in the Outside they knew. And it was true, the 30s were devastating. The Gulf stream collapsed, or reversed, I can't even remember. The UK was stuck with a low thick grey cloud that just wouldn't budge. Every day was the same dull grey. The seasons became indistinguishable. Then it would rain: hard, solid rain that turned the streets to rivers. Humans bunkered in - everything else roughed the Outside. Soon everything else withered away. Turns out the rapidly decreasing biodiversity meant our flora's resilience crashed, becoming increasingly susceptible to any illness.

That's when the SAD displays came in. Even Judit's gardens had been abandoned by then, the

Outside held carcasses of trees and the weeds that had survived the pollinator crisis. So we turned inwards, into this artificial glow that offers us the freedom of the Forum and the chance to forget everything else. I find a dusty photograph. It's the 8 of us that used to live in this house, dressed up for a party outside in our garden. The house got split up. Every room was rented individually once kitchens stopped being used – produce became too expensive and most city folk just order in weekly sets of packaged meals. This is when my partner finally left. She laughed at my hypocrisy: "Whatever happened to the capitalist spectacle! You were the one always pointing out how we were getting more and more isolated, separated from each other, our food, and now even from reality with that stupid game!" All I could say was "I'm so tired." I don't know the people living around me anymore.

In a lot of ways life has become simpler, more comfortable. I fund my meals and my rent with

(Continued) on p. 129

80

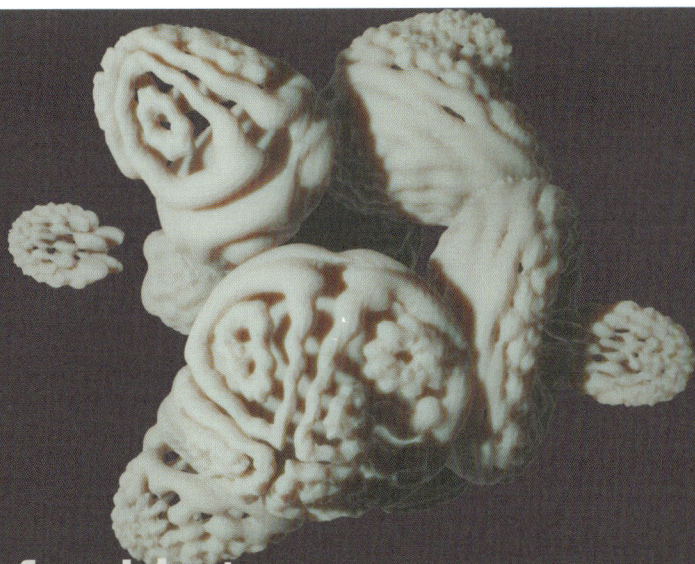

A brief guide to

The 2051 Munich Climate Conference

2051年慕尼黑气候大会

La Conferencia Sobre el Clima de Munich

2051 Мюнхенская климатическая конференция 2051 г. 18-19 September 2021

مؤتمر ميونخ للمناخ 2051

La Conférence sur le Climat de Munich en 2051 ⵜⴰⵙⵉⵍⴰⵍⵜ

The 2051 Munich Climate Conference, 2051年慕尼黑气候大会, La Conferencia Sobre el Clima de Munich 2051, Мюнхенская климатическая конференция 2051 La Conférence sur le Climat de Munich en 2051,

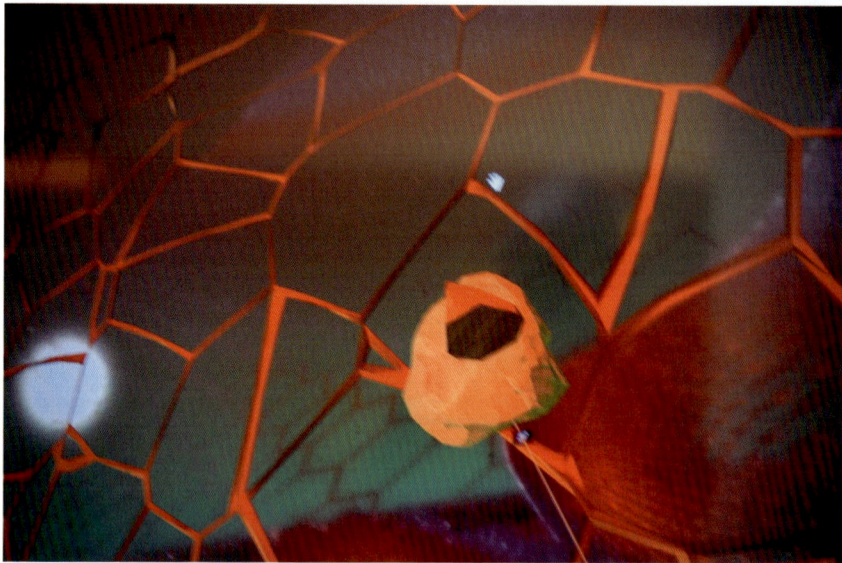

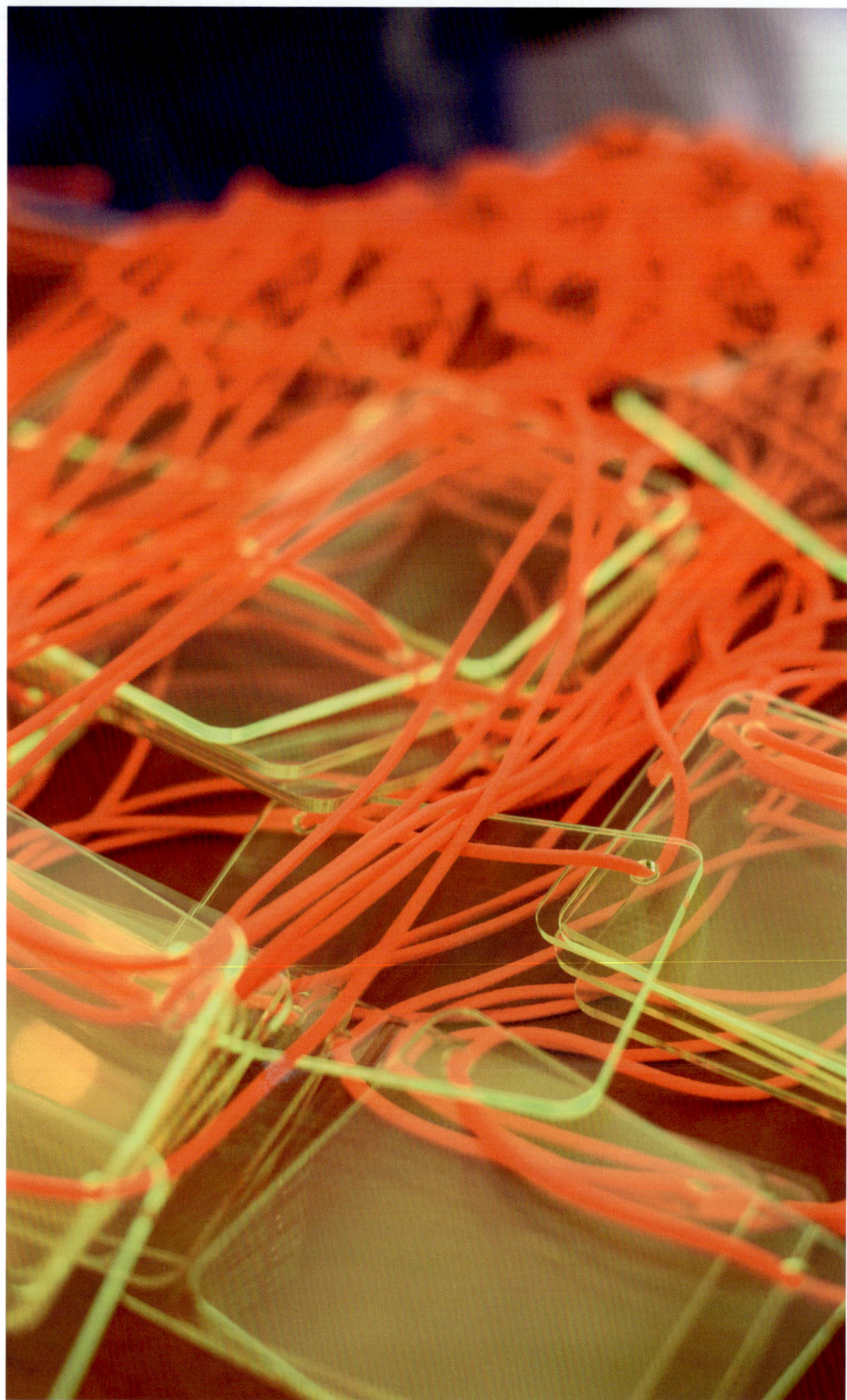

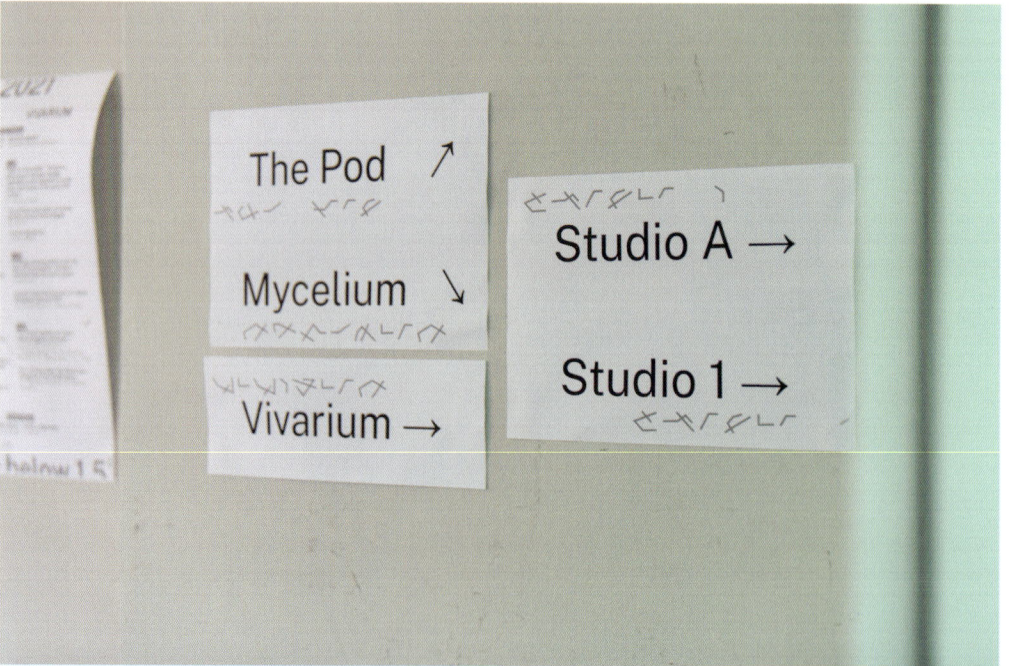

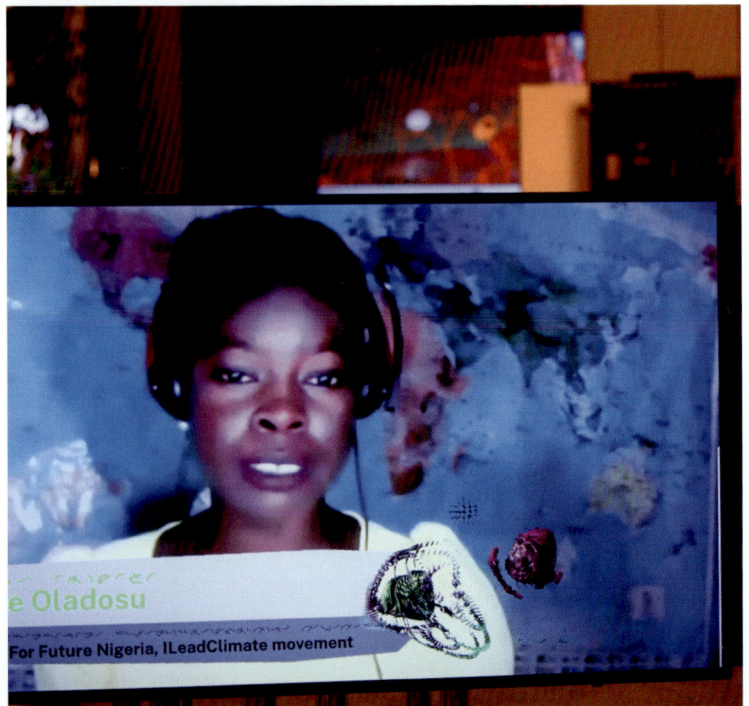

For Future Nigeria, ILeadClimate movement

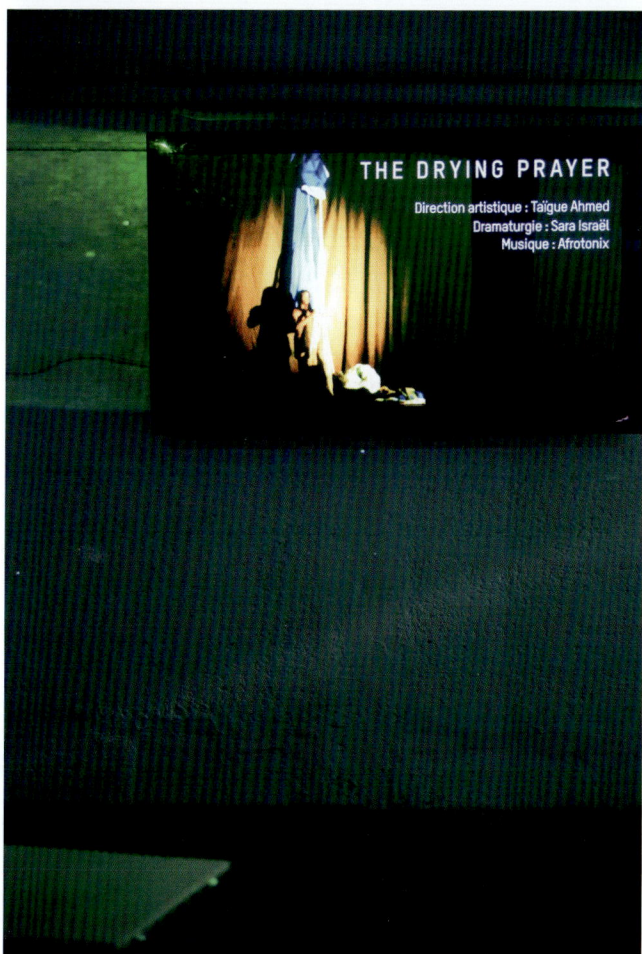

THE DRYING PRAYER

Direction artistique : Taïgue Ahmed
Dramaturgie : Sara Israël
Musique : Afrotonix

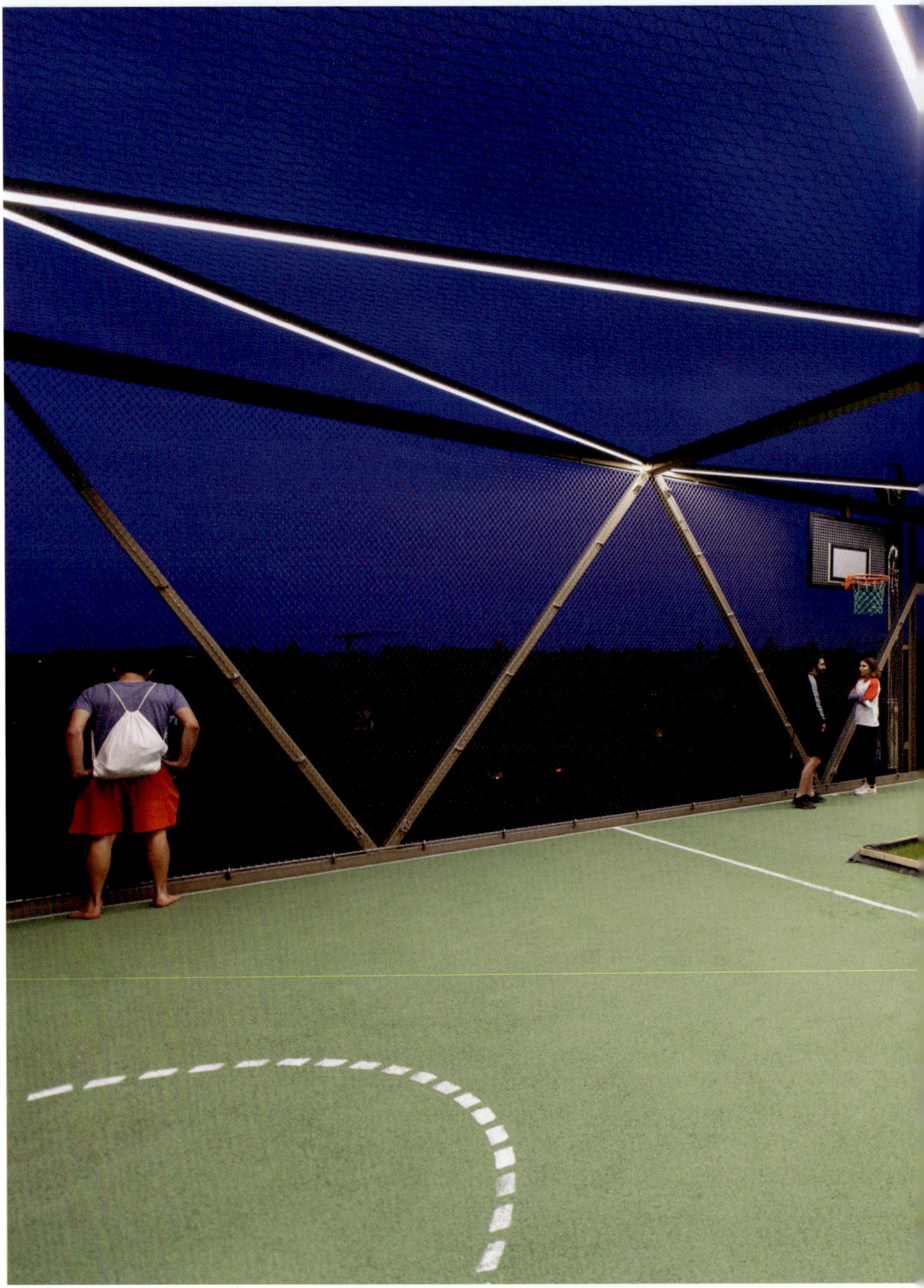

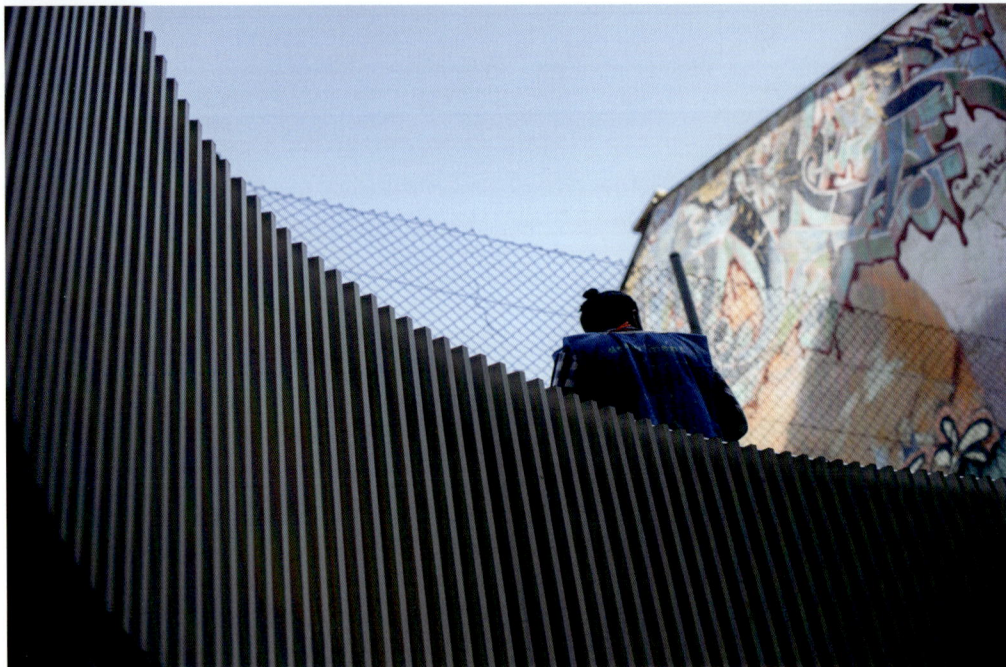

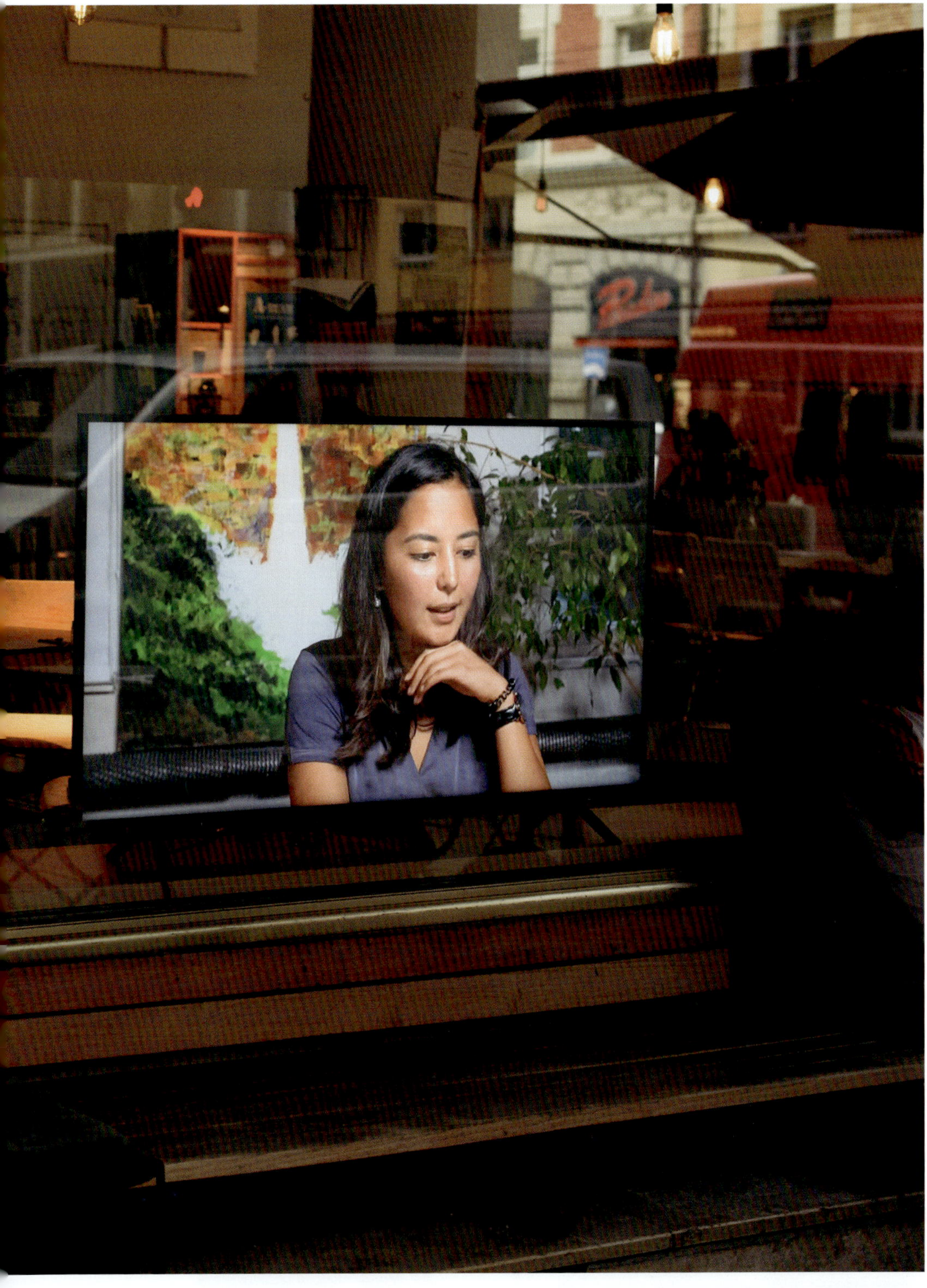

PORTAL

Enter the portal

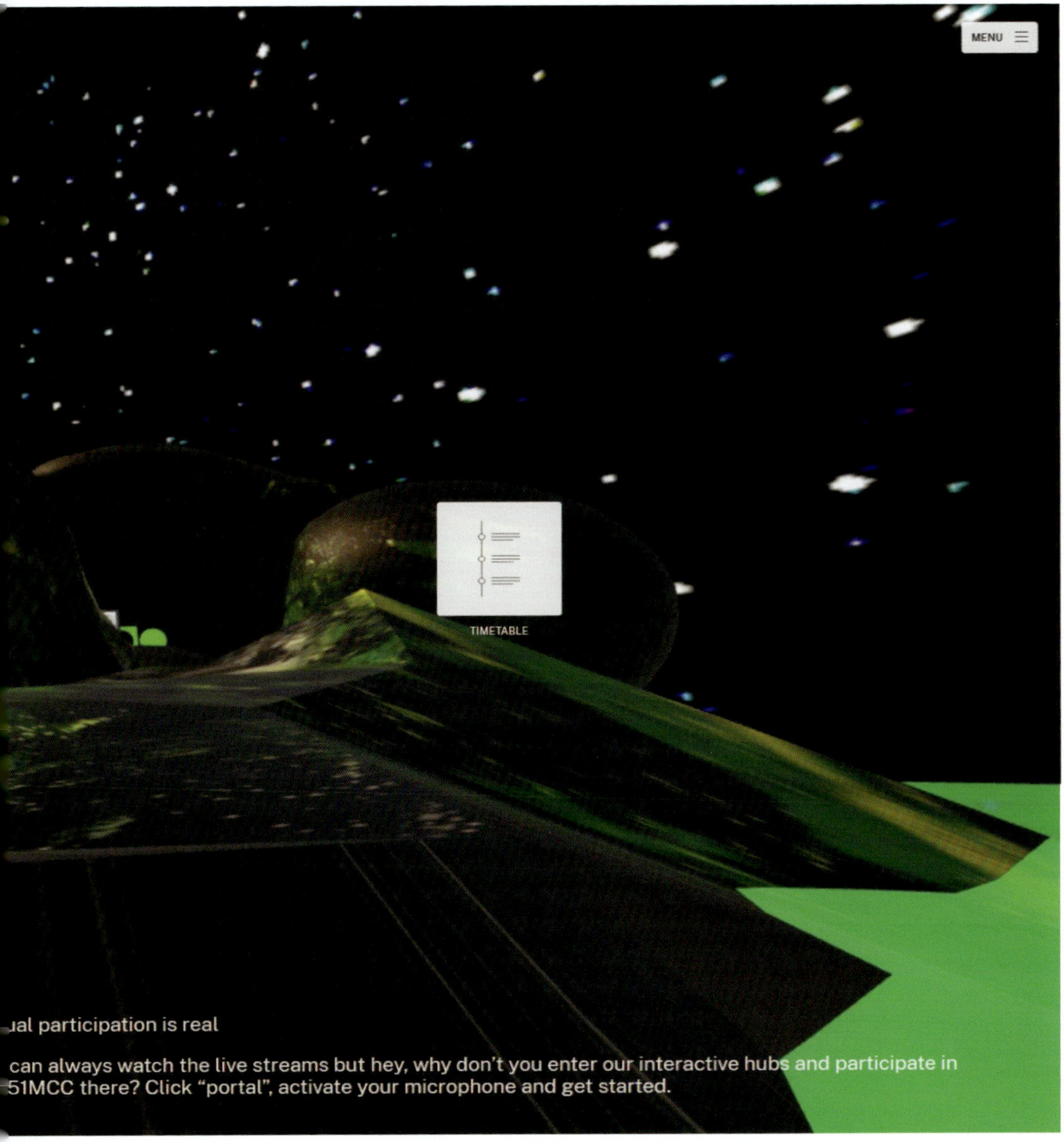

MENU ≡

TIMETABLE

ual participation is real

can always watch the live streams but hey, why don't you enter our interactive hubs and participate in
51MCC there? Click "portal", activate your microphone and get started.

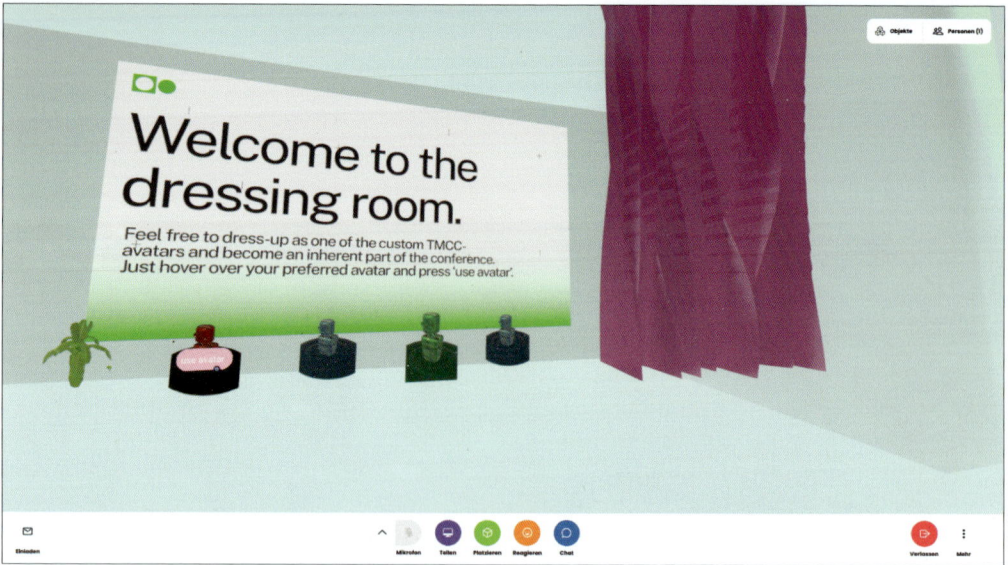

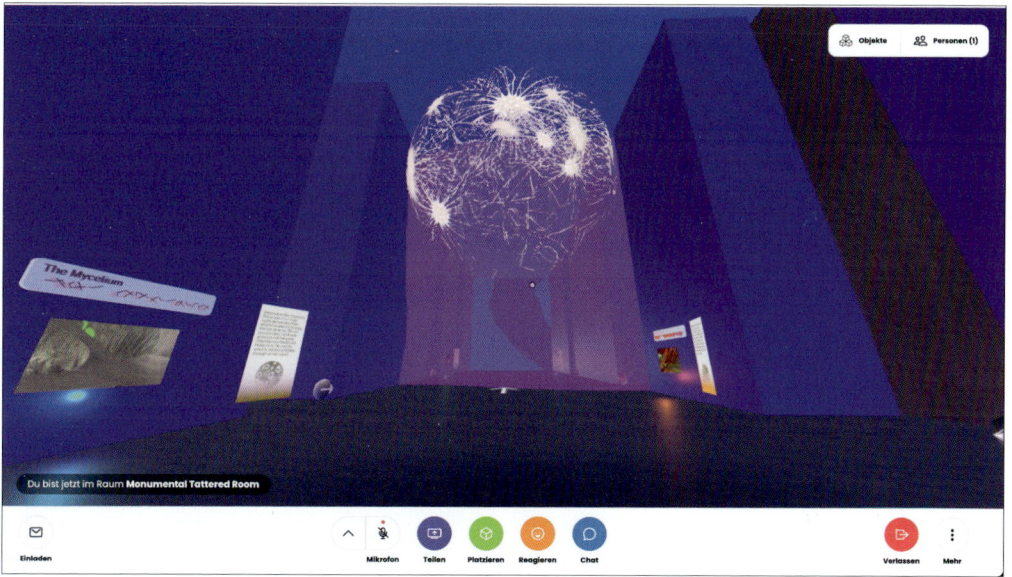

T2051MCC live via Moz͟ılla hubs

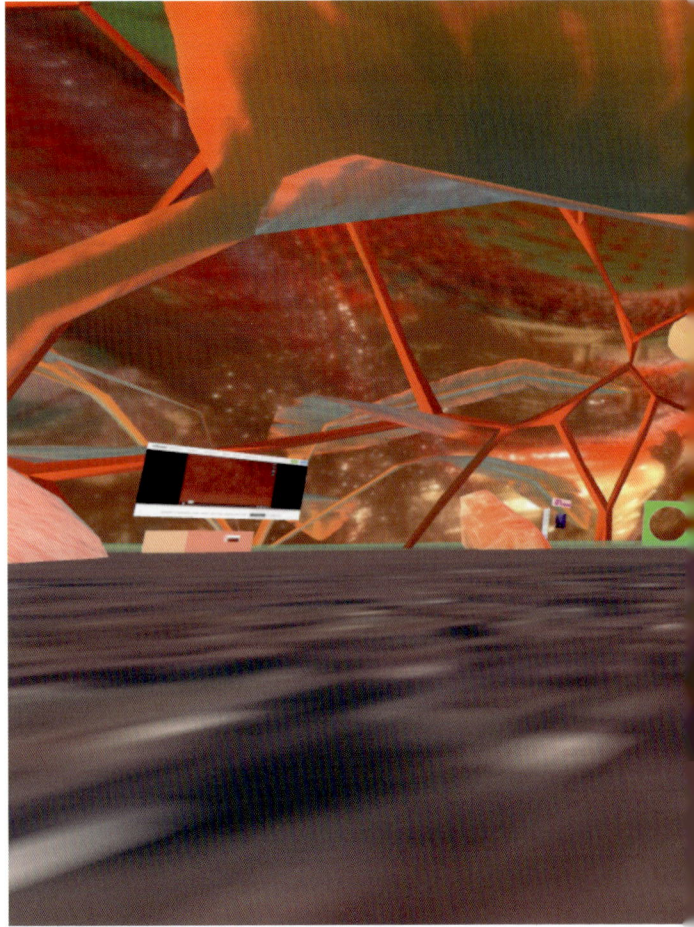

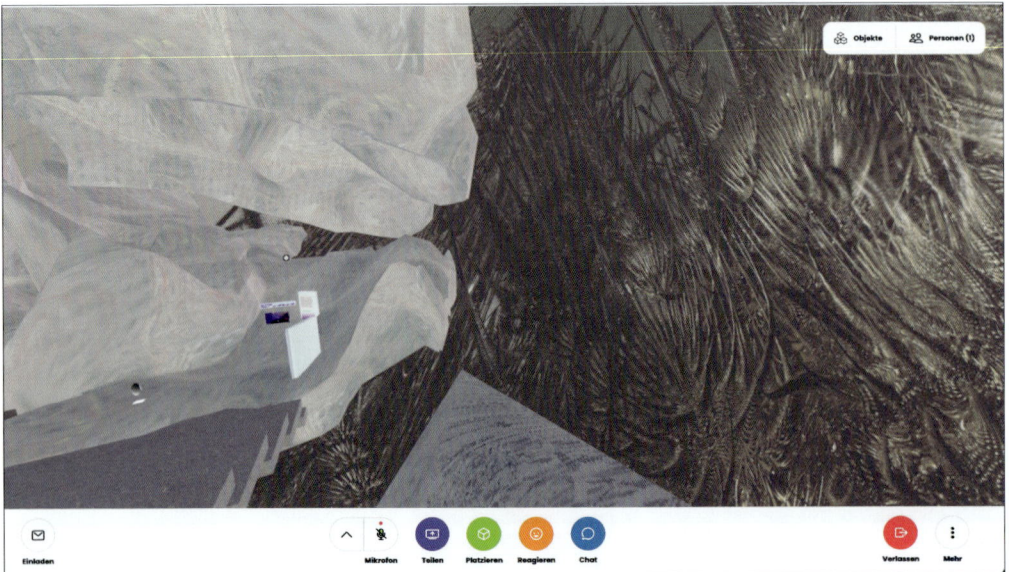

T2051MCC live via Mozilla hubs

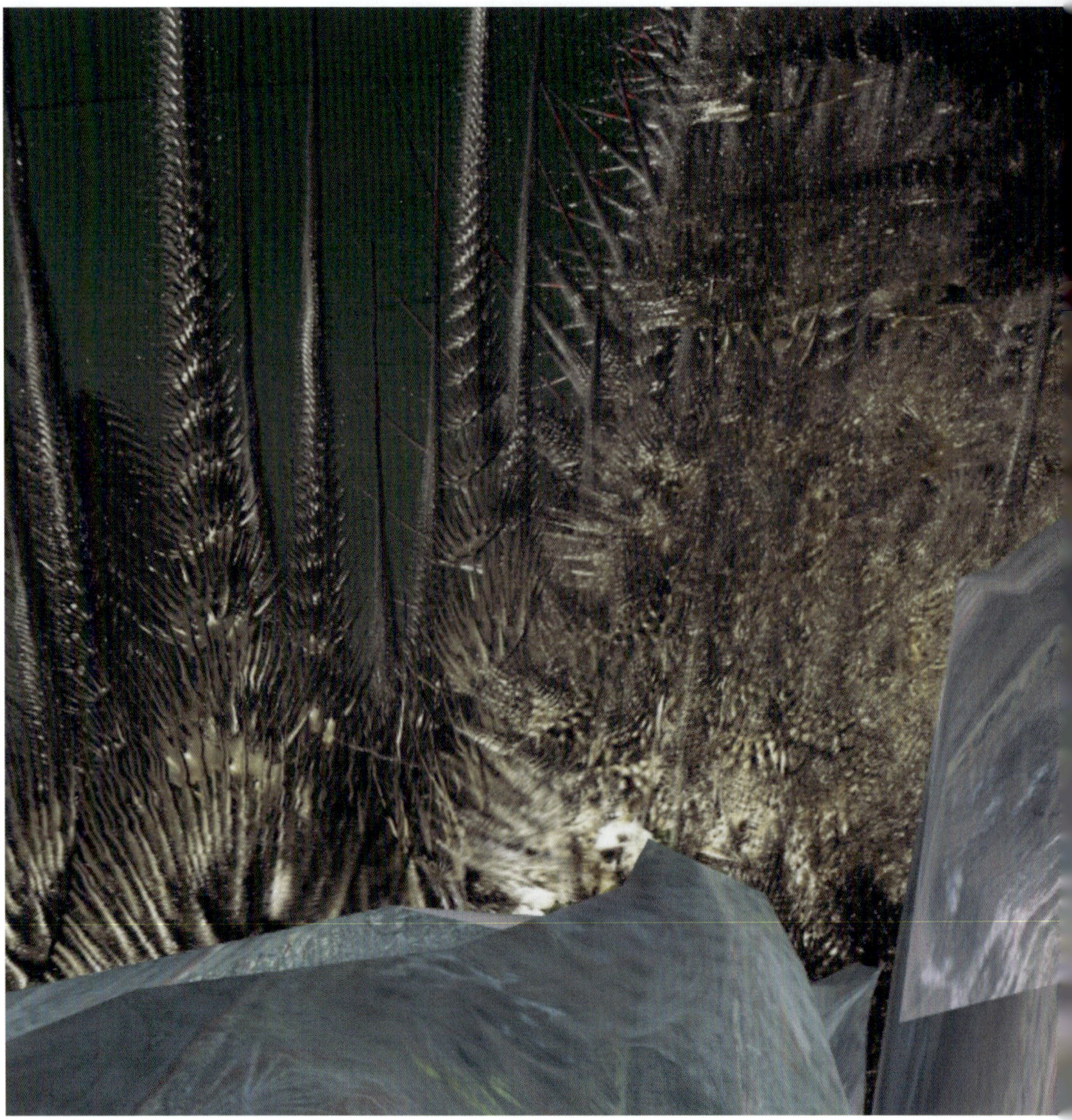

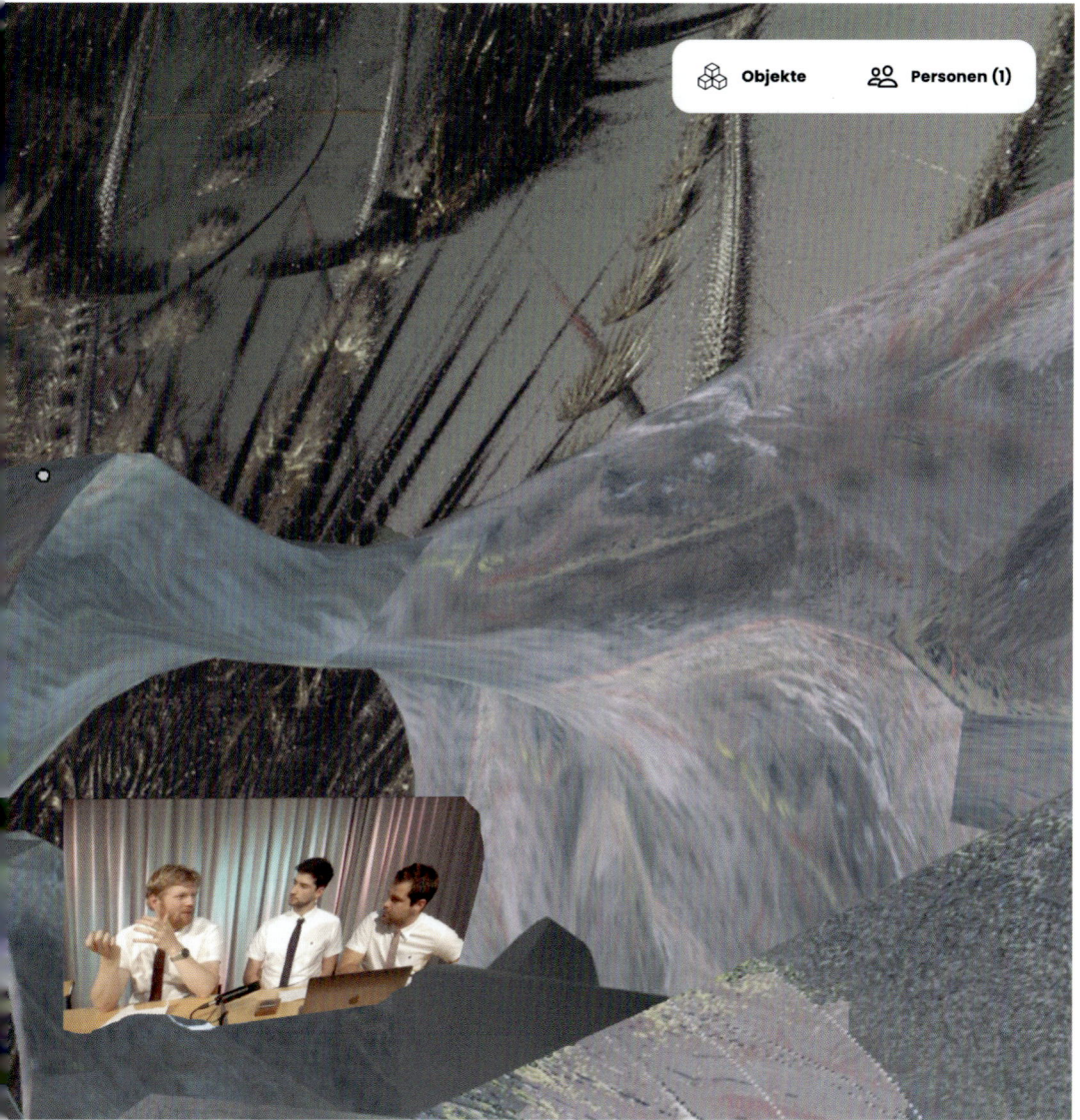

-0	86·0	86·5	85·5	84·0	83·5	84·0	81·5	74·0	67·0	21	Calcutta	·4	1·2	1·4
3·5	55·5	48·5	43·5	42·5	45·0	49·5	55·5	61·5	66·5	1,837	Canberra	1·9	1·7	2·2
7·5	62·5	58·0	55·5	54·0	55·0	57·0	61·0	64·0	67·0	56	Cape Town	·6	·3	·7
3·5	70·5	71·0	70·0	69·5	70·0	70·5	70·0	68·5	68·0	3,418	Caracas	·9	·4	·6
3·5	72·5	69·5	67·0	68·0	70·0				2·5	2,723	Catalão	11·8	10·2	8·8
5·0	47·5	57·5	67·5	73·5	7					823	Chicago	2·0	2·0	2·6
8·0	53·5	48·0	43·5	42·5						32	Christchurch, N.Z.	2·2	1·7	1·9
3·0	49·5	57·5	62·5	65·5						184	Cologne	2·0	1·8	1·8
1·0	82·0	82·5	81·0	81·0						24	Colombo	3·5	3·5	5·8
4·0	84·0	82·0	78·5	77·0	7					97	Darwin	15·2	12·3	10·0
2·5	82·0	92·0	92·5	88·5	86·0				2·5	714	Delhi	·9	·7	·5
1·0	62·5	64·5	67·5	70·5	71·5	71·5	69·5	66·0	62·5	82	Funchal, Madeira	2·5	2·9	3·1
3·0	49·5	57·0	64·0	67·5	66·5	60·5	51·0	42·0	35·5	1,329	Geneva	1·9	1·8	2·2
2·5	65·0	70·0	75·0	79·0	80·0	78·0	74·0	68·5	65·0	151	Hamilton, Bermuda	4·4	4·7	4·8
6·0	18·0	31·5	40·0	47·0	48·0	40·5	31·0	20·0	4·0	49	Hebron, Labrador	·9	·7	·9
	71·0	78·0	81·5	82·5	82·5	81·0	77·0	69·5	63·5	109	Hong Kong	1·3	1·8	2·9

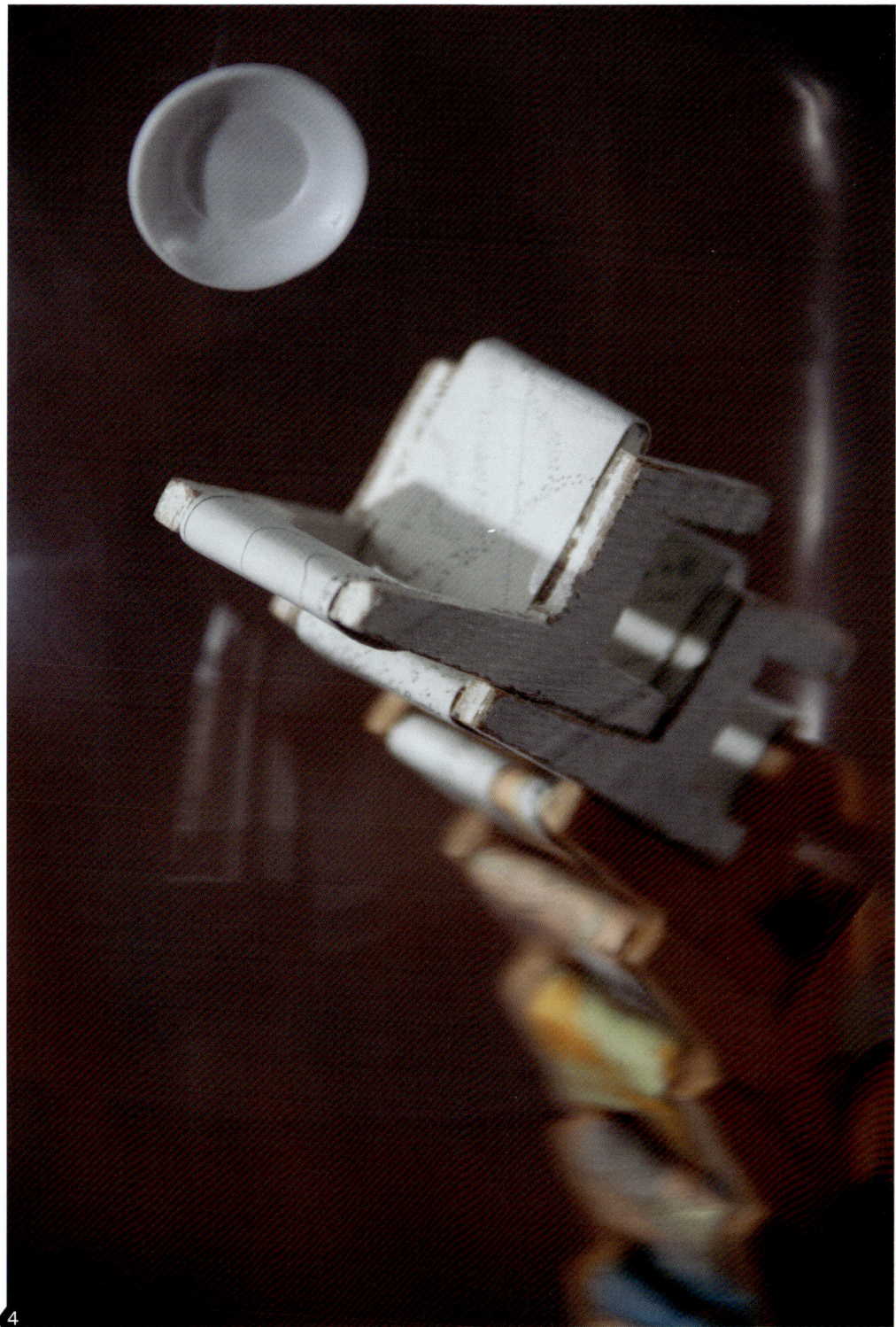

Photos and illustrations from contributors

Photos and illustrations fro   contributors

FAILING IMAGES. HOW THE VISUAL DISCOURSE ON CLIMATE CHANGE CHANGED NOTHING IN THE AGE OF VISUAL COMMUNICATION.

Markus Kink (pp. 38-55)

SHROUD FOR AN ANCIENT SEA.
Sarah Nance (pp. 56-57)

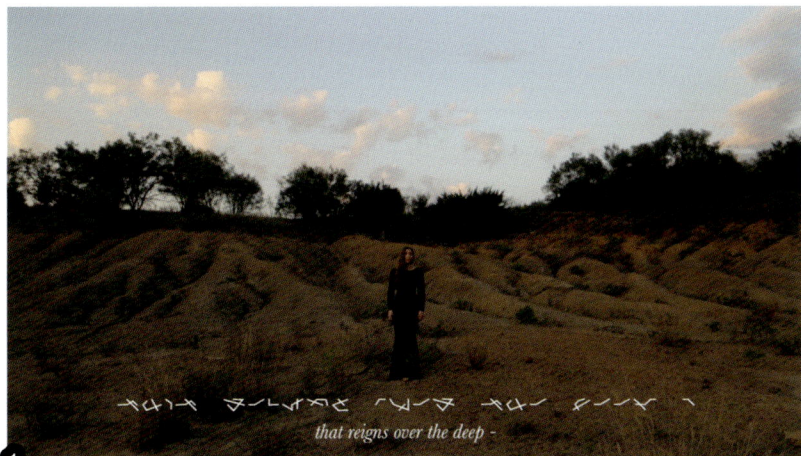

that reigns over the deep -

eternal night,

skagway tidal aria (1945-2081)

There __ is a dark - ness

that __ reigns __ o - ver the deep and __ what __

__ is __ up is what __ is down and __ the qui -

- et ver - ti - go __ in my __ ears __ is the slum - b'ring

turn - - - ing of diff - i - dent __

drip - ping __ black moons __

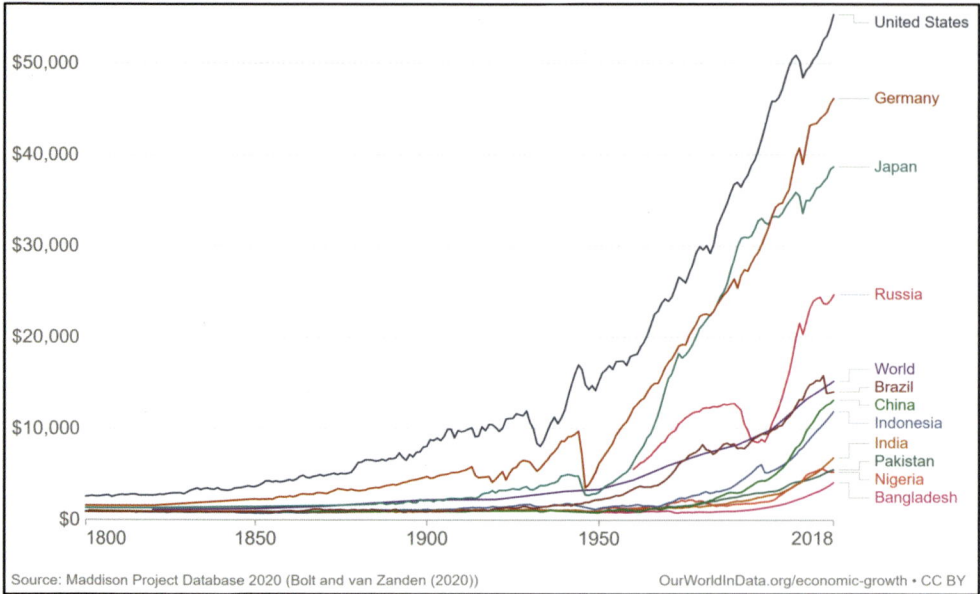

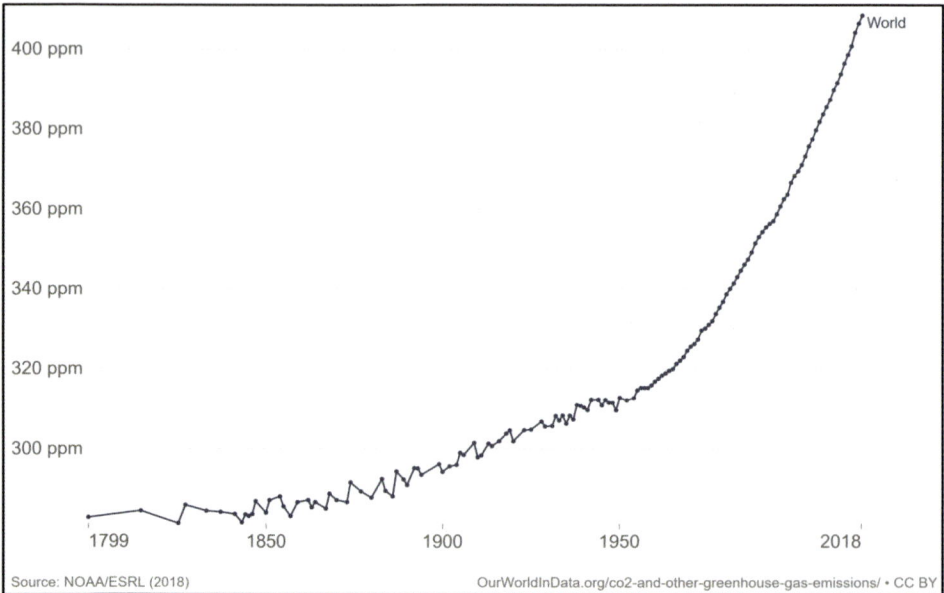

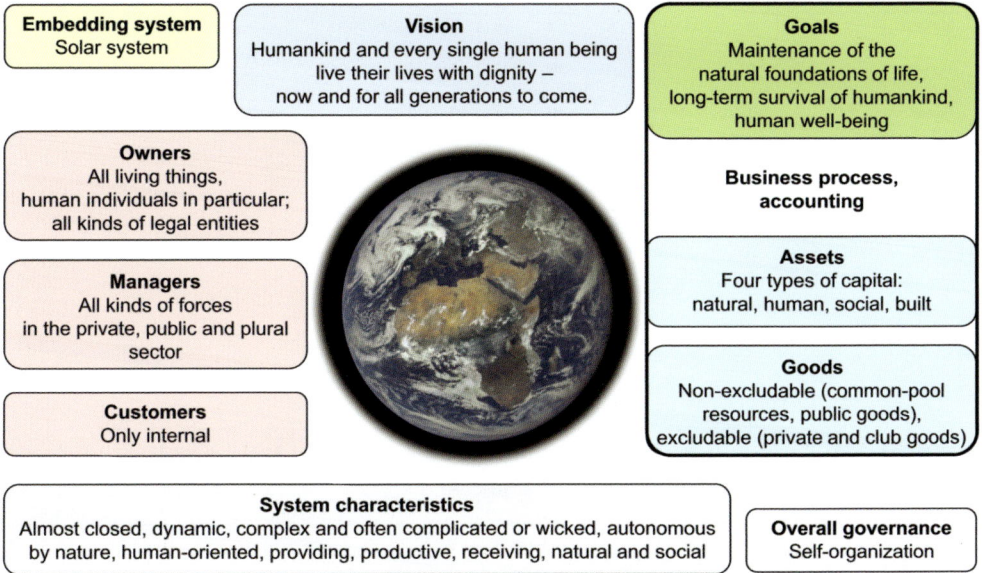

Embedding system	Vision	Goals
Solar system	Humankind and every single human being live their lives with dignity – now and for all generations to come.	Maintenance of the natural foundations of life, long-term survival of humankind, human well-being

Owners
All living things, human individuals in particular; all kinds of legal entities

Business process, accounting

Managers
All kinds of forces in the private, public and plural sector

Assets
Four types of capital: natural, human, social, built

Customers
Only internal

Goods
Non-excludable (common-pool resources, public goods), excludable (private and club goods)

System characteristics
Almost closed, dynamic, complex and often complicated or wicked, autonomous by nature, human-oriented, providing, productive, receiving, natural and social

Overall governance
Self-organization

2

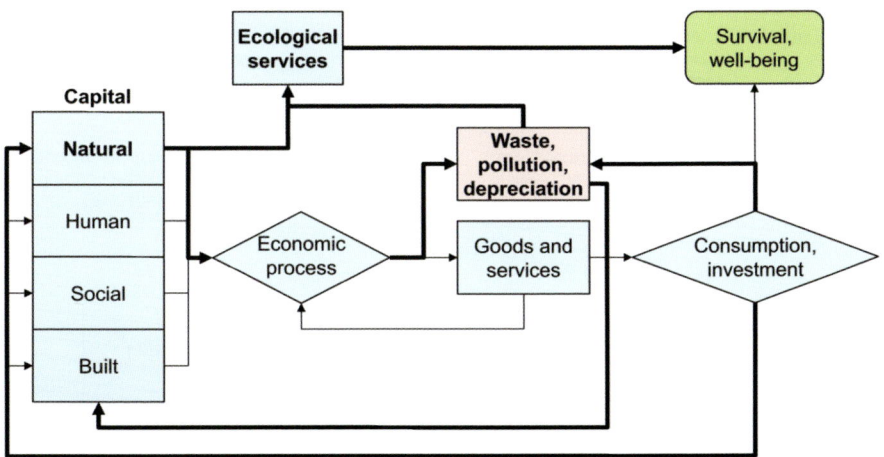

3

Traditional:
Gross Domestic Product

Capital	Value* at		Δ
	t_1	t_2	
Natural	12	12	0
Human	9	9	0
Social	6	7	+1
Built	2	3	+1
Total	29	31	+2

Profit illusion

Conclusion:
business as usual

New:
Planet Earth as a Business

Capital	Value* at		Δ
	t_1	t_2	
Natural	63	58	-5
Human	16	16	0
Social	16	17	+1
Built	5	6	+1
Total	100	97	-3

Real loss

Conclusion:
transform your business

4

Issues	Concepts from management theory or economics	Major findings from transfer and adaptation to PEaaB	Implications for PEaaB managers
Business model	Business model typology [30], managing a hub economy [31]	Platform business, out of balance, humankind as destabilizing superpower	Reduce humankind's value capture and support the other species as ecosystem partners
Generic strategies	Cost leadership – differentiation – focus [32], efficiency – consistency – sufficiency [33], green growth – post-growth – degrowth [34]	Hybrid strategy possible (sequential or simultaneous), right-mix debate	Facilitate the right-mix debate
Organizational structure	Line(-and-staff), matrix, project organization by business functions, product groups, customer industries, projects etc. [35]	If design authority existed: multi-dimensional matrix by economic ecosystems, types of capital, place, forms of life etc.	Cope with PEaaB as a wicked system with unstable structure in a seamless web
Organizational culture	Interrelated set of assumption, values, levers, and evident phenomena [36], global economic ethic [37]	Strongly needed, but still too big differences among too many agents	Emphasize the few common culture elements, seize discontinuities as culture development opportunities
Behavioral innovation	Principles: rhythm, system levers, internal compass, reframing, impulse [38]	Applicable in line with wicked-systems theory	Pursue behavioral, harnessed innovation on sub-wicked system level

5

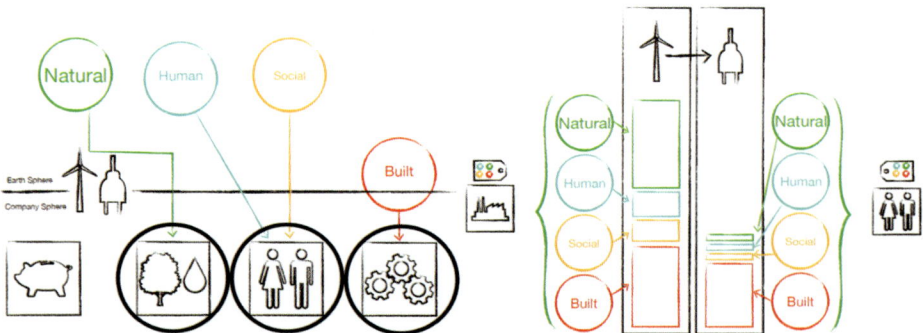

6

EARTH

- No. 1 for life in the entire universe
- 4.6 billion years of success
- Leader in operating complex ecosystems

Humanity has been one of my innovation projects for 2 million years.
For project completion within the next 40 years I am seeking one billion

Earth Operations Managers

in the areas of civil society, politics, business, science, and individuals.

Your tasks:
- Integrate humanity into my proven planetary processes
- Transform human civilization toward sustainability

What I expect from you:

- First experience in dealing with the human species

- Interest in the interrelations between nature, culture, institutions, economy, and technology

- Commitment to my three main goals:
  Preservation of the natural foundations of life – Social equity – Economic efficiency

- At least some of the leadership competencies which have been valid for thousands of years:

+ **Open-mindedness for new approaches** + **Willingness to experiment** + **Ability to cross boundaries** + **Constructive handling of fundamental differences**	+ **Courage and determination** + **Integrity** + **Power of persuasion** + **Mental resilience** + **Long-term orientation (> 1,000 years)**

- Self-determined start as a manager in your current position

Compensation: Lifelong supply to you and all descendants

Reference: Schmitt 2019

7

Level of climate control

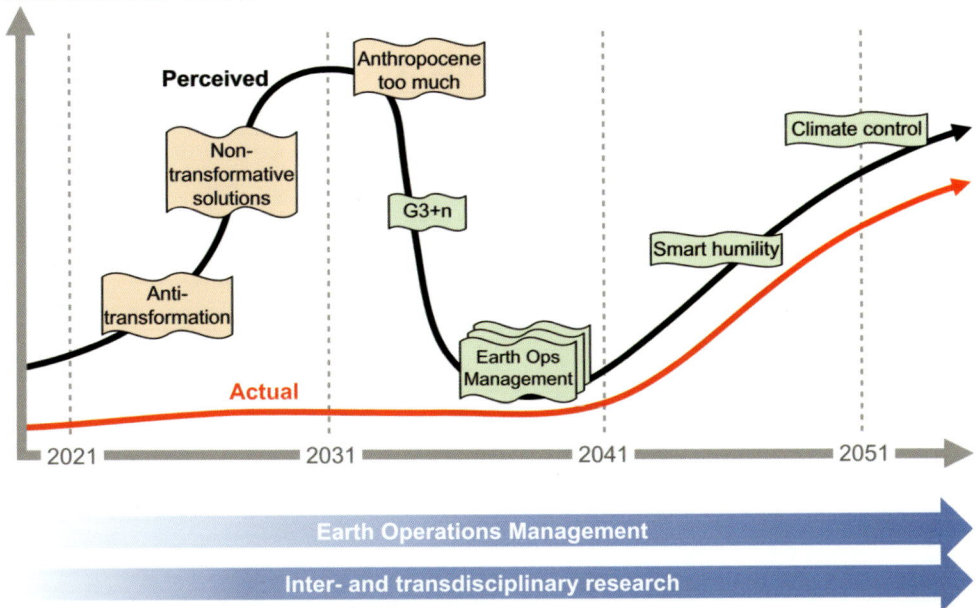

Perceived

Anthropocene too much

Non-transformative solutions

G3+n

Climate control

Anti-transformation

Smart humility

Earth Ops Management

Actual

2021   2031   2041   2051

Earth Operations Management

Inter- and transdisciplinary research

8

LEIKHĒN
AN AUDIOVISUAL EXPERIENCE INSPIRED BY A SYMBIOTIC RELATIONSHIP.
Claudia Robles Angel (pp. 159-163)

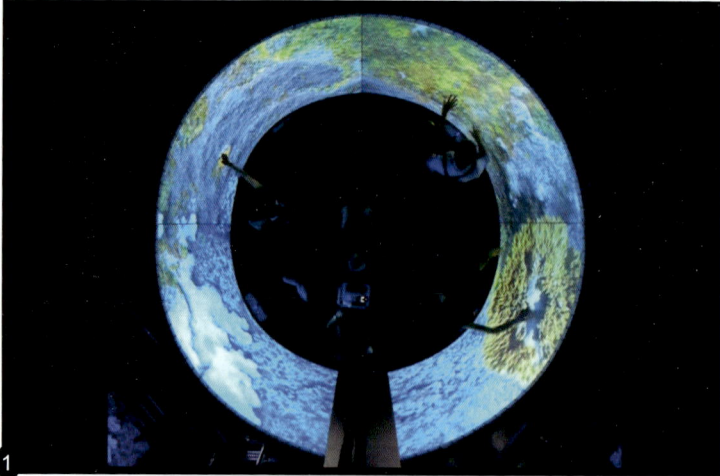

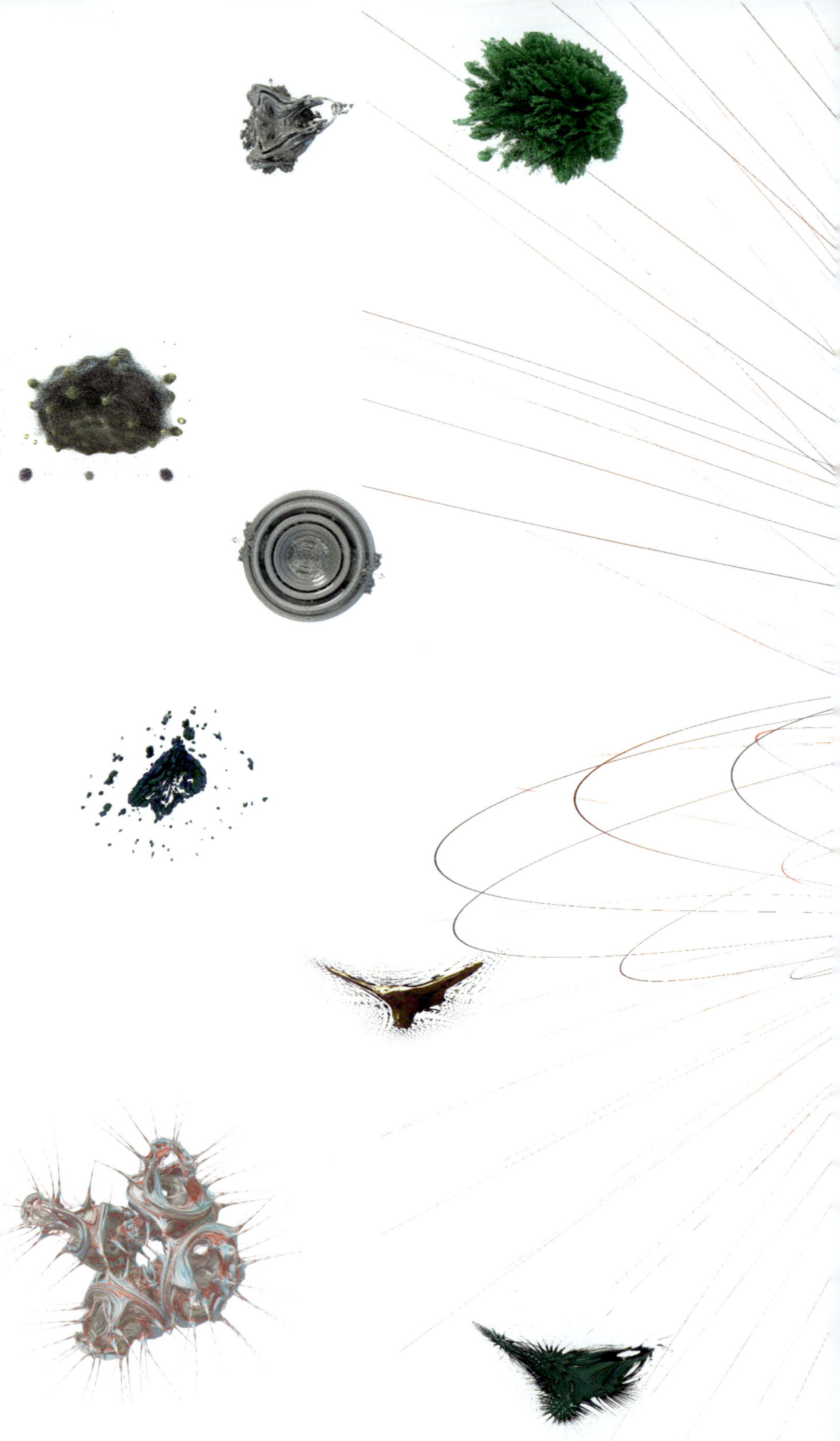

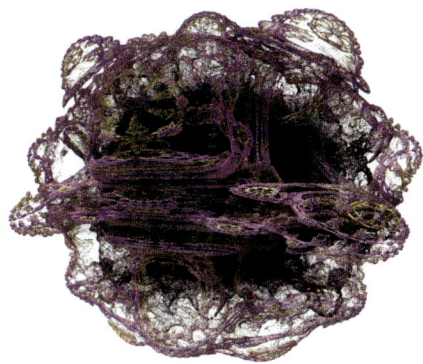

day 1: beyond 2°

	MYCELIUM	VIVARIUM
room		

10.00am

Opening Session

Opening statements | **Keynote speech**
A. Paollucci | z. Akhlaqi | S. Huq

12.00 noon

51-1A
Climate Resilient Development in 2051: For whom?
L. Schipper, E. Carr, S. Eriksen, L. F. Carril, B. Glavovic, C. Trisos

Locked-in: Revisiting coastal adaptation policies in the Maldives
G. Gussmann

51-1B
Why academia was of no help in building a sustainable society
M. Keck

The transformative potential of sociological imagination for eco-social change
L. Schlegel

3.00pm

51-1C
1001 scenarios for a troubled Earth
R. A. Tyszczuk

Proposed silvopastoral management solutions to the environmental and economic problems of the Carpathian Basin after the drought of 1862-1863
A. Varga

51-1D
Failing Images. How the Visual Discourse on Climate Change Changed Nothing in the Age of Visual Communication
M. Kink

Playing it safe or going the risky route: Europe's Emission Trading System as a yardstick for taking (regulatory) risks to address (climate) risks
M. Pahle

5.30pm

51-1E
Shroud for an Ancient Sea
S. Nance

Accelerating towards the Anthropocene: How 2025 transformed the future
M. Kernan

Earth Operations Management
K. Wallner, M. Schmitt

51-1F
A Museum of Carbon Ruins? Ethical and political challenges in historicising an unevenly distributed decarbonisation
P. Graham Raven, J. Stripple, L. Bengtsson Sonesson, R. Hildingsson, G. MacDonald, A. Nikoleris

Agony Aunt Letters: Epistolary notes from an everyday future
N. Powell

7.30pm

Closing Session

Keynote speech | **Artistic statement: Looking Back at "The Drying Prayer" (2021)**
A. Oladosu | T. Ahmed, S. Israel

18 Sep 2021

19 Sep 2021

room

MYCELIUM   VIVARIUM

10.00am

Opening statement **Keynote speech**
Yolande Bönning   Elizabeth Wanjiru Wathuti

12.00 noon

51-2A
Reducing the ecological impact of T2051MCC
S. Börsig, S. Weidacher, R. Geres, S. Brandis, T. Grantner

51-2B
Adapt or Surrender? The policy dilemmas of climate change, habitability and migration in a low-lying atoll nation in the early 21st century.
K. van der Geest

The promise and reality of carbon dioxide removal technologies
M. Jakob

Climate Barbarism
J. Blumenfeld

3.00pm

51-2C
Project Pando: A social network analysis of an early post-Paris Collaborative Habitat Node Station effort
N. Smith

Renaturierung – The human vs nature re-connection
S. Javaid, R. Habeeb

51-2D
Tackling unsustainability with the help of consumption corridors: Transforming the meat system
M. Kanerva

Lessons from the Pioneers of a World Changing Cultural Shift
M. Solveig Siem, H. Naalsund Wille

5.30pm

51-2E
Global cloud control Or: How I learned to stop worrying and love geoengineering
J. Kubečka, V. Besel, I. Neefjes

Lost in the nexus?: The integration-fragmentation of global climate governance in 2015-2045
M. Goldberg

Climate Resilient Development in 2051: For whom?
N. Powell

51-2F
The virtual realities of hydro-meteorological extremes
L. Arnal, M.-H. Ramos, F. Pappenberger, B. van den Hurk, M. Werner, L. Magnusson, H. L. Cloke

First contact after the Blank Days / Delegation from Kathmandu
W. Tuladhar-Douglas, B. Tuladhar-Douglas

7.30pm

Closing Session

Keynote speech   **Artistic statement**
H. Gualinga   C. Robles

day 2: below 1.5°

How will humans in 2051 look back at today?

Discover the answers of 45 scholars at The 2051 Munich Climate Conference

18-19 Sep 2021
T2051MCC.com

Мюнхенская климатическая конференция 2051 г. خانملل 2051 خينويم رمتؤم La Conférence sur le Climat de Munich en 2051 The 2051 Munich Climate How will humans in 2051 Conference 2051年慕尼黑气候大会 look back at today? La Conferencia Sobre el Clima de Munich 2051 Мюнхенская климатическая конференция 2051 г. خينويم رمتؤم 2051 خانملل La Conférence sur le Climat de Munich en 2051 Discover the answers of more than 2051年慕尼黑气候大会 45 academics at خينويم رمتؤم 2051 خانملل The 2051 Munich Climate Conference Мюнхенская климатическая конференция 2051 г. 18-19 Sep 2021 La Conferencia Sobre el Clima de Munich 2051 2051年慕尼黑气候大会 La Conferencia Sobre el Clima de Munich T2051MCC.com 2051

(Continued from p. 80)

the odd jobs I do on Forum. I've been a fisherman, an accountant and a forest ranger. Now I'm teaching at University, running a course for young people on how to make the most of their Forum lives. The most annoying thing is having to constantly wonder whether the people you're interacting with are real. Forum is getting full of very realistic bots. Last month I only realised this woman I was dating was a Bot after the server was closed by the #StopBots campaign. But I get to do what I want. If things start getting nasty, I can just switch server. It's not like everything that has happened is my fault. Not that much has changed anyway. I'm still in the same house.

I guess what I'm trying to ask is: I did the best I could right? All things considered.

I'm sorry. Please repeat.

Dear agony aunt - above 1° celsius

129   Nice Powell

I'm truly grateful to be here, to speak about what it'll look like in 2051. I want to really appreciate the leadership for organising this conference to see how we can whole imagine our world in, in three decades to come.

So this, this is how I'm going to start, you know: There are two schools of thoughts. And one believes that migration in itself should be an adaptation strategy, while the second believes that adaptation is failing, that migration is a failure to adapt.

We are seeing it through the clashes between the farmers and the herders and this it what the climate change crisis poses to us because it's overwhelming our infrastructure. And this is the current happening now that we can no longer adapt to the climate change crisis. And our democracy is at stake now. And probably the lake Chad might have dried out, you know, these are the kind of crises that we are faced with currently. Because the mega Chad lake has a stroke.

Sahara that was once the green Sahara is now known as world's largest and hottest desert. This is a crisis for us to beat. And as time passes by, it becomes nearly impossible for us to take the necessary action since we can't take it now. And now it'll cost us more time to deal with the issue of climate change. Because there are decades of inaction that preceded the decade of action. And also policies that we did not take into account some decades ago cannot suit the present situation.

So more irreversible actions occurred because we did not act the way we should. And that is what brought us to what we have today. That it is becoming unbearable for the world citizen because climate change is making our habitat, our earth or planet inhabitable for the population. First, our agriculture: the agricultural sector is suffering a setback because we are unable to adapt to the current crisis.

We have millions or billions of population to feed, but there is no capacity. People are dying of hunger. People are dying of poverty. More people are in dire need of humanitarian assistance. And that is why we are calling for humanitarian aid so that there can be food on the table of people and they are likely to be sustainable enough for them not to require more aid in dealing with this crisis.

And also talking about our infrastructure: it can no longer take the impact of climate change, because that is what we are seeing currently. That is happening. Our democracy is now at stake because we can no longer have human rights to be the law, because our environment is deteriorating every day. And at the same time, it's affecting human rights. We don't have safe drinking water, and it takes days for us to dig a well for us to get the needed amount of water we need. And now our taps can no longer bear water for us. At the same time, we cannot isolate. No quarantine from the impact of climate change. Climate change is now a pandemic that we cannot get a vaccine for, and that is the most dangerous part of it. That we cannot get a vaccine for climate change crisis. I remember how we dealt with the COVID 19. That everyone, everywhere could afford vaccine for free and the government's trying to make sure that everyone has a vaccine.

The same thing we could have done to climate change to ensure that everyone is able to take action. You know, I have seen where a voluntary action could make an action to be completed, and that is why we can still do something now, but it might be too late. And that is why we have been saying, you know, the youth of yesterday are the adults of today.

And that is why I said that we have to take necessary action now. That we are responsible for not just the future, but also the present because the present action is determining where we are going to. We have had several decades of inaction. Lake Chad has stroke. What do we talk about? The millions of livelihoods that depend on it on a daily basis. What will happen to our rivers now? Many people need water on a daily basis, which is becoming a scarce commodity. And now climate change impact is now causing a reality that we are seeing, and we could not deal with the climate change crisis as it should.

We are now dealing with the multiplying effects. Now it is threatening piece and causing an insecurity issue. And now it has become a big migration issue. That everyone could not stay in the east of our country due to displacement. We are now being faced with an exodus of people leaving their country. Migration is never a choice. Never has being a refugee been a choice. It is due to the impact of climate change. And I'm afraid that in this present situation, many, many more people we have to migrate because currently more than half of the world's population resides in countries that are faced with the greatest impact of climate change crisis. Now we all have the responsibility to take the necessary action or it becomes too late for us to act.

And that is why I've been saying, that every leader should be committed to what it is our leadership can give. We should stop talking about 2030 when we are now here today. Now we can make the necessary decision at this time to talk about what each leadership can give in solving the climate change crisis. Enough of leaders postponing climate into the future because this is the most difficult and dangerous thing to do. To postpone climate change into the future or climate action into the future. And this is now that we need many more people to join climate justice. For us to come together to decide: reimagine the present and the future together.

Because I come from a country where we are faced with the biggest impact of climate change crisis. And today it still continues. Women are, girls are still bearing the burden of the climate change crisis. We want activism to work, but it's motto is: let us be the change we want the world to be.

Everyone has to take action individually, collectively, in groups and different kinds. Coming together, taking the necessary action, because I don't see where we can build climate resilience. And we keep emitting, we keep the increasing emissions. It's not possible. It won't work like this. So in as much as we want to build climate change capacity or adaptation to mitigate climate change, we must keep the coal or the fossil fuels in the ground.

And we must start now. By thinking or rethinking renewable sources of energy that is affordable for all. Making it to be subsidised for everybody in each community to be able to afford it. We are all responsible for a liveable planet, no matter where you are from, no matter the action that we are taking. All what we are concerned with, is where we are going to, or what we want to achieve.

You know, I am also from a region, and I had in my undergrad studies in a region that is prone to the clashes between the farmers and herders due to control of resources that are limited. And I am afraid that in this present time, it's becoming worse. As climate change is affecting our diversity. And I'm afraid that it might lead to no ethno-religious war.

Because that is what the current situation is indicating. So we must act now and act fast because anything we do not take into our account right now, we can't take into accounting in the nearest decades. So we are all responsible to take necessary action and to keep reminding our leaders to take action.

Because the youth of today, we, we will become the adult. And that is why we have to act now. We are saying that the iceberg is melting and these are irreversible actions. We are losing our landscape, green vegetative landscape every day, due to the impact of climate change crisis. At the same time, we are losing our water bodies. They are shrinking and the average temperature in Africa is rising unbearably. And it's becoming unbearable even more, because we are now seeing more, heatwaves, cyclones, wild fires happening around the globe. Record breaking temperature, record breaking reports that we have not seen in the decades past.

This is the only single greatest impact that can affect human existence. Our biodiversity is now at stake. We are losing species every day. And this shows that humanity is in an age of extinction too, if we don't act right now. So every action we take today, we should know that it counts towards making our planet a liveable planet.

And I'm afraid that our democracy, that we cherish so much might also be broken by the climate change crisis. Because democracy should really be defined as a government for the people and the environment by the people and the environment and of the people and the environment. And this way, climate change will not affect our human rights.

And humans will not also intrude into the landscape of our environment and thereby we will have a balanced ecosystem for all. Because right now, our ecosystem has been distorted. A lot is happening, a lot of crises. And the IPCC report is also giving us a warning on every report that they have released for us to take action.

The science is not failing, but we are not listening to the science yet. Because there is no vaccine that we can use to heal or to recover from the impact of climate change. And that is why we are saying that this COVID 19 for us not to recover a green identity is not normal. It is not normal when we have to leave our country to someone else's country or when we have to cross difficult terrain or when we have to be trafficked. And this is a situation that more people will be trafficked or there will be human trafficking of person to the next country in search of livelihood. Every sector that makes up our economy has become vulnerable to climate change crisis. It's now climate sensitive agriculture, housing, building, and every other business. And this is why people's livelihoods are in danger today due to the impact of climate change.

And in Africa, we are an agrarian society that will depend on agriculture for our livelihoods and for employment. You can now imagine the number of people it has displaced from their life. This leads to armed groups of people expanding their reach. And I'm afraid that I might lose my home country if care is not taken due to the impact of climate change posing insecurity and making people to be recruited into Haram group. Because they have lost their livelihoods, lost what they have to do in order for them to be sustainable.

And this is why we have to act now and act fast. 2051. In this day, in this time, we have to reimagine our society. We have to think faster than we do, and we have to increase the force of action. Because those actions that we did not take, we have to find ways of taking them right now, in order for it to suit this prevalent situation in dealing with the impact of climate change. Because if we don't do that climate change might erase many nations in this world as it is happening right now. Thank you.

SEPTEMBER 19, 10 AM. VENUE: VIVARIUM

My name is Elisabeth Wathuti and I'm an environmentalist and climate activist from Kenya and also the founder of the Green Generation Initiative and Head of Campaigns and Daima Consortium Coordinator of the Wangari Maathai Foundation. And for me, when I was younger, I did witness deforestation firsthand, because all of the forests I liked to play in were cut down. And the streams that I used to drink from became flooded with plastic waste. And just that natural wild that my friends and I knew as children changed completely before our eyes. And one thing that really connects me to nature is having grown up in one of the most forested regions in my country. And I say that being in this fight as an environmentalist and a climate activist is actually personal because I have strongly had that connection with nature.

And that means that what hurts nature also hurts me as well. And right now you'll agree with me, that humans have been destroying these priceless global commons for decades and stories of the lost forest, or even poisoned rivers are not in any way unique to my community or even my country. This is something that everyone of us here shares, and I am determined to stop this destruction.

And I'm encouraged to know that I am not alone, like listening to the other speakers. My work has mostly focused on helping children to fall in love with nature so that they may learn to cherish and protect it. And this is what keeps me going every day.

It's actually a very uplifting feeling that I wish everybody the world and our leaders share every time. And when I founded the Green Generation Initiative, I wanted to nurture more young children to love nature and to be environmentally conscious at a young age and especially cause I also got an opportunity to plant my first tree when I was only seven. But along the way, I wanted to go check how the trees we planted as children were doing and I got to this beautiful hill and what I found were tree stumps and tree logs which made me feel so angry. But something I always say is that this anger did not stop at the anger, but it also gave me a hunger to want to do something about challenges like deforestation and climate change.

Right now in the global conversations, nature is receiving insufficient political attention. This is because the discussion about tackling the climate crisis is centring around reducing carbon emissions. But we know that to stay within the 1.5 degrees Celsius, we also need to preserve every remaining natural ecosystem of the planet, as well as planting trees and regenerating nature.

And it's also clear that politicians are out of step with what people want, because there's a lot of allowing the policy to be swayed by the people who have interests and personal interest and especially the big businesses and developers. Just recently, we were trying to save our green spaces in the city of Nairobi, which has scientific reports that it might be uninhabitable in the next 50 years.

So it shows that our cities also play a key role in tackling the climate crisis. And I also reflect as recent surveys in different countries that show that 83% of people want to do much more to protect and regenerate nature. And some of the people are even putting their lives on the line. Just recently, we lost one of us, an environmentalist in Kenya, Joanna Stutchbury.

She was only trying to protect one of the most vulnerable forests in Kenya, Kiambu forest, but she was murdered because of her fight. So this tells us that our environmental defenders are trying to keep all of us safe. And what we need to be doing is keep them safe as well. And there's so many case studies that I have always reflected though I was greatly inspired by professor Wangari Maathai and she fought relentlessly to protect one of the most rich forests in my country. It's called Karura forest. And she was not only fighting alone. She had so many people that were supporting her fight and it is through her efforts that today I can walk into that forest and enjoy the beauty of that forest and it's through high efforts that as well, it remains as one of the most unique green spaces left in Nairobi city. So it tells us that we can do this, the relentless efforts of professor Wangari Maathai and all the people she worked with led to the conservation of the Karua forest in Kenya. And we should definitely take heart in this story, but we cannot leave the conservation of nature to just a small group of educated environmentalists.

This is about the survival of our species. And this moment is calling on each of us to protect every single bit of nature that remains intact. Every time I walk into a school and I have three siblings and I give every child a tree each to adopt and plant in their school compound, it's an uplifting spirit.

And I really wish each and every person will take this very seriously because the impacts of climate change are really affecting so many people right now. And what matters is that while we may all be the same storm, the climate crisis, we definitely not the same boats. Cause there are people that are affected the most and have the least capacity to adapt and also have the least amount of resources to be able to adapt to these crises.

So I'd like to finish with a quote from the late Wangari Maathai that says that: "Those of us who understand and feel strongly must not tire, must not give up. Because the burden is on us, who know, and those who don't know are at peace. It's those of us who know that get disturbed and are forced to take action." Thank you.

SEPTEMBER 19, 12 AM. VENUE: VIVARIUM

Welcome to the year 2051. My name is Dr. Jacob Blumenfeld and I am a postdoctoral researcher at the Institute for the Study of Permanent Catastrophe. I'm here today to talk to you about how we succeeded in keeping global warming below 1.5 degrees Celsius, and in succeeding, failed.

In 2021, there was a common belief that genuine awareness and acceptance of the existence of man-made climate change would automatically lead people to develop political and moral positions which advocate for collective human action towards minimising suffering for all and adapting human societies towards a fossil-free future. This was a mistake. Scientific awareness of the facts of climate change was not enough to motivate a common ethical project of humanity towards a unifying good. Rather, as we now know, climate change awareness can just as well equally motivate heightened divisions of humanity into anti-egalitarian, xenophobic, class-differentiated zones of competitive survival. I call this climate barbarism, and seek to explain its political and philosophical grounds. Climate barbarism is a useful concept for grasping the general tendency towards anti-egalitarian climate politics, but it is too broad a concept to capture the specificity of particularly brutal ideologies of climate despair, like eco-fascism. I will thus develop the concept of climate barbarism in relation to eco-fascism. What do these concepts mean and how can they be challenged? In 2051, climate barbarism has become the norm. Perhaps it is time to look back at how we got here. In the late 2010s and early 2020s, a few authors warned us about this specifically regressive form of climate adaptation. But no one listened. That is why it is imperative to return to them now, to see the options we had at a crucial moment, and the choices we took, for better, but mostly, for worse.

In 2018, Geoff Mann and Joel Wainwright presented four potential global political responses to climate change, each of which expressed a different conjuncture between state sovereignty and global capitalism. These four social formations were split along two axes: planetary sovereignty vs. anti-planetary sovereignty, and capitalist vs. non-capitalist.

They called the planetary capitalist response to climate change Climate Leviathan, which they saw as the most likely scenario going forward. In short, Climate Leviathan named the strategy of global capital adapting to a warmer world so as to maintain free markets, the circulation of commodities, cheap labor, high consumption, and

* An expanded version of this text has been published at Constellations, 2022, Online First, 1-17 https://onlinelibrary.wiley.com/doi/full/10.1111/1467-8675.12596

```
                        Capitalist
                            │
        CLIMATE             │        CLIMATE
        LEVIATHAN           │        BEHEMOTH
Planetary    ───────────────┼───────────────    Anti-Planetary
Sovereignity                │                    Sovereignity
        CLIMATE             │        CLIMATE
        MAO                 │          X
                            │
                      Non-capitalist
```

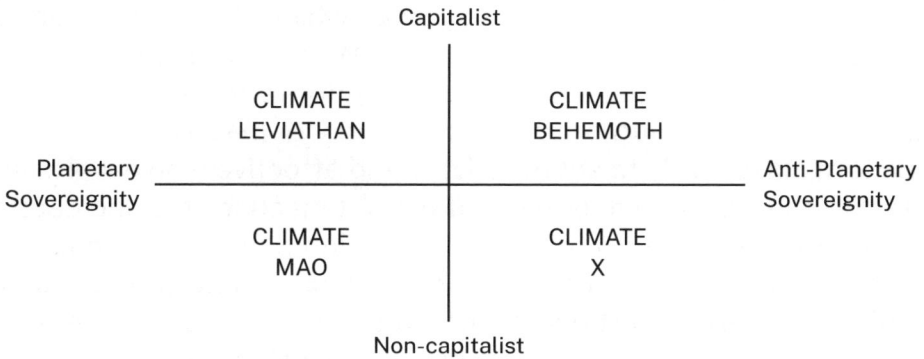

economic growth. This is the path of the Paris Agreement, the UN frameworks, the WTO, IMF, and G8. In homage to Thomas Hobbes, Climate Leviathan designated the new form of sovereignty emerging in response to the climate emergency. This sovereign structure reflected an agreement among the wealthiest and most powerful nation-states to coordinate climate policy through transitional institutions in order to maintain their hegemony while offsetting the costs and burdens to the poor and future generations. Either in the form of green neoliberalism or green Keynesianism, this was the path of green capitalism, a capitalism conscious of the need to organise itself globally to manage the ecological threat to its financial bottom line.

The anti-planetary capitalist response, which Mann and Wainwright feared the most, was called Climate Behemoth. This possible social formation intensified nationalism, protectionism, climate denial, racism, xenophobia, social Darwinism, and international conflict. In this scenario, sovereignty does not expand to the planet in order to confront climate change, but contracts to the protected space of one's own borders. Climate Behemoth is a global state of nature against Leviathan's world order, unregulated anarchy to their managed globe. This social formation incorporates radically different interest groups, like wealthy elites and poor working-class populations, in order to block any climate policy that would impact jobs, industry, growth, in short, "our way of life". Combining scientific denialism with economic protectionism, this anti-liberal deglobalised response to climate change reasserts national sovereignty as the only legitimate source of authority and protection in a world of diminishing returns. Scapegoating immigrants, fortifying borders, withdrawing from international treaties and protecting domestic companies and workers are Climate Behemoth's main policies. In this pathway, the extraction and consumption of fossil fuels are ramped up to the max for the good of our economy, irrespective of its disastrous effects on the planet, on others, on the future, and on ourselves.

The planetary non-capitalist response, which they saw as possible but unlikely, was called Climate Mao. With reference to China in particular, this potential form of sovereignty reflected a conjunction between a strong authoritarian state and a massive revolutionary subaltern class ready to act decisively and effectively on a world stage to tackle climate change outside of market mechanisms and capitalist institutions. Climate Mao reflects a sovereign power which has a clear and immediate interest in radically mitigating climate change since its population is disproportionally affected by extreme climate events, droughts, floods, fires, and famines. As a major geopolitical force, Climate Mao would unite the global south and the non-capitalist bloc in order to implement climate measures from above that circumvent fossil capital and Euro-American hegemony. No more futile UN meetings and G8 gatherings about climate, this is mitigation through the brute force of state power.

The anti-planetary non-capitalist response, which they politically supported but also pessimistically doubted, was called Climate X. This pathway named the unknown trajectory of a radical democratic politics from below which does not sacrifice local communities and transnational solidarity on the altar of economic growth or national sovereignty. Climate X names whatever it is that would meaningfully transcend capitalism and tackle climate change without displacing the costs onto the poor, the future, and the non-human. Combining grassroots forms of communal adaptation with democratic experiments in sovereignty, Climate X brings together climate activists, scientists, farmers, care workers, indigenous communities, urban ecologists, eco-socialists and all those who struggle for a just and equitable carbon-free way of life. This unnamable future was alive in the form of anti-pipeline protests, climate justice movements, degrowth ecology, solidarity economies, and more. Whether it could unite into a formidable force to overcome the power of Climate Leviathan was, at that point, unknown.

In their insightful analysis, Mann and Wainwright focused mostly on Climate Leviathan and why it was likely to prevail, but they also spent ample time on the non-capitalist possibilities of Climate Mao and Climate X. What they tended to skip over was the dangerous power and potential of Climate Behemoth, a somewhat murky concept that needs some more precision to be useful. This was a mistake precisely because something closer to Climate Behemoth won out in the end over Climate Leviathan, with some key differences. Instead of using their specific term, I will develop the concept of "climate barbarism" to help explain the ecological transition to our present, 2051. But even that term is not specific enough, for we also must distinguish between climate barbarism in general and eco-fascism in particular. Thus, there are three concepts that need to be elaborated: climate behemoth, climate barbarism, and eco-fascism. What do these concepts mean and how are they related?

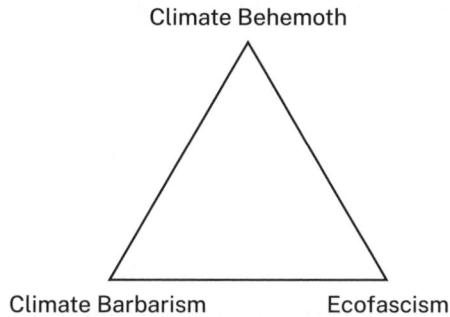

Climate Behemoth

Climate Barbarism   Ecofascism

Recall that Climate Behemoth names a form of anti-planetary, capitalist sovereignty in response to climate change, one that unifies neoliberal climate denial from above with anti-environmental, xenophobic resentment from below. While these forces were still real and powerful in the 2010s, their ideological coherence along the lines of climate denialism was shattered in the 2020s. The reality of climate change imposed itself more and more forcefully and convincingly on all parts of the population due to increased and seemingly constant extreme weather events, explosive IPCC reports and a continuous stream of articles, books, movies, stories, and podcasts. More scientists and journalists were speaking out, more politicians and activists were taking a stand, and even more CEOs, bankers and investors were signalling the end of fossil fuels. Perhaps the most powerful wakeup call came from the uprising of the future generations themselves, that is, the youth, in the form of "climate strikes" and militant mass protests, which only paused for a brief moment during the Covid-19 pandemic. After that, their tactics escalated even more, to a point where no one could turn the eyes away from the ongoing catastrophes and its causes. Everyone agreed that the world was warming and that it had to be stopped. Everyone thought such universal scientific awareness would be enough to motivate a shift of economic and political priorities to a more just, and ecologically sustainable world. Well, the world did become more sustainable, but definitely not more just.

In short, climate denial in the 2020s and 30s was no longer socially acceptable, and moreover, no longer necessary. One could accept the irrefutable truth of climate change without giving up one's love of fossil fuels or hatred of immigrants. Just because one understood the reality of climate-induced migration and the suffering of climate refugees, for instance, did not mean that one was now willing to accept them. Welcome to the new climate world, where action on climate change was by no means "progressive," "left", or "radical". Whether framed in terms of overpopulation or austerity, community or identity, safety or necessity, this kind of ecological politics was a terrifying development and should have been a wake-up call for all those who believed in the basic value of universal human solidarity. This anti-egalitarian, regressive, reactionary transition from climate denial to climate acceptance can be theorised, on my account, as a shift from climate behemoth to climate barbarism. Unlike climate behemoth, this political response accepts the reality of climate change, but not the needs of other human beings.

What is climate barbarism? One of the clearest articulations of this concept comes from Naomi Klein, in an interview from 2019:

> Climate barbarism is a form of climate adaptation. It's no longer denying that we have begun an age of massive disruption, that many hundreds of millions of people are going to be forced from their homelands, and that huge swathes of the planet are going to be uninhabitable. And then, in response to that, rather than doing all the things that are encoded in the UN Convention on Climate Change, which recognizes the historical responsibility of many of the countries that happen to have a little more time to deal with the impacts of climate change — are insulated both by geography and relative wealth — instead says, look, we simply believe we are better, because of our citizenship, because of our whiteness, and our Christian-ness, and we are locking down, protecting our own, pulling aid. (2019b)

For Klein, this indifference towards vulnerable populations outside one's borders (or at the margins within one's borders) was present for a while in the USA and the UK, but it was now particularly ruthless given the West's historical responsibility for climate change. Climate barbarism recognises climate change and adapts to it by withdrawing from any obligations to others, outside of one's own preferred in-group, the boundaries of which can always be narrowed further and further in cascades of violence and disregard. It says: "This is why we need to cut foreign aid, because we don't have enough money to help these other people, we need to help our own" (2019b). For Klein, this forces a choice upon us all, "are we going to live up to the rhetoric of equality and the idea that we actually believe people are of equal value by right of being alive on this planet? [...] Or are we going to double down and get monstrous?" (2019b). The suggestion here is that climate change puts to the test deeply held liberal beliefs in equality, dignity, and human rights, such that one can no longer abstractly profess them as ideals without acting upon them in reality. In short, you either adapt your behaviour or become a hypocrite — no more beautiful souls.

In another interview from the same time, Klein puts it even more succinctly: "We are seeing the beginnings of the era of climate barbarism. We saw it in Christchurch, we saw it in El Paso, where you have this marrying of white supremacist violence with vicious anti-immigrant racism" (2019c). Klein is referring to acts of domestic terrorism in Christchurch, New Zealand and El Paso, Texas in 2019, the perpetrators of which expressed concerns about environmental degradation and climate change on the one hand, and far-right ideology, white supremacy, Islamophobia, antisemitism, and anti-immigrant hostility on the other. These horrific acts of violence were certainly symptoms of climate barbarism, yet they should be further specified as early expressions of ecofascism. In an interview from November 2019, Klein distinguishes more precisely between these two. Whereas climate barbarism refers to governmental policies of anti-solidaristic climate adaptation, ecofascism names a specific far-right ideology that rationalises white supremacist violence by invoking imminent ecological collapse and scarce natural resources. She notes:

> What I'm calling climate barbarism is de facto what is happening at the borders. Politicians know [climate change is] real whether or not they deny it. [..] They have used the specter of the invading "other" as a unifying force for their political project. This is a form of climate change adaptation that we're seeing with these barbaric practices, such as the construction of concentration camps, whether they're in Texas, in Libya, or off the shore of Australia in places like Nauru or Manus; this has been the story of the decade. (2019d)

Ecofascism, in contrast, is a bit different — more brutal, local, radical. It is an "articulated ideology" in which a "sector of the far Right is no longer denying climate change and is using the reality that we are entering a period where more and more people are going to be on the move as a rationale for extreme violence." (2019d) The fear of the "climate refugee" is thus added to the context of delusion in which Muslims, Jews, racial minorities, leftists and cultural elites are all colluding in destroying white civilisation, and thus must be destroyed.

In her 2019 book On Fire, Klein wrote about the rising threat of ecofascism after the Christchurch massacre. Her correct worry was that ecofascism as an ideology would emerge more frequently as a rationalisation for violent action if we failed to live up to our "collective climate responsibilities" (2019a, p. 45). According to this account, the less universal the policy for mitigating and adapting to climate change, the more popular ecofascism will be as an alternative ideology for a particular in-group. And in the same book, with reference to US policies which deny climate aid to vulnerable countries in the global south, she notes:

> Let there be no mistake: this is the dawn of climate barbarism. And unless there is a radical change not only in politics but in the underlying values that govern our politics, this is how the wealthy world is going to "adapt" to more climate disruption: by fully unleashing the toxic ideologies that rank the relative value of human lives in order to justify the monstrous discarding of huge swaths of humanity. And what starts as brutality at the border will most certainly infect societies as a whole. (p. 50)

Climate barbarism takes place "at the border", whereas ecofascism happens within it. Ecofascism, then, would be something like internalized climate barbarism: xenophobia and hate not towards those outside who want to get in but to the "other" inside, those who take what should belong to "us". These are classic expressions of racism and resentment towards "undeserving" parts of the population — phenomena which spike every time the economic pie is seen as shrinking. With a deepening climate crisis and a major recession looming, and no transformative options on the table, this negative strategy of "adaptation" was only intensified.

But ecofascism is not just a recent side-effect of barbaric climate policies. Ecofascism — or far-right ecology in general — is not some strange blend of intrinsically incompatible worldviews. Rather, it has a long history and developed political vocabulary and ideology. It builds from theoretical and political traditions which take seriously ideas such as sustainability, protection of nature, localism, bioregionalism, autonomy, veganism, decolonisation, and even indigeneity. Such concepts may seem to be inherently progressive or even left-wing, but that is an illusion. Nothing about the focus on "locality" or "place", for instance, entails egalitarian principles, beliefs in justice, fairness or even liberal values. To protect nature, respect locality, and support autonomy can (and does sometimes) mean protecting homogeneity from difference, local community from foreign residents, hierarchy from equality, gender roles from feminism, heteronormative families from queer identity, male authority from deliberative democracy, ethno-nationalism from multiculturalism, racist ideas from anti-racist action.

To challenge ecofascism then cannot just entail warding off climate barbarism from infecting society in general, as if the danger was not already inside. And to challenge climate barbarism then cannot just involve criticising anti-immigrant border policies. Almost all border policies around the world are structurally "anti-immigrant", some more than others. What makes climate barbarism specific and deadly is its potential as a real political strategy of adaptation to climate change. This strategy cannot be confronted on the epistemological grounds of climate science vs. climate denial, nor even on the moral grounds of human rights vs. national sovereignty, but only on the grounds of political and social power that can articulate an alternative economic and ecological vision of the future, and actually fight for it.

Or at least, that was what we thought in the 2020s. Klein was more right than she could ever know, as the policy of regressive adaptation occurred throughout the next decades all over the world. Climate policy was implemented, but in a racially differentiated, economically hierarchical, socially unjust way that separated out those who were deemed worthy of protection, from those who were deemed superfluous. The path from 2021 to 2051 was a chaotic one in which some individuals maintained their high costs of livings, while others were forced to give up on basic necessities; in which some select groups were allowed to enjoy life in protected, luxurious zones of high-emission existence, while others had to fend for themselves in abandoned wastelands of industrial ruin. Slowly, as rations were enforced on the majority of the working class, global production levels dropped, emissions lowered, and temperatures stabilised. Most people adapted to needless suffering, and avoidable death, which they already learned how to do during the pandemics of the 2020s. Green nationalism, working-class austerity, strong borders, and harsh immigration policy — these were the mechanisms of the great transition. Floods, fires, and droughts continued to increase, but having the right citizenship or enough money could allow one to weather any storm in the newly built zones of adaptation. Most people couldn't enter these private utopian spaces, but everyone thought that maybe they could one day, if they kept working hard enough, maybe giving up more pleasures for the greater good. They still believe that today.

One conclusion of these thoughts is that climate barbarism should have been taken more seriously as a real possibility of cruel adaptation to the reality of climate change between 2021 and 2031. By 2032, it was too late. The walls were built, and the new zones of exclusion were imposed. Nearly twenty years later, we are living in the world that was

Jacob Blume feld

promised, the world of 1.5 degrees, but not the one we desired. Climate barbarism was an anti-social response to climate change. It did not come shrouded in climate denial. Rather, it was precisely the reality and acceptance of climate change that justified its nationalistic, social Darwinism, which manifested both at the state level of immigration policy and foreign aid and at the local level of popular resentment and white supremacist terror. Although we now live in a world with a stable climate, it is more socially unstable than ever. The technical shifts to a sustainable eco-system are easy when you don't have to think about the moral claims of other human beings, especially those from outside one's community. We should be careful what we wish for.

REFERENCES:
Klein, N. (2019a). On fire. Simon & Schuster.
Klein, N. (2019b). Against climate barbarism: A conversation with Naomi Klein. LA Review of Books. https://lareviewofbooks.org/article/against-climate-barbarism-a-conversation-with-naomi-klein/
Klein, N. (2019c).We are seeing the beginnings of the era of climate barbarism. The Guardian. https://www.theguardian.com/books/2019/sep/14/naomi-klein-we-are-seeing-the-beginnings-of-the-era-of-climate-barbarism
Klein, N. (2019d). Naomi Klein on climate chaos. In These times. https://inthesetimes.com/article/22166/naomi-klein-climatechaos-baby-boomers-capitalism-bernie-sanders-warren
Mann, G., & Wainwright, J. (2018). Climate leviathan. Verso.

Dear Agony Aunt,

Like every first Sunday of the month, today was Tidy Up Action Day. The tradition had started for us as just a way to keep the house clean and dust-free, but now we expanded the meaning of tidy up, and used it as a moment for introspection as well, and to "clean up" any issues existent in the community. It starts with a sunrise walk to the Mound, which is extraordinarily beautiful in the mornings. The birdsong was astounding. After the thanksgiving we tried some chanting, accompanied by the drum my brother brought. He has just sailed in from Spain, embarking from Santander and arriving in Portishead. He told us about how much Santander had changed after so many people from the South of Spain had migrated north escaping the heat, drought, and the creeping desert. The north had taken it well though, and many of the emptying villages in the damp and rich valleys have been regenerated by the movers. The southerners complained about the rain, but my brother said deep down they were grateful.

We walked back towards the house, energised by the morning's procedures. The allotments around here used to be all divvied up but eventually integration and open passage were prioritised and the Ashley Vale Allotment Association replaced the private family allotments. Now we walk across an orchard with the occasional signs of wild boar disruption, there are blueberry bushes and turnips.

The house is an old Georgian build, on the corner where Montpellier meets St Pauls. It is tall and thin and the last one in the terraced street, with a large camel drawn on its side that's always brought the curious to our door. The walls and the design are pretty much the same that would've been built in the early 1800s. Thankfully, we'd been part of its repairing 20 years ago. Now we boast triple glazing, underfloor heating, solar panels and solar water heating. All the houses in the small block, about 30 in total, came together and we brought down the walls dividing up our gardens and liberated the land from its concrete slabs. We collaborated on the design of the new garden: play area, vegetable patch, composting, a more secluded and private corner, picnic and bonfire zone... The idea had come initially from the Yard in St Werburghs and the people from Bright Green Futures who had trialled net zero housing in Montpellier. So when the reparations investment came along, communities in Easton and St Pauls pushed this idea of the "repaired" housing, which gave them almost complete energy independence, larger green spaces to cultivate and where to culturally express themselves.

Our tidying was well underway. 3 of us did the kitchen, the other 2 sorted the bathroom. My brother played more music and kept us going with tales from his home. Once we were done Luke offered to show him his workshop, and I decided to attack my room – I'd been wanting to get at the boxes at the bottom of the storage cupboard for a while. I started digging out all our old paraphernalia. There were my old degree certificates, my love letters and photographs, the folded up posters that used to hang from the walls of the different rooms I've had. My partner and I have been living in this house on-and-off for 30 years, so the collection spans a lot of our lifetime. I find a purple sticker that says:

I Cheered
I Danced
I Shouted
I Toppled Colston

31 years ago the statue came down. Less than a year later the "Atonement and Reparation for Bristol's role in the Transatlantic Traffic in Enslaved Afrikans (TTEA)" motion was passed. It pushed for "holistic repair": including investing in historically marginalised communities to address the city's continuing inequalities. At first it didn't make much noise... but the land justice movement was growing. In 2021 people in the UK had right to roam over only 8% of the land and 4% of the inland waterways. Some of the largest landowning families were directly linked to slavery or plantations. Activists like Guy Shrubsole and Nick Hayes became household names for their continued highlighting of the hypocrisies of land ownership and lack of access. I find a drawing my partner had made in one of the mass trespasses we went to. It shows an abandoned old manor house. The trespasses revealed more and more empty decaying exuberant houses, left to rot by indebted aristocracy.

There's a small envelope full of polaroid pictures. The first ones show Judit in the Gallery Garden, proudly posing in front of the kale and sunflowers. Then there's a big group of us, celebrating outside College Green. That was when Cleo Lake, who was the Green Party Councillor who put forward the reparations motion was elected Mayor in 2025. The Council created a reparations budget, and interpreted it broadly by advocating for resilient communities rich in self-expression and pride of place. The word "repair" took on new meaning. Community organisations got busy repairing, meaning anything from pedestrianising streets to insulating council houses. A lot of the money went into paying salaries to full time community organisers, into their training and empowerment. Reparations was about democratising the everyday, giving voice and tools for people to redefine their own spaces. The next picture shows me smiling in the new electric tram. The city centre had been made mainly car-free, creating more free space for nature. The last set of pictures remind me of the immense sense of pride I felt: there are all our housemates, dancing and running along the newly emptied M32. Cleo Lake became the first Mayor to rewild a motorway, creating a nature corridor straight from the heart of the city's Bear Pit out towards Stoke Park and the Frome Valley. Many would follow suit.

Reparations had become a hugely useful concept. It aimed to repair injustices done to people and their ecosystems, but the conversation was always carried by curiosity, not judgement or vengeance. The history of the city, street by street, slowly unravelled. We surrounded ourselves with ghosts. Not only the ghosts of slaves, neglected women and abused travellers, but also those of lost creeks and brooks, waterways long buried and landscapes forgotten. The histories were weaved through our maps and senses, the city came alive in endless iterations of what had been and what could be.

Hiding behind one of the boxes in the cupboard I find our old hammock. We're 50 years old now and haven't camped in a while, but I'm flooded by memories. The energy started by reparations spilled out of the cities. The festive mass trespasses turned into respectful occupations. Abandoned country properties were "repaired", sometimes with council support. People pilgrimed to the different repaired communities using the Slow Ways maps, which showed walking paths between every city, town, village and hamlet in the UK. My partner and I were youth workers back then, and we travelled around Somerset and Gloucestershire running workshops in the different occupations organised by youth groups, finding anywhere along the Slow Ways to hang up the hammock and rest. Many of the projects didn't last long, and were more of a statement, but the councils supported reparations and regenerative farming after some big wins for the Green Party all across the country. They collaborated with Land In Our Names (LION), making land accessible for people of colour to purchase in collective holdings. Some landlords who's ancestors had amassed wealth from the slave trade donated land to LION, as a symbol of the growing societal consensus that reparations were improving the country for everyone.

By the early 30s the changes to the landscape were evident. Urban farming was here to stay and nature corridors had been prioritised to give biodiversity a chance to bounce back. Alongside many of the Slow Ways land was being set aside for rewilding, creating a network of beautiful paths between towns which produced the revitalisation of old country pubs that offered their gardens as camping grounds. More of us crowded these paths during the summer, with spontaneous festivals set up across the now open access fields. With cultural activity more equally distributed between the rural and urban, farming was re-energised with diversity and made attractive to young people.

Agroforestry, permaculture and other regenerative farming methods were made the norm.

I'd almost finished dusting everything off when underneath it all I found a grenade. It was made of paper, and still had its promotional card clipped on: "SEEDBOM. Throw it. Grow it." I was taken aback. A tear crept out of my eye. We'd bought this as a gift for Judit, and forgot to ever give it to her. She had been the original guerrilla gardener out here, taking over every inch of land she could with hard work and care. I go over to the window. Her face smiles back at me. The portrait had been sprayed on the wall of her favourite garden, where she had greeted anyone who passed with a smile. She created that pause in the busy city life, and had everyone marvel at how the corner was "flourishing", as she would say. Her corner grew into a small city farm, right on this roundabout. The tram whirred silently by as I overlooked her legacy – it was almost hidden by the apple trees she had planted beside the tracks.

But none of this is why I'm contacting you. I write of course with a complaint, and to seek advice. We all met in the garden to wrap up the Tidy Up Action Day. We heard from a neighbour that a lynx has apparently been spotted not far from here. It has followed the M32 into town, presumingly chasing after one of the herds of deer that cross Bristol to get to Ashton Court. I said it was a one in a lifetime opportunity to try to see one. I've only ever seen their droppings on a walk around Godney, close to Glastonbury. I'll admit I was overexcited by the conversation, and was convinced we should take the children and organise a house outing. Amaal thought I was being rude, looking to be a nuisance to a lynx who is minding their own business. "They're not here for your entertainment."

SEPTEMBER 19, 5:30 PM. VENUE: MYCELIUM

INTRODUCTION
As scholar-activists who have worked between anthropology, conservation biology, heritage studies, and Indigenous rights, we saw the project T2051MCC as a rare opportunity to challenge pernicious assumptions in a creative and engaging way. In order to deliver a performance, we had to develop a critically articulated back story rich with details — economic and social collapse, massive ecosystem shifts, new forms of language, scavenged technologies, and an anarchist politics of just collapse, for starters. When we finally came to the moment of delivering our presentation, we had worked out an entire future history. The two characters that occupied the screen had long biographies, and had arrived in Munich through an arduous journey. As with all speculative fiction, from Jonathan Swift through Zamyatin to Ursula LeGuin, we had written out future history in order to engage with problems from the present day, problems which we felt were either invisible in the global heating debate or had deliberately been overlooked. This is comparable to Kim Stanley Robinson use of speculative fiction to explore the importance of outdated economic theories and the disproportionate power of bankers to the environmental crisis in The Ministry for the Future (Robinson 2021); but we are also drawing from a long tradition of storytelling among Urāy, Newar, and other Indigenous peoples.

In this short essay, we will lay out in a more academic fashion the specific problems we were confronting with our performance, why we think an Indigeno-futurist performance was the best tool for analysing and foregrounding these problems, and how we imagine those problems should, or could, be resolved. We write from the perspective specifically of the Urāy, a specific community among the Indigenous Newars.

CHALLENGING THE CONCEPTUAL FRAMEWORK
The actual crisis facing the planet and all its organisms is a trident: pollution, planetary overheating, and extinction of species. These three sharp points are linked in many ways, but they are all three wholly caused by humans. The two agencies that have emerged in the past decades to orchestrate international research and political theatre around this crisis are the IPCC[1], which deals with overheating, and the IPBES[2], which deals with extinction.

1   Intergovernmental Panel on Climate Change
2   Intergovernmental Panel on Biodiversity and Ecosystem Services

Will Tuladhar-Douglas

We chose to start with two problematic assumptions that haunt present climate and biodiversity discourse: First, the belief that it is still possible to keep to the Paris target of no more than 1.5C average warming; and second, the commodification of Indigenous peoples and Indigenous knowledge in conservation biology.

GLOBAL HEATING BELOW 1.5°C?

The most recent IPCC report (AR6[3]) applies a range of social, economic, and technical scenarios to the physical modelling in order to derive possible trajectories for future emissions and global heating. According to the first working group's report, published in August 2021 while the Munich2051 conference was being planned, it is almost certain that the 1.5°C threshold will be passed by 2051 (Allan et al. 2021, p. 14). In fact, the social models used by the IPCC predict a far worse outcome under the SSP3 ('Regional rivalries') model which predicted, with unfortunate accuracy, an increase in war and conflict[4]. The Munich2051 event was constructed around a dichotomy: do you assume an optimistic emissions pathway that stays below 1.5°, or a pessimistic pathway that exceeds 1.5°. To us, though, that was impossible. The only imaginable scenario that went below 1.5C by 2051 was a scenario of collapse, where all the economic sectors that presently contribute to the global crisis — manufacturing, militaries, transport, agriculture, tourism, and domestic consumption — where they all stopped suddenly. That took us towards an apocalyptic vision: widespread disease, war, and a collapse in human fertility all coinciding within a short time span.

PACKAGING INDIGENOUS KNOWLEDGE FOR CONSERVATION EFFICIENCY

The IPPC and IPBES have both claimed to recognise the need to work with "non-Western", and especially Indigenous societies. Studies in conservation biology have shown that territories under Indigenous stewardship maintain biodiversity better than government managed protected areas (Schuster et al. 2019, Dawson et al. 2021). Indigenous knowledge and practices are somehow more effective at stewarding landscapes than the techno-capitalist knowledge marketplace of

3   AR6 was published in three parts, from the three Working Groups: WG1 in August 2021, WG2 in February 2022, and WG3 in April 2022, with a final summary expected early in 2023.
4   Neither SSP3 nor any other social scenario anticipated a large-scale war such as the Russian invasion of Ukraine. The environmental impacts of the Russian invasion are not limited to acts of barbarism on Ukrainian territory; the deliberate rupturing of the Nordstream gas pipeline in the Baltic Sea released at least 220 million cubic metres of methane (Sparkes 2022).

"developed" countries, and thus it becomes necessary to master and appropriate them. The IPCC AR6 part II report is filled with references to Indigenous knowledge as a resource that needs to be tapped (for example, section 9-96: "there is a need to...provide methodological approaches for the incorporation of indigenous (sic) knowledge". Yet the knowledge passed down among various Indigenous communities is not a commodity to be harvested. The warning that Ford et al issued in response to the previous AR5 WGII report (Ford et al. 2016) — that Indigenous knowledge cannot be objectified, is highly diverse, and that the only way for the IPCC or IPBES to find the Indigenous knowledge they seek is to bring Indigenous scientists in as lead authors — seems to have gone unheeded. Indeed, we would argue that Ford et al fail to grasp the real challenge of working with Indigenous scholars and lineages of knowledge: in order to learn from Indigenous scholars, the academic system which legitimates the knowledge production practices at the core of the IPCC and IPBES would have to surrender their claim to authority. There is no single Indigenous knowledge system; instead, there are thousands of distinct linguistic and place-based lineages of knowledge whose experts have, for millennia, honed and transmitted their expertise while also recognising the work and insights of other particularised knowledge practice lineages. Hence to learn from these experts, the IPCC and IPBES would have to renounce the colonial knowledge commodification industry that authorises their work — the system through which academics find jobs, publish papers, win grants, and generally succeed in their jobs — and accept a partial and incomplete, but also collaborative and open, approach to discovering reliable knowledge.

There are numerous Indigenous scholars who, from their side, have engaged with what we might call International Academic Knowledge, including Robin Wall Kimmerer (Kimmerer 2013), Kim TallBear (TallBear 2019), Linda Geniusz (Geniusz 2009), and many biologists and conservation professionals within the ICCA collective[5]. Jim Enote is a distinguished museum curator and archaeologist form Zuni, New Mexico, who has challenged colonial museum paradigms. Non-Indigenous ally scholars such as Helen Verran (Verran 2013), Sandra Harding (Harding 2015), and John Law (Law 2004) have theorised how to work within multiple non-coherent traditions of knowledge. Further,

5 The ICCA Consortium (www.icca.org) is a global collective of scientists and activists, Indigenous or recognised allies of Indigenous people, who work to protect and extend Indigenous and Community Conserved Areas, now usually referred to as Territories of Life. The ICCA is an active participant in discussions at the IPBES, UNESCO, Convention on Biological Diversity (CBD), and other global policy bodies, but its primary role is to share skills and mobilise solidarity to protect ICCAs under threat.

Will Tuladhar-Douglas

ILK isn't just baskets, navigation, agroecologies, and fishing: it's also governance, civil engineering, and diplomacy. The Newars—the Indigenous community central to our story—were masters of urban architecture; for centuries, before they ever were colonised and became "Indigenous", they evolved an inclusive and ecologically sustainable civilisation; and they are still the most skilled and sought-after sculptors of sacred Buddhist images in Asia. Hence in our narrative we decided that, in order to survive the economic collapse, diseases, earthquakes, and surrounding wars, our protagonists would rely on almost-lost Indigenous knowledge practices to adapt and build a new society in the ruins.

CHOOSING A SETTING

We chose to set our future history in Nepal Mandala, which is the Newar name for their homelands: the Kathmandu Valley and the surrounding valleys. As scholars we are very familiar with the history, sociology, and ecology of this region[6], and it was all too easy to imagine a trajectory for social and economic collapse there. We have seen the population of the region swell from half a million to four million or more, overwhelmed by air, water, and soil pollution, over-development, corruption, and a failing water supply. The present development trajectory is a nightmarish mixture of cutting down the urban forest and bulldozing ancient structures and whole villages in order to build unnecessary roads that simply contribute to further pollution. The ancient hydraulic architecture, which supplied clean water from surrounding hills into neighbourhood communal taps, has been crushed, and common green spaces and pools that were used for rituals and markets have been enclosed and sold off for shopping malls. Every urban planning mistake of the late 20th century is being repeated—with copious international development funding. Because it is a high-altitude bowl, air and water pollution simply accumulate in the valley; and the intricate system of irrigated terraced fields that once supplied clean air, water, and food to the valley has been lost to uncontrolled urban sprawl. It is now one of the most polluted and overcrowded cities in Asia: the perfect setting for an environmental apocalypse.

INDIGENO-FUTURISM

Indigeno-futurism is a hopeful borrowing from Afro-futurism, a term that refers to speculative fiction, music, and performance which

6   Among other publications: (Tuladhar-Douglas 2008, 2010, Mallarach *et al.* 2018, Tuladhar-Douglas and Tuladhar-Douglas 2018)

acknowledges the structural oppression of Africans worldwide, and specifically as Black peoples living in the countries of their former enslavers, while appropriating the tools of their oppressors to imagine — and perhaps so to construct — a better future-in-the-present. Some of its better known practitioners include Octavia Butler, Samuel R. Delaney, Sun Ra, and Nnedi Okorafor. As with Afro-futurism, Indigeno-futurism is intended to counter the appropriation and commodification of Indigenous people, their bodies, symbols, knowledge, culture, and arts; and it points directly towards a strong appreciation of Indigenous knowledge in a science that responds to present and future crises. Under this label, we propose to challenge the stereotypical portrayal of Indigenous people as rural, non-literate, non-technological, having crafts but not fine arts, and having kinship but not governments.

Mark Dery, seeking to understand Afro-futurism, asked 'Can a community whose past has been deliberately rubbed out, and whose energies have subsequently been consumed by the search for legible traces of its history, imagine possible futures?' (Dery 1994, p. 181) With Indigeno-futurism, we must ask: how can the innumerable, very different, communities who were colonised, enslaved, missionarised, driven from their homelands, who had their languages destroyed and their artwork sold...how can an alliance of such irreducibly plural and diverse communities seek to imagine futures?

Nonetheless, we have a wonderful legacy of storytelling, dance drama, horror stories, and theatre to draw upon. Mark Whyte wrote a remarkable essay on Native American storytelling and speculative fiction as a tool with which to confront, undermine, and resist colonial narratives of the Anthropocene (Whyte 2018). He points out that Indigenous communities have already undergone an apocalypse and continue to suffer both physical and epistemological violence in the present day — and that Native American communities have a rich tradition of apocalyptic stories. Newars, for their part, have a rich performance, artistic, and literary culture filled with demons, gods, Bodhisattvas, and end-of-the-world narratives. Monastic courtyards are draped with long narrative painted scrolls (paubha) that depict otherworldly journeys, flesh-eating demons, and nested recursive visionary tales that put the Arabian Nights to shame. Newar performances include both formal storytelling rituals, such as the Buddhist fasting and storytelling ritual of dhalāṃ dhānegu, and the ornate endowed multilingual costume dance performances such as pyākhā. The irresolvable contradiction between the ongoing cultural production, and the unending colonial oppression, creates the conditions for Indigeno-futurist storytelling and performance.

Will Tuladhar-Douglas

CHOOSING KERNELS TO THINK WITH

Once we understood our project — to create a performance of a presentation to the Munich2051 conference in the character of elected representatives from our imagined future society — we set about completing that imaginary future. We filled many pages with notes, sketches, designs, food webs, weather patterns, and ideas for scavenged technologies. From all this we had to select enough to give depth to a ten minute presentation, and we here list some of the particular kernels around which we scripted our performance.

VULTURES

The horrific population crash in Gyps vultures across South Asia that began in the 1990s (Cuthbert et al. 2016) was, in many ways, a precursor to the many and multiplying pandemics affecting plants and animals now – chitrid fungus, white nose disease, pine borer beetles, Dutch elm disease, ash dieback, African swine fever, avian influenza, and so on. Our scenario required a mass die-off of humans, and this in turn left us room for a bit of ecological justice: we imagined that the vulture population of the central Himalayas would rebound, and that vultures would become an integral part of the corpse management system in the Kathmandu Valley as the survivors struggled to create a clean, safe living space.

SACKING THE MUSEUM

Following on the same theme of restorative justice, we wondered how we could best represent a rupture with the colonial-extractive model of Indigenous knowledge-as-resource. "Let's sack the museum!" said Bhavana, and sack the museum we did. It was the most satisfying answer we could find to the two dominant models of repatriating Indigenous items under ongoing colonial oppression: digital repatriation, and repatriation to a museum that reinforces the local colonial relations. All of these past and present events required us find a way to take our items back from the museum to teach our children. We Newars do not belong in the forest and do not belong in the museum's walls or inside someone else's text books. It is time to pose our own questions and concerns and open up all the 'hidden drawer [s]' (Migwans et al. 2016, p. 226) at the museum where our ancestral items are kept to make money for the looters. Museums offering us 'digital surrogates' (Boast and Enote 2013, p. 197) are simply not good enough. For example, the Zuni leaders who were offered digital repatriation project were rather confused thinking about digital repatriation (Boast and Enote 2013, pp. 110-11). Jim Enote spoke for the Zuni. 'If digital surrogates were so good, Enote reasoned, why didn't the institutions researchers, and scholars keep them, and return the original, non-digitised, analog object to the community instead?' (Bell et al. 2013, p. 197). This shows the imbalance of power in academia, museums and society: who holds the power, and for whom? We simply have to sit and hope that a museum approves our repatriation request, that it approves us as legitimate people...and even then we are not to have that which is ours. If we are lucky we might be offered our own objects with terms and conditions in place, or they might be given to a national museum — not our museum. The question is, how long can we wait for things to be just? Government policies, violent education systems, climate crisis, and now Covid have killed many of our elders and children. Soon those items will be nothing but items only, stripped of their cultural, ritual, and symbolic lives. What is the point of having such items later? Were talks about attempting to repatriate artefacts to the Nalik- speaking people of northern New Ireland , Papua New Guinea, who have been heavily missionarized. When finally, a museum decided to repatriate their malangan, a complex set of funeral rite objects incorporating clan totems and designs, objects which are ritually polluted/dangerous because they should have been destroyed at the end of the ritual, they were refused. The Nalik no longer cared about these items — their material culture had been looted and their rituals and worldviews destroyed (Were 2015, pp. 157-60).

Sacking the museum is our only hope to teach our people before we disappear into academic text books. We plan to teach anyone who is interested, without regard to class, caste, or any other marker. According to Smith, 'When indigenous peoples become the researchers [or protecter or activists] and not merely the researched, the activity of research is transformed. Questions are framed differently, people participate differently, and problems are defined differently, people participate on different terms' (Smith 2012, p. 196). We want to produce human beings where we are not producing and re-producing knowledge for only one kind of people. We want to give equal opportunities to all genders and people with disabilities. This way we may be able to re-claim our stolen voices (Chew et al. 2015, p. 74). We welcome people who are oppressed to make their own tools to be a protector or to be an activist or to be a scholars whose job really is to help everyone. However, it also imposes a strong sense of moral, ethical, political or parental responsibilities to hold an activists stance (Scheper-Hughes 1995).

APPROPRIATE TECHNOLOGIES
In imagining our society, surviving among the ruins, after the museums had been broken open, we thought about scavenged technologies and

Will Tuladhar-Douglas

low-tech solutions. We sketched out how old phones and small solar panels could be used to broadcast WiFi network names as beacons to mark which buildings were dangerous, and which had already been cleared out. We worked with artists here in Scotland to work out how printing presses could be rebuilt from spare parts found in the ruins. We asked what kinds of computer networking would be possible when the satellites and optic fibres failed. We developed lightweight hoist and pulley arrangements to lift corpses onto the top of derelict buildings as offerings for the vultures. We researched both the ancient Newar water filtration and supply systems, and the gigantic, over-budget, and incomplete Melamchi water project. We considered decontaminating the soils in the rubble-strewn terraces. We worked with a colleague at the University of Aberdeen to imagine a small, portable methane capture unit that could insert a deep tap into deserted megacity tips in order to produce hydrogen and electricity, and hypothesised that it could be used as a fuel and gas source for a convoy of airships travelling west across the ruins of Eurasia from Kathmandu to Munich. And we imagined the Fever Bindi, which we were able to prototype and send as part of an exhibit for the conference.

The Fever Bindi combines the South Asian practice of wearing an ornamental sticker on the forehead with thermochromic materials, materials which change their colour within a defined temperature range. Some people may remember these as mood rings or as forehead fever strips. In our imagined society, everyone from small children up, of whatever gender or persuasion, wears one or more thermochromic stickers on their forehead — and in so doing, makes the presence or absence of a fever public knowledge. To hide a fever would be as shaming as being publicly naked. We also looked at how ancient Newar quarantine practices had been revitalised in response to the Covid pandemic (The ancient practice of self-isolation 2020).

GOVERNANCE
Before the Newar city-states were colonised by the expanding Gorkha kingdom, they formed a remarkably inclusive society that welcomed wave after wave of refugees from political turmoil in South and Central Asia. They were also monarchies or oligarchies, rather than representative democracies; but for modern Newar activists, the image of that society is a pointer to a better model of society than the present intolerant and hierarchical Hindu state of Nepal. Building on this, we imagined a literal refugee state, a polity built on a strong sense of hospitality and inclusion. We wrote up plans for how quarantine against disease, and a crash course in compassionate civil society and syndicalist responsibility, were equally part of receiving refugees that

somehow found their way to the Valley. We designed citizenship papers, invented bureaucratic terms in a rapidly changing new Newari language, and developed representative biographies for families and individuals who were survivors within the valley or refugees who contributed their love, skill, and energy to creating a society that would not repeat the horrific mistakes that destroyed the world outside.

WHERE NEXT
After months of inventing people, landscapes, diseases, ecosystems, stories, rituals, laws, technologies, and dreams, we had to make a short presentation at T2051MCC over a video link. We would like to extend this project into a continuing series of exhibits and stories: we have brainstormed on an exhibit of posters made with salvaged equipment, a wifi landscape where all the network names encode a ruined landscape in the process of salvage, perhaps storytelling sessions or graphic novels, perhaps a grammar and dictionary of this imagined language and culture.

REFERENCES

Allan, R.P., Cassou, C., Chen, D., Cherchi, A., Connors, L., Doblas-Reyes, F.J., Douville, H., Driouech, F., Edwards, T.L., Fischer, E., Flato, G.M., Forster, P., AchutaRao, K.M., Adhikary, B., Aldrian, E., and Armour, K., 2021. Summary for Policymakers. In: Climate Change 2021: The Physical Science Basis. Contribution of Working Group I to the Sixth Assessment Report of the Intergovernmental Panel on Climate Change. Cambridge, UK: Cambridge University Press.

Bell, J.A., Christen, K., and Turin, M., 2013. Introduction: After the Return. Museum Anthropology Review, 7 (1–2), 1–21.

Boast, R. and Enote, J., 2013. Virtual Repatriation: It Is Neither Virtual nor Repatriation. In: P.F. Biehl and C. Prescott, eds. Heritage in the Context of Globalization: Europe and the Americas. New York, NY: Springer, 103–113.

Chew, K.A.B., Hicks Greendeer, N., and Keliiaa, C., 2015. Claiming Space: An Autoethnographic Study of Indigenous Graduate Students Engaged in Language Reclamation. International Journal of Multicultural Education, 17 (2), 73.

Cuthbert, R.J., Taggart, M.A., Saini, M., Sharma, A., Das, A., Kulkarni, M.D., Deori, P., Ranade, S., Shringarpure, R.N., Galligan, T.H., and Green, R.E., 2016. Continuing mortality of vultures in India associated with illegal veterinary use of diclofenac and a potential threat from nimesulide. Oryx, 50 (1), 104–112.

Dawson, N.M., Coolsaet, B., Sterling, E.J., Loveridge, R., Gross-Camp, N.D., Wongbusarakum, S., Sangha, K.K., Scherl, L.M., Phan, H.P., Zafra-Calvo, N., Lavey, W.G., Byakagaba, P., Idrobo, C.J., Chenet, A., Bennett, N.J., Mansourian, S., and Rosado-May, F.J., 2021. The role of Indigenous peoples and local communities in effective and equitable conservation. Ecology and Society, 26 (3), art19.

Dery, M., 1994. Black to the Future: Interviews with Samuel R Delany, Greg Tate, and Tricia Rose. In: M. Dery, ed. Flame Wars: The Discourse of Cyberculture. Durham, NC: Duke University Press, 179–222.

Ford, J.D., Cameron, L., Rubis, J., Maillet, M., Nakashima, D., Willox, A.C., and Pearce, T., 2016. Including indigenous knowledge and experience in IPCC assessment reports.

Will Tuladhar-Douglas

Nature Climate Change, 6 (4), 349–353.

Geniusz, W.M., 2009. Our knowledge is not primitive: decolonizing botanical Anishinaabe teachings. Syracuse: Syracuse University Press.

Harding, S., 2015. Objectivity and Diversity: Another Logic of Scientific Research. University of Chicago Press.

Kimmerer, R.W., 2013. Braiding sweetgrass: indigenous wisdom, scientific knowledge and the teachings of plants. Minneapolis, Minnesota.

Law, J., 2004. After method: Mess in social science research. Routledge.

Mallarach, J.M., Frascaroli, F., Tuladhar-Douglas, W., Liljeblad, J., Borde, R., Bernbaum, E., and Verschuuren, B., 2018. Implications of the Diversity of Concepts and Values of Nature in the Management and Governance of Protected and Conserved Areas. In: B. Verschuuren and S. Brown, eds. Cultural and Spiritual Significance of Nature in Protected Areas: Governance, Management and Policy. London: Routledge.

Migwans, C., Corbiere, A., and Racette, S.F., 2016. Pieces left along the trail. In: C. Andersen and J.M. O'Brien, eds. Sources and methods in indigenous studies. London: Routledge.

Robinson, K.S., 2021. The ministry for the future.

Scheper-Hughes, N., 1995. The Primacy of the Ethical: Propositions for a Militant Anthropology. Current Anthropology, 36 (3), 409–440.

Schuster, R., Germain, R.R., Bennett, J.R., Reo, N.J., and Arcese, P., 2019. Vertebrate biodiversity on indigenous-managed lands in Australia, Brazil, and Canada equals that in protected areas. Environmental Science & Policy, 101, 1–6.

Smith, L.T., 2012. Decolonizing methodologies: research and indigenous peoples. London: Zed.

Sparkes, M., 2022. Nord Stream pipes leaked 'enormous' amount of methane into atmosphere. New Scientist.

TallBear, K., 2019. Feminist, Queer, and Indigenous Thinking as an Antidote to Masculinist Objectivity and Binary Thinking in Biological Anthropology. American Anthropologist, 121 (2), 494–496.

The ancient practice of self-isolation, 2020. BBC.

Tuladhar-Douglas, B. and Tuladhar-Douglas, W., 2018. Working Together to Carry Water: Research Ethics when One of Two Parents is Indigenous. Ethnobiology Letters, 9 (1).

Tuladhar-Douglas, W., 2008. The Use of Bats as Medicine among the Newars of Nepal. Journal of Ethnobiology, 28 (1), 68–91.

Tuladhar-Douglas, W., 2010. Collusion and bickering: landscape, religion and ethnicity in the central Himalayas. Contemporary South Asia, 18 (3), 319–332.

Verran, H., 2013. Engagements between disparate knowledge traditions: Toward doing difference generatively and in good faith. In: L. Green, ed. Contested Ecologies: Dialogues in the South on Nature and Knowledge. Cape Town: HSRC Press, 141–61.

Were, G., 2015. Digital heritage in a Melanesian context: authenticity, integrity and ancestrality from the other side of the digital divide. International Journal of Heritage Studies, 21 (2), 153–165.

Whyte, K.P., 2018. Indigenous science (fiction) for the Anthropocene: Ancestral dystopias and fantasies of climate change crises. Environment and Planning E: Nature and Space, 1 (1–2), 224–242.

SEPTEMBER 19, 7:30 PM. VENUE: MYCELIUM

ABSTRACT
This paper introduces the interactive audiovisual installation LEIKHĒN, which combines biomedical signals within an immersive interactive environment. This artistic work is inspired by lichens, very resilient organisms and extremely sensitive to human pollution, hence of unvaluable importance for the ecosystem, because they are indicators of climate and global change. The installation was developed in the frame of an artist in residence invitation at the Immersive Lab (IL), ICST -Institute for Computer Music and Sound Technology, Zurich University of the Arts (ZhdK).

Installation // Interaction // Bio-interfaces // BCI // Brainwaves // Audiovisual // Immersive Environment // Symbiosis

INTRODUCTION
The project is inspired by the composite organism of lichen (from Greek: leikhēn), the result of a hybrid partnership between a fungus and an alga. The installation takes place in an audiovisual space, specifically in the Immersive Lab (IL) at ICST Zurich and represents a reflection not only upon the interaction and mutualistic relationship between two organisms, but also upon how this union impacts on their behaviours.

The IL is a space developed by Daniel Bisig and Jan C. Schacher at the ICST Institute for Computer Music and Sound Technology, Zurich University of the Arts (ZhdK), which consists of a panoramic video made by four video screens arranged in a cylindrical form with a diameter of approximately 4 meters and a 10.3 meters long screen with a height of 1.5 meters, in addition to a full-scale interaction surface, which tracks the visitors' touch from behind the screens using infrared cameras. The audio components inside the IL consist of 16 loudspeakers arranged behind the screens in two levels, and two subwoofers. The IL serves therefore as a platform offered to artists to experiment and develop audio-visual interactive installations combining three senses: Sight, Hearing and Touch. (Schacher & Bisig, 2017, p. 243).

LEIKHĒN INSTALLATION: DESCRIPTION
LEIKHĒN consists of an interactive audiovisual environment, in which a central figure or host (who, depending on the circumstance, could be either a designed performer or a member of the audience) interacts with images and sounds through a Brain Computer Interface (BCI hereafter), in order to create a habitat (the audiovisual environment)

Claudia Robles ...gel

LEIKHĒN

with his/her own emotional states. Visitors (up to ten visitors at a time) are invited to enter the immersive space and interact with the environment and the central figure by touching the screens (p. 120, fig. 1).

Apart from the central figure or host, sitting in the middle of the panoramic video space and whose brainwaves' values are collected via a BCI in order to influence the audio-visual environment, there is also a second type of participant, the guest(s), represented by visitors who, by touching the screens, influence the host's emotional states and consequently, also the audiovisual environment. Additionally, a TENS (transcutaneous electrical nerve stimulation) device and tactile transducers are attached to the chair where the central figure or host is seated, and whose function is explained in the next paragraph.

The touch screen sensors at the IL consist of a tracking system composed by four infrared cameras behind the screens operated by a camera-based system (OpenCV in OpenFrameworks), which surveys the whole panoramic screen (Schacher & Bisig, 2017, p. 247). This system measures the duration of each touch and registers the number of touches. LEIKHĒN uses these values by constantly sending them to the MAX software, where they are mapped into different sound frequencies and sent back to the host's body through the afore-mentioned tactile transducers: as soon as the screens are touched by visitors, the host will feel that touch or presence in his/her own body.

Hence, the interaction between visitors and environment happens through the host as an intermediary, where visitors touch the screens, each touch sends data transformed in frequencies to the tactile transducers, which are received by the host, influencing his/her emotional reactions and consequently, his/her mental processing (brainwaves). As changes in body reactions are reflected in changing brainwave activity, these values are captured by the BCI and transmitted to the MAX software, which through different algorithms and effects alter both visual as well as audio aspects of the environment. In this manner, a feedback loop emerges, where the host is affected by the audience's actions, whilst the audience is simultaneously affected by the host's reaction measured via his/her brainwaves, all of which changes the audiovisual environment.

In this way, the screens become the skin of the host - a simulation of the body sensor system in which when the touch receptor in the skin is stimulated, electrical impulses are sent to the brain - these frequencies will not only stimulate the brain but also the host's body, as mentioned by Elsenaar & Scha, who quote experiments by Caldani and Fontana in the XVIII century in which a muscle group can be externally activated by the stimulation of the nerves via an external electrical signal (Elsenaar & Scha, 2002, p. 22), which in this case will be the transducers attached to the host's chair.

As soon as guests touch the screen, a lichen appears on the point touched: if the touch remains for a certain period of time, the image of that particular lichen increases substantially in size (p. 120, fig. 2) while additionally, low frequencies are sent to the back of the chair of the host via a tactile transducer, producing a pleasant massage feeling; if the touch is quick/short and/or nervous, a lichen appears, but does not increase in size and disappears immediately after the hand is retrieved from the screen, while frequencies sent to the host are converted via a TENS in a subtle electrical current, which is felt as unpleasant by the host. The manner in which the guest touches the screen produces a reaction on the host and this reaction determines how both image and sound will change. The reaction produced on the host could be either relaxing or disturbing, and this emotional state will be reflected on the audiovisual environment, as both image and sound will react accordingly, inviting guests to be aware of their behaviour towards the host's habitat.

AUDIOVISUAL ELEMENTS: INSPIRED BY NATURE

The purpose of this audiovisual installation is twofold: on the one hand, it reflects upon the interaction and mutualistic relationship between two organisms and how this union impacts on their behaviours within a created audiovisual space; on the other hand, it invites visitors to raise their awareness about these composite organisms which are so vital to the ecosystem. **In order to achieve these goals, both visual and sound elements have been carefully selected, as described below:**

Visuals: vital to understand the hybrid significance of this project is the inclusion of close-up images from diverse lichen species, which are the only visual elements utilised in LEIKHĒN. Lichens are the product of a mutualistic relationship between a fungus and an alga. As described by the British Lichen Society, there are strong indications that this symbiosis in the lichens is mutualistic because both organisms profit from the exchange, instead of other types of similar relationships, such as parasitic or commensalistic, which do not show any type of mutual profit. Lichens are those small organisms growing on tree barks, leaves, stones, etc. to which usually not too much attention is paid but whose importance to the ecosystem is essential due to the vital role they play in biodiversity, as they can resist very harsh environmental conditions, and additionally, they are extremely sensitive to human pollution. Their diversity in shapes and colours is often ignored (p. 120, fig. 3) , but they play a key role in ecology, as thanks to their plasticity and biodiversity, they are used as indicators of air quality and have even inspired scientists for alternative highly sustainable ways of life, for example, strategies to manage the water content or temperature changes. Lichens are also very resilient and have revival capabilities, while they also contribute with organic matter to the soil, enriching its formation so that other plants could grow there.

Sound: the acoustic part of the environment is composed by field recordings including crickets, cicadas and thunder sounds that together with the lichen images recreate a nature reserve. Thunders are used only for the moment in which a visitor's touch remained for a certain period of time, that moment in which a lichen increased in size and then sends low frequencies to the tactile transducer attached to the host's chair, Crickets and cicadas are used for the whole environment and the variations of the effects (such as e.g. filters, changes of pitches, etc) is constantly modified by the data received from the host's brainwaves. Furthermore, the sound environment goes from a quiet night nature environment (with sounds of crickets) to a sunny midday, when cicadas are more active. The more relaxed the host is, the quieter the acoustic space becomes.

CONCLUSION

The audiovisual environment LEIKHĒN is a hybridisation of host and guest, where the guests' actions impact on the internal reactions of the host, transforming together the audiovisual environment in a mutualistic relationship. The main intention of the artist in this interactive installation is to extend the awareness to "the other' and therefore to the habitat (environment).

The reason for the creation of LEIKHĒN in an immersive space such as the IL lies in the intention of inviting visitors to experience the installation's audiovisual environment, capturing their attention, sharing their emotions and arising awareness about behaviours in regard to the other, in a similar but not such extreme approach as in, for example, Yoko Ono's Cut piece from 1964, where each participant from the audience was invited to cut a bit of her suit with scissors placed on the floor, or in Marina Abramovich's Rhythm 0 performance (1974), in which her life was in the hands of the audience during 6 hours.

To finalise, it should be noted that LEIKHĒN has not been created as an artificial experience working with synthetic images and sounds. On the contrary, the visual and sound materials are concrete images and sounds from nature. The majority of the visual elements consist of extreme close-up images not easily perceived in our daily lives.

REFERENCES

p. 120, fig. 1. LEIKHĒN @ Immersive Lab. ©2018-2022 Claudia Robles-Angel / VG Bild und Kunst Bonn

p. 120, fig. 2. LEIKHĒN @ Immersive Lab. Foto: Daniel Bisig ©2018-2022 Claudia Robles-Angel / VG Bild und Kunst Bonn. https://tube.switch.ch/videos/b561415b

p. 120, fig. 3. Selection of lichens for the installation LEIKHĒN. ©2018-2022 Claudia Robles-Angel / VG Bild und Kunst Bonn

British Lichen Society (2018, January 27). Retrieved from http://www.britishlichensociety.org.uk

Elsenaar, A. & Scha, R. (2002). Electric Body Manipulation as Performance Art: A Historical Perspective. Leonardo Music Journal

12, 12-28.

Schacher, J. C. & Bisig, D. (2017). Haunting Space, Social Interaction in a Large-Scale Media Environment. Proceedings of the

International Conference on Human-Computer Interaction - INTERACT 2017, Bernhaupt, R., Dalvi, G., Joshi, A., Balkrishan,

D., O'Neill, J., Winckler, M., (Eds), 242-262.

Hi. Thank you all for, for being here and taking part of this conference. My name is Helena Gualinga. I come from a small community called Sarayacu in the Ecuadorian Amazon. Because of the threats and the persecution that my community has lived, because of the threats of the oil industry that that we had when I was a child, I-from a very young age - was involved and advocating for the Amazon and for the rights of indigenous people. When I was growing up in the Amazon, my community constantly faced the threats of the oil companies entering and ever since we have been fighting. In 2002, my community received an attack - I would say it's an attack - when they, without our consent landed on our beaches with helicopters and said, we're gonna dig oil here. After that a long process of fighting begun. The people of my community had to go out to the cities, leave their families behind, leave their traditional way of living behind, to go to the cities, to fight these people in these industries in their own spaces. Because that's what we had to do. We had to go to all these offices, to the lawyers, to courtrooms, to be able to keep them outside of our territories. Because it wasn't enough anymore to just keep them out of our territory with our bodies. We had to take other steps.

So a very long process of fighting began. A 10 year legal battle against the Ecuadorian government because they allowed this to happen to my people. And because of all the atrocities that happened during this time, we were able in 2012 to win a historic lawsuit against the Ecuadorian government.

Which now has led to a lot of communities to do the same thing because now the courts in Ecuador have to support indigenous communities. Which didn't really happen before this case went to an international level. So this happened in 2012, but we understood as a community that, that wasn't enough: keeping the oil companies outside of our own territories wasn't enough. And we also needed another layer of protection because even though we had this very powerful sentence that benefited us that wasn't really a guarantee for my community to be safe. Because the governments change every four years and depending on the government, that was what our existence depended on.

So we understood that we have to do something else, something bigger, think outside what is seen as normal in the modern world. And we came to the answer which was very simple and very easy, and it's the way that we see life and how we needed to share that with the world so that people would understand why is it that we are protecting our territories and why we are. We almost risk our lives and put our own bodies there to defend it for other people to be able to see the why we needed to share how we view the world and how we live in balance and in harmony with nature.

So we made it public, our Cosmovision, our vision of life. This is something that the elders used to tell us and something that we live every day. So it wasn't something that we created. It was something that was always there. And it's called Kawsak Sacha, which in my language means "the living forest". So we created this proposal that is called the living forest, and we deeply believe that it was gonna be the answer to or the solution to everything that was happening in the world.

So as the name says "the living forest", we believe that everything in the forest is living and that indigenous people - or not just indigenous people - we're not something that is opposite to nature. We are nature and we are part of it. So the Kawsak Sacha is universal and proposes a legal recognition and vindication of territorial rights and mother earth, which is necessary and essential for the balance of the planet and preservation of life.

And what this means for us is that we believe that when we go out to the forest, the trees, the mountains, the waterfalls, they all have a being as we. We are beings. And that is how we have this mutual respect of being able to live in harmony with nature, because we do not see them as something that is inferior to us or something that is opposite to us.

We see it as something that we are part of, so we can have this balance and being, seeing life that way is what has permitted us to protect and to fight. That is what has inspired us and what has been pushing us to protect it because, you know, this is also something that is very extremely, extremely sacred to us the relationship with the natural world.

So today in 2051 I'm so happy to be announcing a lot of good news for my people, for the Amazon and for the entire world. Cuz when something good happens to the Amazon, it's something that benefits the entire world. The first one is that it's the five year anniversary of the Kawsak Sacha proposal being recognised by the Ecuadorian government, which means that we can now actually use this as a legal tool because within the proposal we understood also that we need to translate this proposal into this world that we're living in, which means that we need to create laws around it.

There's legislation that needs to be changed. And after the implementation of the proposal of the way that we live on a state level, we were finally seeing the results. And that brings me to the second item of news. Item of good news. And it is that indigenous people in the Amazon are no longer being persecuted by governments and extractive industries, the transition to renewable energies and this shift in our mindset and perspective have completely changed our existence and our fight. We're finally seeing the fruits of this fight. It was never in vain and we are understanding now that the solution that we put out is finally working. This is something that comes from years and years and years and years of fighting

There's a long way to go still. But I truly believe that this is a huge step for a better world. So I thank you for listening to me. And thank you for the space.

MINIMISING GREENHOUSE GAS EMISSIONS AND WASTE OF THE 2051 MUNICH CLIMATE CONFERENCE

STARTING FROM SCRATCH

When the idea for T2051MCC came up, we agreed relatively quickly that organising a climate conference and travelling by plane were irreconcilable. One can certainly disagree with this. There is hardly any problem of our time in which the exchange between experts and government officials of all countries is as important as for discussing solutions of the climate crisis. But unlike the big UN conferences, T2051MCC would not be about negotiating and deciding on measures and paths of action. What we planned was just an experimental format at the intersection of science and art, an attempt at scientific retrospection from imagined versions of the future. So we agreed, our way of working should also be experimental.

We also wanted to address the ecological harm T2051MCC would cause in a systematic way. It is becoming more and more common that institutions in the cultural field take on the task of determining the carbon footprint of their activities, and therefore knowledge is also increasing on how they can, or could, avoid CO_2 emissions. For the independent theatre scene however (at least in Munich), we are not aware of any project that has attempted this task. That is not surprising. The projects are in competition with each other. Year after year a jury has to decide how a limited amount of money is spent. Why should one diminish one's chances here by planning for seemingly unnecessary costs? A bit reminiscent of the problems on a global level, I'm afraid.

We were lucky to find a sponsor in FutureCamp Climate who not only supported us financially, but also took on the task of professionally assisting us in analysing our CO_2 emissions.

We found another sponsor in Bürgerstiftung München and another partner in Rehab Republic, with whom we were able to address a second important issue: the avoidance of waste.[1]

In both areas, we – as well as our partners - have learned a lot and hopefully, also achieved a little.

MINIMISING WASTE

To minimise waste, we asked Rehab Republic if they were up to this particular challenge. Rehab is a Munich-based association in which a group of enthusiasts joined forces in 2012 to develop projects for a more sustainable city. Their slogan reads "Sustainability - with YEAH

---

1   For the sake of transparency, we would like to point out that the author of this article has worked for FutureCamp for many years and was a member of Rehab Republic's strategy advisory board.

instead of BOO!" and this positive attitude is evident in their work. Rehab have started numerous remarkable projects. They have successfully created the first zero waste label in Munich and were part of a consortium that was commissioned by the municipality to develop a zero-waste concept for Munich.

In the following, we summarise the work Rehab Republic did to minimise waste at T2051MCC. A report can be downloaded from the conference website (see page 13). It was written with the intention of helping other organisers meet the challenges of creating a zero-waste event. They characterise the report as follows:

> It is important to say that our work is not perfect at all. It was a first try to get an insight into the waste perspective at an event as T2051MCC. We would change many things if we would do it again. But this is not the point. We want to share our experiences. What was the challenge? What did we achieve and where did we fail? We do not want to write another greenwashing report. We are convinced that a transformation is only possible when we honestly face these points. We will keep this document as a „living document". This means, that we keep it open to adapt this document again and again and to feed it with new findings. (Rehab Republic 2021)

Rehab had a number of basic thoughts we found very convincing: Resources should be kept in the cycle instead of burning them with the goal of shifting "from a linear to a circular economy" (ibid.). Focussing on an event made sense because events produce large amounts of plastic waste – things that are newly purchased and thrown away after a one-time use. Methodologically, their approach started with the refusal of everything that was not really wanted. The list of things to buy should then be reduced to the necessary things and amounts only. Reuse is preferable to buying new, and anything that could subsequently be reused should be fed into this cycle. Non reusable stuff should be recycled and all organic materials composted ("rotted"). The approach can be summarised as "the five r's": refuse, reduce, reuse, recycle, and rot. Finally, it is noteworthy that when we speak of zero waste, we talk about an utopia. Reaching it today is hardly possible, but we should aim high (or rather: low) to achieve as much as possible.

In their project, Rehab identified four fields of action: the participants, the office(s), catering, and the art installations and costumes. They interviewed the responsible people of every field to learn, which products and materials would be used and to estimate the resulting waste.[2] Rehab then researched sustainable alternatives for every waste position and proposed them to our team.

A significant amount of work was put into the art installations at the conference centre and the costumes:

> We made a list of all the things they needed and researched sustainable alternatives for them. For example, we asked a garden company for roots (a waste product for them). We also contacted an animal shelter if they want to take the straw we do not use anymore after the event. [...] The challenge in this field was that the artists' plans changed several times and at short term. Moreover, it was sometimes difficult to estimate how much material would be used. It was not possible to constantly adjust our results. At some point, time is pressing, so the quick solution may be to buy without looking at the waste. (ibid.)

With regard to the offices the main challenge was that all of us – due to the pandemic – worked from home, and that the team was constantly growing. Rehab made sustainable proposals that could reduce office trash by 77%. While it was not possible to evaluate the success, they felt that they were met with a lot of understanding.

For participants, both on site and online, Rehab created a guide and added signs all over the conference centre to raise awareness. They had also prepared an online questionnaire but unfortunately not too many participants filled in the form.

With regard to catering, cooperation was really difficult. While the manager of the Bellevue café was interested in the topic, she and her team had hardly any capacities to deal with it. Gastronomy still suffered heavily from the pandemic with high fluctuations of staff and many extra tasks due to the hygiene rules. Therefore, it was planned to facilitate a workshop for the café's team sometime after the conference. This approach matches our and Rehab's goal of focussing on sustainable effects rather than optimising the numbers of a short, singular event.

Rehab's conclusion motivates the reader to try out zero waste. It reminds them of how crucial communication is and that it is crucial to know your boundaries. The main focal point should be the big leverage while accepting your own limits. The most rewarding path is choosing digital workflows as well as reusable materials and products. Rehab concludes: "Overall, we hope that we do not need guidelines like this in

2   Future readers of the report might wonder why sanitary products and face masks ranked so highly among participants. Be reminded that T2051MCC took place in the middle of a pandemic.

2051 since it has become natural to implement zero waste measures in every event organization." (ibid.)

MINIMISING GREENHOUSE GAS EMISSIONS

To determine and minimise the contribution of T2051MCC to global heating we partnered with FutureCamp Climate GmbH. FutureCamp is a Munich-based consultancy company that has been active in the field for more than 20 years. While they are utterly experienced in carbon footprinting, the unconventional format of T2051MCC came with new challenges. As a sponsor of T2051MCC, FutureCamp was happy to take on the task of advising us on reduction measures, calculating the carbon footprint, and carrying out the compensation of unavoidable emissions.

In the following, we summarise the work FutureCamp conducted to determine, minimise, and compensate greenhouse gas emissions related to T2051MCC. A report can be downloaded from the conference website (see page 13). It describes their approach, their steps taken and summarises their results.

In their approach the consultants followed the strategic guidelines of the Greenhouse Gas Protocol. Priority was given to emission reductions in four identified areas of action: energy, mobility, accommodation, and food. With regard to energy-related emissions, all involved parties were asked about their use of electricity and heat. The latter played a minor role for T2051MCC as it did not take place in the heating period yet, but our approach was always to look beyond the event and help involved institutions to expand their knowledge about climate-related aspects of their activities. This focus on capacity-building among our partners was even more important because Büro Grandezza had no direct influence on the procurement of heat and energy themselves. With regards to mobility, it was difficult to identify further mitigation options: flights were excluded as part of the conference concept, while the conference centre, located in the heart of Munich, was very easy to reach with public transport and a nightmare for automobile lovers. The field of accommodation proved to be more complex. FutureCamp made a substantial effort researching eco-friendly accommodations. Different price and comfort levels were included. The results were handed to the supporting local cultural management bureau Rat&Tat with the request to pass on this knowledge and use it for other projects, too. With regard to food, the Bellevue café already realises the most relevant mitigation options: all food is vegan or vegetarian, coffee is fair-trade, and all dishes are reusable.

In a second step, systematic boundaries for the footprint calculation were determined and a data query was performed. Organisational and thematic boundaries were differentiated. Data was then collected and evaluated. Regarding waste the number of replies to questionnaires was lower than expected. Hence, assumptions had to be made for the missing data. In a next step, emission factors were matched with the data provided. Emission factors are coefficients that aim to represent the amount of CO_2 equivalents caused by a certain activity. Most emission factors can be found in specialised databases. But with its heavy reliance on online streaming and virtual conference rooms, T2051MCC was an unconventional challenge for the footprinting experts. While video streams make up a very large part of global data streams in the internet, significant uncertainties remain about their climate impact. FutureCamp conducted a review of available studies and tried to collect data from the providers of services like Mozilla hubs, which T2051MCC relied upon heavily. The devices of participants were identified as the most relevant and influenceable source of emissions regarding virtual participation. Therefore, measurements were undertaken to understand the effects of Mozilla hubs and Youtube on electricity consumption of a laptop. We won't dive into details of 2D vs 3D, GPU vs CPU here, but recommend the report that is available online. The research conducted here, alongside all other data and emission factors gathered, formed a solid base to calculate the carbon footprint of T2051MCC. As one might expect for a conference with no participants travelling by plane, with vegan and vegetarian catering, and a heavy reliance on virtual participation, the resulting emissions were very low for an academic conference. They amounted to less than 6 tonnes of carbon dioxide – less than the annual emissions of one person living in Germany. Nevertheless, FutureCamp compensated the emissions through a forest protection project in Brazil that "aims to reduce the illegal logging and forest destruction in the area as well as generating alternative sources of income for the local community. The project is certified under the Verified Carbon Standard and the Climate, Community and Biodiversity Standard." (FutureCamp 2022). Additionally, the same amount (6 tonnes of CO_2) was reduced within reforestation projects of the "Menschen für Menschen"-foundation in Ethiopia. The foundation aims to enable people in rural Ethiopia to improve their livelihoods by providing aid to self-help at eye level. One aspect of the foundation's work is integrated reforestation, which creates alternative sources of income and enriches ecosystems. All in all the remaining emissions were reduced (or compensated) double in other parts of the world.

As expected, excluding flights by design was the biggest lever to reduce emissions. Offering only plant-based food was the second most important step. But the whole project offered more takeaways than this, as FutureCamp summarise:

> While all event partners were willing and interested to cooperate to determine their emissions related to the conference, the knowledge and capacities to report the required data was sometimes lacking in the cultural field. (ibid.)

ABOUT BEING CONSISTENT, OR TRYING TO

T2051MCC had a very low carbon footprint - mainly due to deciding not to accept participants to come by plane. This needed no expert analysis but just the most basic knowledge about climate change. As an art collective we were free to make such a radical decision. The interesting thing about excluding flights is that the decision has fundamental consequences for the dramaturgy of the project. How could we make virtual and in-situ participation equally attractive? This question became central for our work over three years. We did try-outs[3] to test ideas for the setting, work on site and with our streaming partner and sponsor MediaBox TV. During the conference they worked with a crew of 10 people at a time. We were also lucky to find a sponsor for the online part in the Edith-Haberland-Wagner foundation. In Moby Digg we found a digital design studio that was keen on the task and made a significant effort in the development of our virtual rooms. One single decision led to a substantial effort on the organisational and the artistic side of the event. It was necessary to be consistent but it led us to unknown roads. Within the realm of waste avoidance, we have not yet been so consistent. Maybe that has to be the next step.

BACK AT THE AIRPORT

To be consequential, I want to add an epilogue and I know it might sound like an apology.

In 2019, I travelled to the UN World Climate Conference (COP) in Madrid to spread the word about our planned conference. Because nobody had ever heard of T2051MCC we wanted to do everything we could to increase the odds that enough promising submissions would have landed in our mailbox once our call for papers had ended. I also was invited to participate in a conference on sustainability in the arts in Amsterdam right before my COP visit.

I am quite regularly travelling long distances in Europe by train and I am used to plan trips through several countries using different rail companies. I enjoy making these plans. You can leave Munich in the

3 A particularly interesting one was „Displaced by Climate Change". While it resembled the later conference in many aspects, we were not allowed to have a live audience due to Covid-19 rules: https://www.youtube.com/watch?v=tncDVc8n97I

morning and be in Copenhagen for dinner, or in Edinburgh for a drink later in the evening. You can travel to Sicily in two nights, spending a full day in Rome in between. I had my longest sleep in a while on a night train from Budapest to Miercurea Ciuc in Transylvania.

Planning a trip from Munich to Madrid via Amsterdam however got me frustrated. To reduce travel emissions, Spain offered low-cost tickets on high-speed trains for conference participants, thus the availability of tickets was problematic. In France, a train strike was planned. It was impossible to plan the trip, even if this is sort of a hobby for you. There were bus connections of around 28 hrs, if I remember it properly, and I don't recall why that was no option for me. In the end, I booked a flight.

Travelling to Madrid by plane felt frustrating. But it reminded me that nobody stands outside the system. You cannot reduce your ecological footprint to a sustainable level. Sometimes this might have an assortment of reasons as they compiled here, where personal planning requirements and available logistics collide. By living in an industrialised country alone there is a residual environmental impact that is unsustainably high-even if you are a homeless person, a toddler, or a Buddhist monk, as a team at the MIT once illustrated. Nevertheless, I wonder if I could have been more consequential here. The feeling of personal guilt remains, and it is one of the dilemmas we are faced with again and again.

Further Contributions to T2051MCC
Watch them in the recorded livestreams (see page 13)

SEPTEMBER 18, 12 AM. VENUE: VIVARIUM
MARKUS KECK
Why academia was no help in building a sustainable society
In 2051 the global temperature has increased by more than 2°C above pre-industrial level. Extreme weather events such as heat waves, heavy rainfall and hurricanes are commonplace around the world, causing countless casualties every year. Markus Keck investigates why academia in the early 2020s was no help in building a sustainable society. He collects eyewitness reports by sustainability researchers, which provide highly intimate insights into the logics of science at that time.

SEPTEMBER 18, 12 AM. VENUE: VIVARIUM
LISA SCHIPPER, EDWARD CARR, SIRI ERIKSEN, LUIS FERNANDEZ CARRIL, BRUCE GLAVOVIC, CHRISTOPHER TRISOS
Climate Resilient Development in 2051: For whom?
Climate resilient development are pathways that emerge through efforts to achieve sustainable development while avoiding dangerous climate change. Looking back at 2021, Schipper, Carr, Eriksen, Carril, Glavovic and Trisos realise that climate resilient development is much more complicated than first assumed. It is an uncertain process that involves value-laden and ideologically charged decision-making. How can climate resilient development be fair, just and sustainable? And for whom?

SEPTEMBER 18, 3 PM. VENUE: VIVARIUM
MICHAEL PAHLE
Playing it safe or going the risky route: Europe's Emission Trading System as a yardstick for taking (regulatory) risk to address (climate) risks
What is the crucial factor that could have taken climate policy to a new and really "serious" level in the 2020s? According to Michael Pahle the fundamental issue was the degree of risk society was willing to take to tackle climate change. Discussing the European Emissions Trading System (EU-ETS), he illustrates the risk in relying on markets to combat climate change. The upside? It could trigger disruptive technological and social innovation at a much larger scale and speed.

SEPTEMBER 18, 3 PM. VENUE: MYCELIUM
ANNA VARGA
Proposed silvopastoral management solutions to the environmental and

economic problems of the Carpathian Basin after the drought of 1862-1863

Researching on silvopastoral management solutions in the Carpathian Basin after the drought of 1862-1863, Varga discovered that papers from the 19th century were often more developed than those in the early 21st century. In a present the answers that are already there are often overlooked. Varga will look back at what can be learned from the 19th century papers she studied from a day on a pasture land in 2051.

SEPTEMBER 18, 5:30 PM. VENUE: MYCELIUM
MARK KERNAN
Accelerating towards the Anthropocene: How 2025 transformed the future
On the 22nd of April 2025 the global temperature has risen to 1.5°C. How did we get there so quickly and how did we deal with it? Kernan looks back on all the mistakes and problems that lead to the climate tipping point much earlier than the community of scientist had expected. How could we have done things differently in attempting to address the ominous erosion of earth's life-support system?

SEPTEMBER 19, 12 AM. VENUE: VIVARIUM
KEES VAN DER GEEST
Adapt or Surrender? The policy dilemmas of climate change, habitability and migration in a low-lying toll nation in the early 21st century
In 2020, the territory of the Marshall Islands was less than 2 meters above sea level. Most Marshallese people strongly resisted the idea that their islands could become uninhabitable. In the late 2020s and 2030s, climate negotiators from small islands states managed to turn the narrative from one of 'climate refugees' and hopelessness to a more positive narrative of fighting to keep their countries habitable for future generations. Kees van der Geest looks back on the methodologies and actions that led to this turn around.

SEPTEMBER 19, 3 PM. VENUE: MYCELIUM
RIYAN HABEEB, SANA JAVAID
Renaturierung – The human vs nature re-connection
Since the pandemic in 2020, nature-based solutions were researched to both combat rising temperatures and increasing water woes but also to include humans centrally in the entire course of action. Now, in 2051, the exclusion and injustice that climate change inflicted s effectively encountered. Javaid and Habeeb speak from a future, where climate action happened through a change in lifestyle and basic measures like planting and fostering urban trees.

SEPTEMBER 19, 3PM. VENUE: VIVARIUM
MINNA KANERVA
The short history of consumption corridors and the transformation of the meat system
In the early decades of the 21st century, consumption was increasingly named as the root cause of the twin crises of climate change and ecology. Therefore, transferring societies towards sustainability was eventually seen to require strong sustainable consumption governance, rather than merely steering consumers towards "better choices". Kanerva looks back at the developments from the early 2020s onwards regarding consumption corridors and the transformation of the meat system.

SEPTEMBER 19, 3 PM. VENUE: VIVARIUM
SOLVEIG MARIE SIEM, HAKON NAALSUND WILLE
Lessons from the Pioneers of a World Changing Cultural Shift. A Historical Analysis of the Commercial Beginnings of the Mycelium Initiative Concept
Today, in 2051, the majority of the world's leading historians recognize the 'Mycelium Initiative' as the 2020s catalyst for the mass cultural shift towards a holistic ecological mentality. Solveig Marie Siem and Håkon Wille identify the beginning of it all in a project for local climate action in a small Norwegian town that eventually developed in a global network. The 'Mycelium Initiative Centres' allowed the public to access tools and information to support the creation of their own climate projects.

SEPTEMBER 19, 3 PM. VENUE: MYCELIUM
NATHAN SMITH
The Pando Consortium: Science Fiction Prototyping for Conservation Technology
In order to develop a future where we achieve the goals of the Paris Agreement, we need to leverage not only the technology, policy, and economic tools at our disposal, but also, of course, our collective imagination of a better future. Using a science fiction prototyping methodology, Smith is developing a future scenario where all of the above can converge and where, in 2051, we have analysed the outcomes. Critical to this scenario is The Pando Consortium, a platform where scientists, artists, engineers, investigators, and others can interact, collaborate, and develop solutions that utilise today's cutting edge technology and thinking, as well as what's on the horizon.

SEPTEMBER 19, 5:30 PM. VENUE: VIVARIUM
LOUISE ARNAL, MARIA-HELENA RAMOS, FLORIAN PAPPENBERGER, BART VAN DEN HURK, MICHA WERNER, LINUS MAGNUSSON, HANNAH L. CLOKE
The virtual realities of hydro-meteorological extremes
Throughout the last decades, rapid changes in the Earth System have led to unequal effects of climate change across the planet. As a result, there has been an increase in social inequalities. The predictability of extreme hydro-meteorological events such as e.g. droughts and floods is now very variable across the globe. Arnal et 6 al look back from a future where technologies such as virtual reality are mainstream and can be used to forecast and anticipate extreme events as well as warn those at risk.

SEPTEMBER 19, 5:30 PM. VENUE: MYCELIUM
VITUS BESEL, JAKUB KUBECKA, IVO NEEFJES
Global cloud control Or: How I learned to stop worrying and love geo-engineering
Besel, Neefjes and Kubecka imagine a world in which during the 2030s artificial intelligence has become so advanced that we gave it full control over the weather in order to stay below 1.5°C. It came at a great cost, but humanity is still going, and we may have just ensured another few decades to our existence.

SEPTEMBER 19, 5:30 PM. VENUE: MYCELIUM
MATTI GOLDBERG
Lost in the nexus?: The integration-fragmentation of global climate governance in 2015-2045
'Nexification' is understood as a tendency to seek connections. Goldberg witnesses that in 2015-2045, the more connected things became, the less responsible key-actors in the realm of climate change felt to change. Based on actual interviews with international civil servants and secondary literature, this study describes the intensified nexification of global climate governance in 2015-50.

LOUISE ARNAL

University of Saskatchewan, Centre for Hydrology, Coldwater Laboratory, Canmore, AB, Canada
Dr. Louise Arnal is a scientist with a lifelong love of art. She is a postdoctoral fellow at the University of Saskatchewan (Canada) with the Global Water Futures programme, where she studies how far ahead we can predict river flows across North America. As well as using scientific tools on her computer, Louise enjoys exploring water-related topics using a diversity of artistic media (from watercolour paintings to multi-sensory immersive installations). Louise is the creator and lead curator of the Virtual Water Gallery science and art pilot project, a space that brings together artists, water experts and the public, to collectively reflect on water challenges we all face.

VITUS BESEL

Institute for Atmospheric and Earth System Research, University of Helsinki, Finland
Vitus completed his bachelor's degree in biochemistry at the Ludwig Maximilians University Munich after which he moved to Helsinki to study the master's track of Theoretical and Computational methods. Already simultaneously to his master's degree he started working as a research assistant for the computational aerosol physics group in which he continued with his doctoral studies after graduating in 2020. While his master focused on the clustering of sulfuric acid and ammonia in the atmosphere, he moved to research the utilization of machine learning and big data to understand the role of compounds and their oxidation products emitted by vegetation. Additionally to his research, Vitus has always had a passion for art, especially music. He has been playing the guitar and has been singing since he was a teenager, and in recent years also turned to music production. Most recently he won the Dance your PhD contest 2021 with the Molecular Clusters song together with Jakub Kubečka and Ivo Neefjes.

STEFANIE BÖRSIG

rehab republic e.V., Munich
Growing up on a farm, Steffi learned to live in harmony with nature, to appreciate and care for it. It was only logical that she wanted to pass on the message and also include it in her professional life. Steffi studied economics and sustainability as well as business ethics in Stuttgart, Istanbul and Dresden and has already gained a lot of practical experience. Always driven by the will to do something good for the world, she has been involved in student environmental organisations and supported refugees in their job search. She has also developed integrity trainings for employees at Daimler AG and set up a sustainability platform at Sparda-Bank München. Since last year, Steffi has been putting her energy into rehab republic, where she is responsible for zero waste projects. For example, she is supporting the city of Munich on its way to becoming a zero waste city. For this purpose, she is developing a Zero Waste concept for Munich with other partners – a good exercise to now create the Zero Waste concept for the Clima Conference 2051.

JACOB BLUMENFELD

Carl von Ossietzky Universität Oldenburg, Germany
Jacob Blumenfeld is an Assistant Professor of Practical Philosophy at the University of Oldenburg, and a researcher in the interdisciplinary DFG project "Structural Transformations of Property". Before coming to Oldenburg, he taught at FU Berlin, The New School, and CUNY. He has had research stays at Humboldt University Berlin, Technical University Darmstadt, and the Goethe University of Frankfurt. He completed his PhD in philosophy at the New School for Social Research in New York with a dissertation on the concept of property in Kant, Fichte and Hegel. His research areas are political philosophy, critical theory, and German Idealism, with a special focus on property, ecology, and freedom. He is the author of All Things are Nothing to Me (2018), and a translator of Rosa Luxemburg's complete works. He is currently writing a book on climate politics.

SEBASTIAN BRANDIS

Stiftung Menschen für Menschen – Karlheinz Böhms Äthiopienhilfe

Dr. Sebastian Brandis has been Executive Director since December 2016 and Board Spokesman of the Menschen für Menschen Foundation since April 2019. Before his appeal, Sebastian Brandis was managing director at e-shelter facility services GmbH (today NTT Group), which develops and operates data centers in Germany, Austria and Switzerland. From 2001 to 2010 he held several managing positions at BT Group (BT Germany and BT Global services), starting 2008 he functioned as Executive Director of BT Germany (Munich). Further stations included VIAG INTERKOM (1998 to 2001) and Booz Allen &Hamilton (1995-1998), as well as private investor and founder of social and cultural initiatives. Dr. Brandis is responsible for communication, fundraising, and development cooperation for the Menschen für Menschen foundation.

HANNAH L. CLOKE

University of Reading, UK; Uppsala University, Sweden; Centre for Natural Hazards and Disaster Science, Sweden

Prof. Dr Hannah L. Cloke OBE is a physical geographer, natural hazards researcher, climate scientist and hydrologist specialising in earth system modelling, flood forecasting, catchment hydrology, applications of Numerical Weather Predictions and science communication. Hannah advises government, forecasting authorities and humanitarian agencies on flooding and provides expert commentary in the media. She is currently a Fellow of the European Centre for Medium-range Weather Forecasts (ECMWF) where she is researching Earth System modelling, land surface processes and flood forecasting. Hannah's research also partners with many other climate services, forecasting agencies and humanitarian actors. Hannah was appointed Officer of the Order of the British Empire (OBE) in 2019 for services to flood forecasting and the development of hazard early warning systems. She has also been awarded the 2018 Plinius Medal of the European Geosciences Union and the 2019 British Hydrological Society's President's Prize. Hannah obtained a BSc (1999) and PhD (2003) in Geography from the University of Bristol, UK. She then worked at the European Commission Joint Research Centre in Ispra, Italy on the European Flood Alert System and then from 2004 lectured at in the Department of Geography at King's College London, UK. In 2012 she moved to the University of Reading.

KEES VAN DER GEEST

United Nations University Institute for Environment and Human Security (UNU-EHS) in Bonn , Germany

Kees van der Geest (PhD) is Head of the "Environment and Migration: Interactions and Choices" (EMIC) Section at United Nations University Institute for Environment and Human Security (UNU-EHS). As a human geographer he studies the impacts of climate change, human mobility, environmental risk, adaptation, livelihood resilience and rural development. Key features of his work are the people-centred perspective and the mixed-method approach combining quantitative and qualitative research tools. His work has contributed substantially to expanding the empirical evidence base on migration-environment linkages and impacts of climate change beyond adaptation ("loss and damage"). Kees has extensive fieldwork experience in the Global South, mostly in Ghana (5 years), but also in Burkina Faso, Vietnam, Bangladesh, Nepal, Marshall Islands and Bolivia. Kees has also been active as documentary film maker. His first, award-winning, documentary (Shit & Chicks) was screened at over twenty prestigious international film festivals worldwide. His second documentary (Hunt & Play) received a nomination for the Holland-doc Jury Award of the Dutch Film Festival, and has been watched more than 3 million times on youtube.

ROLAND GERES
FutureCamp Climate
Dr. Roland Geres, managing partner of the FutureCamp Holding GmbH, is co-founder of FutureCamp. Since 2001, he has been in charge of all consulting and service activities in the business domains of emissions trading and climate protection. He has broad experience involving all regulatory, economic and organisational aspects of climate protection, emissions trading and project-based mechanisms. He actively shapes the development of the latter and participates regularly in international climate negotiations, as well as in national events. He furthermore leads a work group at the interface between the German industry and the German government. Before joining FutureCamp, Dr. Geres worked as a business consultant at Mannesmann Pilotentwicklung and as officer at the German Federal Armed Forces. He studied governance and public policy with focus on environmental law and economics at Universität der Bundeswehr, where he received his doctoral degree.

BRUCE C. GLAVOVIC
Massey University, New Zealand
Bruce has degrees in economics and agricultural economics, environmental science, and urban and environmental planning. He has worked in academia, environmental consulting and Government, chiefly in New Zealand, South Africa, and the USA. Bruce's research centres on how governance shapes social choices in the Anthropocene. His focus is on coastal communities, cities and settlements, and bridging the science-policy-practice nexus in the face of global change. He explores the roles of environmental planning, reflexivity and deliberation, and conflict transformation and citizen engagement, in confronting the sustainable development problématique. He is co-Editor-in-Chief of Ocean & Coastal Management, Senior Editor for the Oxford Research Encyclopedia of Natural Hazard Science, and on several other Editorial Boards. He was Coordinating Lead Author of the sea-level rise chapter in the IPCC's 2019 Special Report on the Ocean and Cryosphere in a Changing Climate. He is a Lead Author of the Climate Resilient Development Pathways chapter, and Cross-Chapter Paper Lead on Cities and Settlements by the Sea, in the IPCC's Working Group II contribution to AR6. He led the team that designed and facilitated South Africa's coastal policy formulation process that culminated in the Government's White Paper for Sustainable Coastal Development in 2000 and the world's first Integrated Coastal Management Act.

MATTI GOLDBERG
Technical University of Darmstadt, Darmstadt, Germany
Matti comes from Finland and studied international relations, environmental studies and social anthropology at the Universities of Munich, Glasgow and Alicante. Since 2008 he has been a part of a community of professionals helping the governments of the world develop global climate change agreements, including the Paris Agreement of 2015. Since 2017, he is working on a PhD project on the efforts to link climate change and security policy. The project has triggered a broader interested of studying the formation of "nexuses" of issues in international politics. He lives in Bonn, Germany with his wife and two young children. On his rather limited spare time, he practices jazz piano, runs, and tries to indoctrinate his children to love the Beatles.

THORSTEN GRANTNER
OmniCert Umweltgutachter
As founder and Managing Director of OmniCert Umweltgutachter GmbH Thorsten Grantner specialized in certifying agricultural biogas plants and sustainable management systems. After obtaining his degree in environmental and technical engineering he then worked for well-known companies such as Siemens AG. Since 2009 he is an environmental auditor accredited by Deutschen Akkreditierungs- und Zulassungsgesellschaft für Umweltgutachter mbH. As member of the advisory board of environmental auditors for the Federal German Government he also engages himself in further implementing the European environmental management

system EMAS and setting standards for environmental auditors in general. Thorsten Grantner and his team review over 1.000 agricultural and industrial biogas plants as well as heat and power plants every year. In addition, OmniCert validates operational safety standards and compliance with water legislation for these plants as well as management systems such as EMAS, ISO 50001 and ISO 40001 for companies and NGOs from various business areas.

GERONIMO GUSSMANN
Global Climate Forum e.V., Berlin, Germany
Geronimo is a political economist and postdoctoral researcher at the Global Climate Forum in Berlin. He holds a Bachelor's degree in Economics, a Master's degree in International Relations and is currently completing his Ph.D. about coastal adaptation governance in the Maldives at Humboldt Universität zu Berlin. Geronimo is an empirical social scientist and works on questions relating to how rules and politics at the coast emerged, how they developed, and how sea-level rise changes them.

RIYAN HABEEB
Dresden Leibniz Graduate School / Leibniz Institute for Ecological Spatial Development (IOER), Technical University of Dresden, Germany
Riyan is a PhD research scholar at Faculty of Architecture, TU Dresden, Germany under DLGS Fellowship funded by Leibniz Institute for Ecological Spatial Development. Prior to this he was working as an urban planner and architect in the field of research, academia and professional practice in India. His work focuses on action-based research on climate change adaptation and resilience through nature-based solutions and alternative building technologies integrating social and ecological responses in urban planning, policy and praxis. When not around desktop, he can be found trying new recipe in the kitchen or hiking around the trails.

BENNO HEISEL
is an independent theatre maker from Munich working mainly as musician, author, director and dramaturgue. Productions with and by Benno Heisel were invited to more than 20 Festivals nationally and internationally, including the Festival Spielart in Munich, 21st Century Theater in St. Petersburg and Souar Souar in N'djamena. One of his main achievements was being founder and Co-Director of the HochX – Theater and Live Art in Munich, for which he continues to work as a freelancer (having quit his directors position after the birth of his daughter). He was founder and CEO of the Netzwerks Freie Szene München e.V. (the Munich independent Arts Union).

BART VAN DEN HURK
Deltares, MH Delft, The Netherlands
Bart van den Hurk has a PhD on land surface modelling, obtained in Wageningen in 1996. He has worked at the Dutch Meteorological institute KNMI in model development for numerical weather prediction, as climate scenario developer, and as head of the department on model development and climate research. He is Lead Author of the 6th IPCC Assessment Report (WG-I). Currently he works as strategic research manager at Deltares, Delft. Deltares is a Dutch knowledge institute on water and subsoil. It develops hydrological forecasting systems and future outlooks.

MICHAEL JAKOB
Mercator Research Institute on Global Commons and Climate Change (MCC), Berlin, Germany
Michael Jakob is a research fellow at the Mercator Research Institute on Global Commons and Climate Change (MCC) in Berlin. He holds a PhD in economics from the Technical University of Berlin and has obtained degrees in physics, economics, and international relations from universities in Munich, St. Gallen, and Geneva. His research interests include climate change mitigation in developing countries, the political economy of climate policy as well as the interlinkages between environmental policy and human well-being. Michael has advised

governments, international organizations as well as NGOs and served as contributing author to the IPCC's Fifth Assessment Report.

SANA JAVAID
Chair for Strategic Landscape Planning and Management, Technical University of Munich (TUM), Freising, Germany
Sana is currently pursuing PhD from the Technical University of Munich, Germany. Trained as an architect she has previously worked both in the industry and academia for over three years in her home country, India. She is a two time recipient of DAAD scholarship for her research endeavours in urban green infrastructure based climate adaptation and climate responsive design. Her interests also lie in participatory planning, justice, inclusivity and accessibility in cities. Her PhD research is based on the impact of vegetation on the urban climate, co-linking the multi-sectoral benefits with a special focus on the environmental and social benefits. Sana likes to divide her time between research, art, travel, writing and photography pursuits.

MINNA KANERVA
artec Sustainability Research Center, University of Bremen, Germany
Minna Kanerva comes originally from Finland. She has lived and worked in the United States, the United Kingdom, and the Netherlands before moving to her current home city of Bremen in Germany. As a researcher, she worked for five years at UNU-MERIT, University of Maastricht, the Netherlands, where she also did her Master's degree on Science and Technology Studies (STS). At UNU-MERIT, she worked on topics related to climate change, innovation, eco-innovation and pharmaceuticals, mostly funded by the European Union. Since 2011, she has been a researcher at artec Sustainability Research Center at the University of Bremen where she in 2019 defended her PhD thesis entitled "The role of discourses in a transformation of social practices towards sustainability: The case of meat-eating related practices". Since then, she is working at artec as a senior researcher in Sustainability Science. Her current research interests include sociology of meat, strategic ignorance, linking practices with discourses, consumption corridors, transformation of the meat system, and the larger sustainability transformation.

MARKUS KECK
University of Cologne, Global South Studies Center, Köln, Germany
I am a geographer working on the sustainability transformation of agri-food systems in the countries of South Asia and in Germany. I am interested in how contemporary agri-food systems are being altered through major societal processes such as globalization, global environmental change, urbanization, and technological innovation and examine the socio-economic and socio-ecological consequences that are linked to these processes. I draw on a variety of analytical traditions including political ecology, practice theories, and science and technology studies. My goal is to contribute to crafting socio-economically just and ecologically sustainable futures. I am currently principal investigator of a DFG-funded project working on genetically engineered cotton in India and will soon act as speaker of the transdisciplinary project NutriAIDE, funded by the Federal Ministry of Food and Agriculture (BMEL), which aims at developing an app-based approach to transform the food environments of overweight and obese consumers in urban India towards sustainable and healthy nutrition. I am author of two monographs and about 40 scientific articles and book chapters. Currently, I am affiliated to the University of Göttingen as Guest Researcher at the Faculty of Geoscience and Geography, and to the University of Cologne as Postdoctoral Associate of the Global South Studies Center.

MARK KERNAN
University College Cork, Cork City, Ireland
My journey into academia has been an unfamiliar and unorthodox one. I have lived and worked in Dublin, London, Dubai, India, and I now live in Ireland again. I have had many jobs in my career: I have been a journalist for a Tibetan newspaper in northern India, a chef in Harrods, London,

and in Dubai, in the early 2000s, and I once spent a summer in a monastery in France helping monks to build coffins which taught some interesting lessons about death. My carbon foot print is too high. In 2009 I came back home to Ireland and studied for a degree in international development. In 2014 I completed a master's degree in international human rights law. As a result of this change of direction, I now teach climate change and sustainability to undergraduates, adults, and professionals in a variety of degree courses, diplomas, workshops and seminars. Now, in 2021, there is nothing more important than struggling with the reality of global warming, whether by teaching, telling stories, or even by shouting out loud occasionally. I am now a lecturer, a writer (Open Democracy, The Ecologist, Global Policy Journal), researcher; and a father, the last one being the most important.

MARKUS KINK
Independet researcher (political & social sciences), journalist, filmmaker, musician, Munich, Germany
Dr. phil. Markus Kink studied political science (with a focus on international relations), sociology and media law at the University of Munich (LMU). He earned his doctorate with "Die Sprache des Krieges" (The Language of War) under Prof. Dr. Christopher Daase in Munich and worked as a lecturer at the LMU and as a research assistant at the Political Science Department at the Technical University of Munich (TUM). The trained TV journalist and filmmaker currently works as a freelance author and artist as well as a managing and creative director of a TV, film and video production company in Munich (mediaBOX TV GmbH), where he is responsible for the conception and creative realization of film and video projects as well as business development and the overall management of the company and its team. He is also involved in the independent art and culture scene in Munich at the association Büro Grandezza e.V. In addition to working on content, he is also involved in the conception and implementation of the visual representations of the Büro's theater and art projects. His current interest in research is focused on the field of visual politics and visual representations of conflict and contested political topics.

LEA KLAUSMANN
FutureCamp
Lea Klausmann is a master student in Sustainable Resource Management at the Technical University of Munich. Since last year she also works for the company FutureCamp in the areas of carbon footprinting, policy advising and research. After her degree, she hopes to start a career in sustainability consulting or environmental policy advising. She completed her Bachelor in Governance and Public Policy at the University of Passau and wrote her thesis analyzing the local climate policy network in her hometown Karlsruhe. In her freetime she enjoys travelling, hiking and playing the flute.

JAKUB KUBEČKA
University of Helsinki, Finland
Since his childhood, Jakub has been playing with chemicals. His late teenage experiments and exploded lab table ended his experimental career, so he became a computational quantum physical chemist instead. He completed his Bc thesis and Ing diploma in Physical and Analytical Chemistry at the University of Chemical Technology, Prague, and parallelly Bc thesis and Mgr diploma in Physical Chemistry at the Charles University in Prague. He came to Helsinki (Finland) in 2018 to continue studies in computational aerosol physics in the Division of Atmospheric Sciences, Department of Physics at the University of Helsinki. His interests are computer calculations with the main focus on theoretical and computational quantum chemistry. He has been studying configurational sampling, structure, and stability of molecular clusters in the context of atmospheric new-particle formation. He did publish several scientific articles but mostly, he very much likes to popularize science, especially when it comes to educating the next young generation of scientists.

Contributors

LINUS MAGNUSSON
European Centre for Medium-range Weather Forecasts, Reading, UK
Linus Magnusson obtained his PhD from Stockholm University in 2009 and joined ECMWF shortly after. He started his work on ocean initialisation and ENSO forecasting and he also worked on sea-ice modelling. For 2011 he is working on diagnostics and forecast evaluation. His research interests include model climate and variability diagnostics, medium-range forecast error propagation, diagnostics for processes in the Arctic and severe weather around the globe such as tropical cyclones.

SARAH NANCE
Meadows School of the Arts, SMU, Dallas, TX, USA
Sarah Nance is an interdisciplinary artist based in installation and fiber. She works within the entanglements of geologic processes and human experience, exploring archived, constructed, and speculative landscapes. Her time spent living in the geologies of the Driftless Area, Oregon, Iceland, and eastern Canada has been significant in the development of her research, much of which continues to be based in these regions. Nance is currently Assistant Professor of Interdisciplinary Art at SMU in Dallas, TX. She previously held professorships in Fibres & Material Practices at Concordia University (Montréal, QC) and Virginia Commonwealth University (Richmond, VA). Her performance work has been featured in the Overburden symposium in Nelson & Castlegar, BC; Ferrara Sotto Le Stelle Festival in Ferrara, Italy; and at Washington-Grizzly Stadium in Missoula, MT. Exhibitions include Galerie Octave Cowbell in Metz, France.

IVO NEEFJES
Institute for Atmospheric and Earth System Research (INAR) – University of Helsinki, Helsinki, Finland
Ivo Neefjes is a theoretical and computational chemist. His research is focused on the development of theoretical models to predict fundamental properties of chemical systems. Throughout his research, he has applied quantum chemistry methods in a variety of different fields, from material science to atmospheric studies. Ivo Neefjes graduated from the KU Leuven with an Erasmus Mundus Master in Theoretical Chemistry and Computational Modelling Summa Cum Laude with congratulations from the board of examiners in 2019. He currently works as a doctoral student in the computational aerosol physics group of the University of Helsinki. His doctoral research is focused on the development of a computational model to determine the fate of atmospheric clusters inside mass spectrometers. The change of atmospheric cluster composition between intake and detection is a key hurdle in accurately measuring the exact concentration of clusters in the atmosphere and thus building reliable atmosphere models. In his free time, Ivo Neefjes is an avid filmmaker, having completed a Bachelor in Audiovisual Arts Cum Laude in 2013 at the Luca School of Arts in Brussels. He has created several short films that have been shown at film festivals around the world.

MICHAEL PAHLE
Potsdam-Institute for Climate Impact Reseeearch (PIK), Potsdam, Germany
Michael Pahle holds a PhD in economics and is head of the working group "Climate and Energy Policy" in Research Domain 3 at the Potsdam Institute for Climate Impact Research (PIK). His research focusses on emission trading and decarbonizing the power sector. He is regularly involved in projects to support policy implementation by state and federal agencies in Germany, covering topics such as coal phase out, power market design, and the EU-ETS reform. In 2019 he coauthored a study on carbon pricing in reform options commissioned by the German Council of Economic Experts on behalf of the Federal Government, for which he was lead author of the EU-ETS chapter.

FLORIAN PAPPENBERGER

European Centre For Medium Range Weather Forecasts, Reading (UK) / Bonn (Germany) / Bologna (Italy)

Dr. Florian Pappenberger is Deputy-Director General and leader of the Forecast Department at the European Centre for Medium-range Weather Forecasts. He is an international leading expert in the operational delivery of weather and climate forecasts and the forecasting of weather driven natural hazards such as floods, droughts, windstorms, forest fires and impacts on human health. He is the author of over 150 scientific publications and has won several scientific awards. He is a Fellow of the Royal Geographical Society and the Royal Meteorological Society as well as member of several other professional bodies including HEPEX, British Hydrological Society, EGU, AGU, EMS, AMS. He has been on the editorial board of several international journals and regularly advises on international committees including WMO, International Red Cross and Crescent Societies, World Bank and World Health Organisation.

NICHOLAS POWELL

University of Edinburgh – MSc Environment, Culture and Society, Edinburgh, UK

Nicholas has recently graduated from a Masters in Edinburgh, receiving the Best Dissertation Prize for his work: learning the trip: a method for the Anthropocene. Inspired by the wide scope of the Environmental Humanities, he developed a playful and experimental transdisciplinary method defined by its tentacular approach to thinking-with the issues at hand.

He is now a freelance writer in Bristol, UK. There he collaborates with numerous community gardening initiatives and rewilding projects, believing strongly in the revolutionary potential of everyday multispecies encounters.

His next academic project (PHD) draws from his interest in the geographies of liminal spaces between the urban/rural and core/periphery binaries, as well as the effects of unplanned rewilding in Spain – to hopefully deliver an ethnographic account of some scenes of "awkward flourishing" in the so-called Emptied Spain. Its working title is: Anthroposcenes in the Emptied Spain: mapping the emergence of the new rural.

MARIA-HELENA RAMOS

National Research Institute for Agriculture, Food and Environment (INRAE), France

Maria-Helena Ramos is a research scientist in hydrology and hydrometeorology. She also lectures on hydrology and water resources at universities and engineering schools in Paris. She started her career in Brazil, where she was awarded a BSc in Civil engineering in 1993 and a MSc in Environment and water resources in 1998. She moved to Grenoble, France, and was awarded a PhD in Atmospheric and Earth Sciences in 2002. She carried out research on hydrometeorological forecasting at the Joint research center of the European Commission in Italy before joining INRAE in France in 2007. Since then, she has focused her research on methods to improve flood and drought forecasting, to communicate forecast uncertainty and to inform decision making in water resources management under present and future climate conditions. She has organized several workshops and training courses on forecasting and co-authored games for teaching and training on the use of probabilistic predictions in hydrology. She was co-chair of the Hydrological Ensemble Prediction Experiment (HEPEX) from 2014 to 2018, and is currently the president of the Hydrological Sciences Division of the European Geosciences Union (EGU) and member of the Scientific Steering Committee of the World Weather Research Programme (WMO).

PAUL GRAHAM RAVEN
Lunds Universitet, Sweden
Dr. Paul Graham Raven is (at time of writing) a Marie Skłodowska-Curie Postdoctoral Fellow at Lund University, Sweden, where he researches the narrative rhetorics of sociotechnical and climate imaginaries. His doctoral thesis proposed a novel model of sociotechnical change based on social practice theory, and a narrative prototyping methodology for infrastructure foresight. He's also an author and critic of science fiction, an occasional journalist and essayist, a collaborator with designers and artists, and a (gratefully) lapsed consulting critical futurist. He currently lives in Malmö with a cat, some guitars, and sufficient books to constitute an insurance-invalidating fire hazard.

CLAUDIA ROBLES-ANGEL
An interdisciplinary artist living in Germany, whose work and research cover different aspects of visual and sound art, extending from audiovisual compositions to performances and installations interacting with biomedical signals via the usage of interfaces such as the BCI (Brain Computer Interface) measuring brain waves activity. She has been artist-in-residence in several outstanding institutions, for example at ZKM (Karlsruhe) and at the ICST-ZHdK in Zurich. Her work is constantly featured in not only media and sound-based festivals/conferences but also in group and solo exhibitions around the globe, for example, the ZKM Karlsruhe; KIBLA Centre Maribor, Bauhaus Museum Berlin; Festival de la Imagen Manizales, DRHA2010 Sensual Technologies London; SIGGRAPH Asia Yokohama; Re-New Festival Copenhagen; New Interfaces for Musical Expression NIME Oslo; ISEA Istanbul, Manizales, Durban, Gwangju and Barcelona; at CAMP audiovisual concert - Salon Suisse, Official collateral event of the 55th Venice Biennale, Audio Art Festival Cracow, Harvestworks Digital Media Arts Center New York City, Museum of Contemporary Art MAC Bogotá, MADATAC Madrid, ADAF Athens, Heroines of Sound Berlin and Museum Gerdau Belo Horizonte. www.claudearobles.de

LISA SCHIPPER
Environmental Change Institute, University of Oxford, Oxford, UK
Dr. Lisa Schipper is an Environmental Social Science Research Fellow at the Environmental Change Institute at the University of Oxford. Her work focuses on adaptation to climate change in developing countries, and looks at gender, religion and culture to understand what drives vulnerability. By examining how development affects the extent to which people are likely to be affected by climate change, she seeks to address the question of whether fair and just development is possible in a changing climate.
Lisa is currently Co-ordinating Lead Author of Chapter 18 of the Working Group 2 contribution to the Sixth Assessment Report of the Intergovernmental Panel on Climate Change (IPCC) ('Climate Resilient Development Pathways') and a Lead Author of the UNEP Adaptation Gap Report 2021. She is also co-Editor-in-Chief of the journal Climate and Development (Taylor and Francis). Lisa holds a PhD in Development Studies and an MSc in Environment and Development from the University of East Anglia, and a BSc in Environmental Science from Brown University.

LENA M. SCHLEGEL
Rachel Carson Center for Environment and Society, Ludwig-Maximilians-University, Munich
Lena Schlegel holds a B.A. in Political Science and Sociology and a M.A. in Peace Studies and International Relations from the University of Tübingen. For her Master's thesis titled "Decarbonising the human – a posthumanist critique and more-than-human ethics for low-carbon transitions" she received the Sustainability Award for Dissertations. After finalizing her M.A. in 2019, she worked as a research associate in an interdisciplinary EU project on disaster management at the International Center for Ethics in the Sciences and Humanities (IZEW) Tübingen. In 2021, she received a doctoral scholarship from the Heinrich Böll Foundation within the thematic cluster "transformation research" and joined the doctoral program in "Environment and Society" at the Rachel Carson Center for Environment and Society, Munich. In her doctoral project she explores the role of human-nature relations for climate (in-)action in

context of the Australian Black Summer. Her research interests are situated at the interface of Environmental Sociology and Environmental Ethics, especially focusing on Feminist New Materialism, Relationality and Care. She also teaches B.A. and M.A. courses in the Political and Social Sciences at the Universities of Tübingen and Augsburg.

MARKUS SCHMITT

Landshut University of Applied Sciences, Department of Electrical and Industrial Engineering, Landshut, Germany

Markus Schmitt is a professor of business and management. In his teaching he covers the principles of business administration, sustainability in economics and business, technology and innovation management, and corporate and business strategy.

Markus graduated in mathematics and business from Friedrich-Alexander University Erlangen–Nürnberg (Germany), then he was a research assistant at the Institute of International Innovation Management at the University of Berne (Switzerland) where he received a doctorate in economics. After four years in consulting for technology companies, he worked at Degussa (a specialty chemicals group, today named Evonik) for six years, including four years in executive positions. In 2004 Markus joined the Landshut University of Applied Sciences as a professor, where he is also the director of the degree programs in engineering and management. Since 2007 Markus has been a member and since 2017 the chairman of the advisory board of a mid-sized industrial group.

He has published comprehensively, e.g. on behavioral innovation (see the book „Verhaltensorientiertes Innovationsmanagement") and sustainability in business and management. His current research focuses on how the power of management can contribute to global sustainable development and whether it helps to interpret planet Earth – besides being so much more – as a business.

SOLVEIG MARIE SIEM

Solveig Marie Siem (1992) is a museologist with an MA in Museology and Cultural Heritage Studies from the University of Oslo. She has a BA in History and Anthropology from the University of California, Berkeley and a Postbaccalaureate certificate in Psychology from UC Irvine. Solveig wrote her master's on a series of co-creation workshops she facilitated herself at the Norwegian Museum of Science and Technology in preparation for their Klima2+ exhibition. In the spring of 2020, she also worked as a research assistant for the Anthropogenic Soils Collaboratory in the newly established Oslo School of Environmental Humanities. She is passionate about utilizing museological methods to tackle issues related to ecological disaster, social inequality, and mental health. The concept of the Mycelium Initiative was heavily inspired by a similar idea she developed with another project team for the Reimagining Museums for Climate Action international competition. She aims to continue fostering a post-disciplinary approach in all her future endeavors connected to museums, academia, and the public sector.

Solveig currently works as a full-time research assistant at the Department of Education at the University of Oslo. She is assisting several projects with research on the history of the national and international use of intelligence testing as a pedagogical and diagnostic tool.

NATHAN SMITH

University of Maine, Orono, Maine, USA

Nathan is pursuing a PhD in Communications at the University of Maine. He is focused on marine conservation, climate change, and seafood. At UMaine he researches public perceptions of climate change and aquaculture risks at local, national, and international levels. As a social scientist and systems thinker, he looks for scalable and transferable solutions to social-ecological challenges. He is a lifelong maker and artist who believes that the most rewarding work as a researcher is to build bridges between disciplines, industries, and professions. In his free time he can be found slowly and intentionally restoring his 1901 cape on the coast of Maine, cooking with his wife, or making dust in his wood shop.

THERESA SPIELMANN

Theresa Spielmann (*Johannesburg, SA) is an independent theatre maker from Munich, currently living and working in Birmingham, UK. She recently did a Masters by Research in theatre studies at the University of Warwick in the United Kingdom (2021-2022). For her Bachelor studies in theatre studies, she attended Ludwig-Maximilians-University Munich (Bachelor of Arts, 2017-2021). During her studies in Munich, she worked as a set coordinator and Assistant Director for the TV network Bayerischer Rundfunk (2019-2021) and interned as well as assisted in productions at Münchner Kammerspiele (2019). Theresa Spielmann is a founding member of the theatre review blog theatertanten.com.

Her focus in practical as well as academic work lies on eco-theatre, with a particular focus on posthumanist practices and theories. For her master's dissertation she researched "Posthumanist Thought and Aesthetics in Eco-Theatre: Entanglement of Humans and Non-Humans in an Anthropocentric Medium".

She joined Büro Grandezza in 2021, specifically for the project The 2051 Munich Climate Conference.

JOHANNES STRIPPLE
Dept. of Political Science, Lund University, Sweden

Prof. Dr. Johannes Stripple is an Associate Professor in Political Science at Lund University, Sweden. His research has traced the governance of climate change through a range of sites, from the UN to the everyday, from the economy, the urban, and the low carbon self. He has edited Governing the Climate: New Approaches to Rationality, Power and Politics (2014) and Towards a Cultural Politics of Climate Change (2016), both at Cambridge University Press. Johannes has in the last years worked on a set of initiatives that through experimentation, narratives and speculative design unlock imagination and portray the possibilities of meaningful life in a fossil-free future. Examples of these are the low carbon mobile laboratory, a tourist guide to a fictional decarbonized European city, the Carbon Ruins exhibition, Memories of the Transition. Years (A soundwalk set in Malmö), and a climate fiction writing contest.

BHAVANA & WILL TULADHAR-DOUGLAS
Situgyan Consulting

Situgyan Consulting is Bhavana Tuladhar-Douglas and Will Tuladhar-Douglas. Situgyan Consulting Ltd. is driven by research and led by values. Bhavana (M.Res, Anthropology, Aberdeen) is an Indigenous activist born in Kathmandu, Nepal, who studies heritage and cultural survival. Will (D.Phil, Asian Studies, Oxford) is a professor who works between classical texts, ethnography, and ecology. As a team, we 'see with two eyes', using a both-and approach to build synergies from complementary approaches such as local/cosmopolitan, social/ecological, dis/ability, or biodiversity/livelihoods.

RENATA TYSZCZUK
The School of Architecture, University of Sheffield, UK

Renata Tyszczuk holds the Chair in Architectural Humanities at the University of Sheffield, UK. She is an academic and artist whose work explores questions concerning global environmental change and provisionality. She has been awarded a British Academy Mid-Career Fellowship (2013 – 2014) for work in this area, which led to the monograph Provisional Cities: Cautionary Tales for the Anthropocene (Routledge, 2018). For her current research project on Collective Scenarios she has been awarded a Leverhulme Trust Major Research Fellowship (2019 – 2022). She convenes Culture and Climate Change, a framework for projects and initiatives that explore the cultural dimensions of climate change.

ANNA VARGA
Environmental Humanities Research Group, Department of European Ethnology and Cultural Antrophology, University of Pécs, Hungary

Anna Varga is a biologist, weaver, forest pedagogue and former Rachel Carson Fellow (2019-

2020). She works on ethnobiology and environmental history topics in the Carpathian Basin. She is passionate about finding and understand the link between historical and present environmental phenomenon and landuse systems. Her current research work is focusing on the forest and pasture commons and enclosures during the 18-19th Century (NKFIH PD 135651).

In her Ph.D., she worked on traditional ecological knowledge, landscape history, and vegetation science of the Hungarian silvopastoral systems. She was actively involved in the forest grazing policy work, as a result of it was possible to graze again legally after 56 years. She was the Student Representative of the International Society of Ethnobiology' Board between 2012-2014 and the Board member of Society for Conservation Biology – Europe Section between 2018-2020. She was the leader of the Hungarian Association for Land and People NGO for 15 years.

KLAUS WALLNER
Rosenheim Technical University of Applied Sciences, Rosenheim, Germany

Klaus Wallner is a professor at the faculty of Management and Engineering. His lectures in the Bachelor's programme cover the basics of business administration, cost accounting, investment accounting and financing. Within the master's programme he covers lectures in business and sustainability as well as entrepreneurship. Klaus completed a banking apprenticeship and studied business administration at the Catholic University of Eichstätt-Ingolstadt (Germany). He received his PhD from the Technical University of Munich with a thesis on the financial valuation of CO_2 sequestration in forest projects within the Kyoto Protocol.

As a freelancer for TÜV Süd Carbon Management Services, he assessed the financial additionality of projects under the Kyoto Protocol. Afterwards he was a consultant at FutureCamp Climate, focusing on emissions trading systems and CO_2 compensation projects as well as climate strategy. In 2015 he joined the Rosenheim Technical University of Applied Sciences as a professor.

He published on topics related to the European Emissions Trading System and Forest Economics. His current research focuses on different aspects of combining management and sustainability.

ANDREAS WEHRL

Andreas Wehrl (birth name Kohn) is a climate policy analyst and independent theatre maker based in Munich and Bregenz. In his policy work his long-term focus has been on climate policy instruments, the transition to a climate-neutral economy, and international capacity building. As a theatre maker he has collaborated in numerous productions as author and director. Many of his works focus on the interface between dramatic arts, science, and the individual. Andreas Wehrl is a founding member of Büro Grandezza (since 2019) and a supervisory board member of Bellevue di Monaco (since 2019). He was a strategy board member of Rehab Republic (2020-22) and a board of directors member of the Munich independent arts union (2018-21).

CHRISTINA WEHRL

Christina Wehrl was born in Upper Austria. She studied Spanish and German at the University of Vienna and arts and communicative practice at the University of Applied Arts. Already during her studies, which she completed 2018 with a master's thesis focusing on media studies, she worked in publishing and was a teaching member in a collective for open German courses from 2016 to 2017. In 2019, she went to Munich for a traineeship, stayed there for three years at a publishing house as a project manager and made books (with a focus on history, book design, and typography). Since 2022, she lives in Bregenz where she works as a secondary school teacher.

SENGÜL WEIDACHER
FutureCamp

Sengül Weidacher is working with FutureCamp since 2006 with an emphasis on Carbon Footprinting and emissions compensation. In addition to project management, this entails the coordination and development of internal processes and monitoring of relevant national and international developments. She has numerous years of experience in the development and implementation of climate strategies and the conceptual design and implementation of information events and workshops. Sengül studied Business Administration with an emphasis on environmental and resource economics and in 2005 completed her diploma thesis on the topic of "The Voluntary Emissions Trading Market", which at that time, was still being developed.

HÅKON NAALSUND WILLE
Håkon Wille has just finished his MA in Cultural Heritage Management at the Norwegian University of Science and Technology. He received international recognition for his master thesis on the role of workshop seminars in the preservation of traditional craft. He also attained a BA in History from Aberystwyth University, Wales. Håkon fostered an interest in pedagogy and conservation in practice while working as a teacher and archivist in his hometown of Ålesund, Norway – the town where the fictitious Mycelium Initiative concept is first established. He is interested in the use of cultural heritage as a part of the solution for modern societal challenges, such as climate change and mental health.